TRENDS IN GOVERNMENT FINANCING

NATIONAL BUREAU OF ECONOMIC RESEARCH

STUDIES IN CAPITAL FORMATION AND FINANCING

Trends in Government Financing

MORRIS A. COPELAND

CORNELL UNIVERSITY

A STUDY BY THE

NATIONAL BUREAU OF ECONOMIC RESEARCH

PUBLISHED BY

PRINCETON UNIVERSITY PRESS, PRINCETON

1961

Printed in the United States of America

This monograph is part of a larger investigation of trends and prospects in capital formation and financing made possible by a grant from the Life Insurance Association of America. The Association is not, however, the author, publisher, or proprietor of this publication, and is not to be understood as approving or disapproving by virtue of its grant any of the statements made or views expressed herein.

Relation of the Directors
to the Work and Publications
of the National Bureau of Economic Research

1. The object of the National Bureau of Economic Research is to ascertain and to present to the public important economic facts and their interpretation in a scientific and impartial manner. The Board of Directors is charged with the responsibility of ensuring that the work of the National Bureau is carried on in strict conformity with this object.

2. To this end the Board of Directors shall appoint one or more Directors of Research.

3. The Director or Directors of Research shall submit to the members of the Board, or to its Executive Committee, for their formal adoption, all specific proposals concerning researches to be instituted.

4. No report shall be published until the Director or Directors of Research shall have submitted to the Board a summary drawing attention to the character of the data and their utilization in the report, the nature and treatment of the problems involved, the main conclusions, and such other information as in their opinion would serve to determine the suitability of the report for publication in accordance with the principles of the National Bureau.

5. A copy of any manuscript proposed for publication shall also be submitted to each member of the Board. For each manuscript to be so submitted a special committee shall be appointed by the President, or at his designation by the Executive Director, consisting of three Directors selected as nearly as may be one from each general division of the Board. The names of the special manuscript committee shall be stated to each Director when the summary and report described in paragraph (4) are sent to him. It shall be the duty of each member of the committee to read the manuscript. If each member of the special committee signifies his approval within thirty days, the manuscript may be published. If each member of the special committee has not signified his approval within thirty days of the transmittal of the report and manuscript, the Director of Research shall then notify each member of the Board, requesting approval or disapproval of publication, and thirty additional days shall be granted for this purpose. The manuscript shall then not be published unless at least a majority of the entire Board and a two-thirds majority of those members of the Board who shall have voted on the proposal within the time fixed for the receipt of votes on the publication proposed shall have approved.

6. No manuscript may be published, though approved by each member of the special committee, until forty-five days have elapsed from the transmittal of the summary and report. The interval is allowed for the receipt of any memorandum of dissent or reservation, together with a brief statement of his reasons that any member may wish to express; and such memorandum of dissent or reservation shall be published with the manuscript if he so desires. Publication does not, however, imply that each member of the Board has read the manuscript, or that either members of the Board in general, or of the special committee, have passed upon its validity in every detail.

7. A copy of this resolution shall, unless otherwise determined by the Board, be printed in each copy of every National Bureau book.

(Resolution adopted October 25, 1926
and revised February 6, 1933 and February 24, 1941)

CONTENTS

TABLES

Foreword

By Simon Kuznets

I

This monograph is part of an inquiry into trends and prospects in capital formation and financing initiated by the National Bureau of Economic Research in 1950, with the financial assistance of the Life Insurance Association of America.[1] The inquiry examines long-term trends in capital formation and financing in the United States and is organized primarily about the principal capital-using sectors of the economy—agriculture, mining and manufacturing, the public utilities, residential real estate, and governments. The analysis for each private sector summarizes the major trends in real capital formation from 1870 (or the earliest years for which data are available) and in financing from 1900 (the earliest practicable date), and the factors determining these trends, and, so far as possible, suggests the significance of these factors for the future. For governments, the subject of this monograph, the emphasis, for reasons indicated by Professor Copeland, is not so much on real capital formation as on financial requirements. In addition to the five sector studies, the inquiry includes two others. One, already published, deals with trends in financing channeled through intermediate financial institutions and attempts to link the major types of institutions with the various groups of capital users. The other, ready to be prepared for press, utilizes the results of all the other studies, within a framework provided by country-wide estimates of national product and relevant components and of country-wide estimates of total financing.

Some of the findings have been presented in part or in preliminary form in a series of Occasional and Technical Papers.[2] This monograph,

[1] Monographs already published, by Princeton University Press for the National Bureau of Economic Research, are: *Capital Formation in Residential Real Estate: Trends and Prospects*, by Leo Grebler, David M. Blank, and Louis Winnick, 1956; *Capital in Agriculture: Its Formation and Financing since 1870*, by Alvin S. Tostlebe, 1957; *Financial Intermediaries in the American Economy since 1900*, by Raymond W. Goldsmith, 1958; and *Capital in Transportation, Communications, and Public Utilities*, by Melville J. Ulmer, 1960; *Capital in Manufacturing and Mining: Its Formation and Financing*, by Daniel Creamer, Sergei P. Dobrovolsky, and Israel Borenstein (1960).

[2] Leo Grebler, *The Role of Federal Credit Aids in Residential Construction*, Occasional Paper 39 (1953); Daniel Creamer, *Capital and Output Trends in Manufacturing Industries, 1880–1948*, Occasional Paper 41 (1954); Raymond W. Goldsmith, *The Share of Financial Intermediaries in National Wealth and National Assets, 1900–1949*, Occasional Paper 42 (1954); Melville J. Ulmer, *Trends and Cycles in Capital Formation by United States Railroads*,

like those preceding it, presents the full results of a specific study, together with the supporting data.

II

The weight of every type of government activity in the country's economy has increased markedly since the beginning of the century. The share of governments in the labor force and in total tangible durable assets rose sharply, and so did their share in net and gross national product. Perhaps even more important, the total volume of government transactions—the magnitude of taxes and other receipts plus borrowing, and the magnitude of disbursements, either on commodities or services or in transfers—has grown at rates much greater than those of the country's total economic activity. As a result, the distinctive characteristics of governments—the substitution of social and political criteria for those of the market place, making for disparity between the price of government services to recipients and the cost of these services, together with other associated consequences—have had increasingly ramifying effects throughout the economy.

Professor Copeland's monograph is a valuable contribution to the understanding of one trend in the complex that reflects the increased weight of governments in the economy—the long-term rise in the importance of governments as borrowers. A few figures clearly illustrate the magnitude of this rise. At the end of 1900, liabilities of the government sector amounted to about 9 per cent of total liabilities in the national balance sheet; and the results are no different if we limit liabilities to payables, mortgages, bonds and notes, and securities (i.e. if we exclude currency, deposits, and insurance and pension reserves). By the end of 1955, governments accounted for 28 per cent of total liabilities (and almost 46 per cent of liabilities excluding currency deposits and various insurance reserves).[3] A similar result is indicated by data on the share of governments in external financing. Of the total volume of external financing over the period from 1900 to 1955, 45 per cent is accounted for by governments, the proportion being particularly high in periods dominated by wars and major depressions.[4] It is this large share of governments in total borrowing

[3] See Raymond W. Goldsmith *et al.*, *A Study of Saving in the United States*, Princeton 1956, Vol. III, pp. 42–43 and 56–57, and *Financial Research and the Problems of the Day*, 37th Annual Report of the National Bureau of Economic Research, May 1957, p. 36.

[4] See Simon Kuznets, *Capital in the American Economy: Its Formation and Financing*, Table 47.

1870–1950, Occasional Paper 43 (1954); Alvin S. Tostlebe, *The Growth of Physical Capital in Agriculture, 1870–1950*, Occasional Paper 44 (1954); Israel Borenstein, *Capital and Output Trends in Mining Industries, 1870–1948*, Occasional Paper 45 (1954); David M. Blank, *The Volume of Residential Construction, 1889–1950*, Technical Paper 9 (1954); all published by the National Bureau of Economic Research, New York.

that tripled the ratio of government liabilities to the total within the country from 1900 to the recent years.

To be sure, with the rise in the share of governments in capital formation and in the stock of tangible wealth, we would expect their share in borrowing to increase—as it would for the private sector. But in the case of governments there is no close connection between their capital formation and their borrowing. The rise in their share in total borrowing is far greater than the rise in their share in tangible assets or in capital formation. Dr. Goldsmith's estimates, already cited, show that at the end of 1900 governments accounted for 9 per cent of all tangible assets, excluding consumer durables. By the end of 1955 the share had increased to 17 per cent—as compared with the rise from 9 to 28 per cent in their share in total liabilities. Likewise, the monograph referred to in footnote 4 shows (Table 45) that of the cumulative total of gross capital formation over the period 1900–1955, the share of governments was 16 per cent—as compared with a 45 per cent share in total borrowing or external financing.[5]

Second, when we distinguish between state and local governments, on the one hand, and federal government on the other, we find further disassociation between capital formation and borrowing. Thus, in Dr. Goldsmith's estimates, the share of state and local governments in total liabilities *declines* from 4.2 per cent at the end of 1900 to 3.6 per cent at the end of 1955, whereas their share in total tangible assets, excluding consumer durables, *rises* from 5.6 per cent to 10.5 per cent over the half-century. By contrast, while the share of the federal government in tangible assets increases from 3.0 to only 6.3 per cent over the period, its share in total liabilities increases from 4.7 to 24.4 per cent. And similar differences in the movement of the shares in capital formation and in external financing would be revealed were we to use the data in the monograph referred to in footnote 4.

Because of the greater rise in the governments' share in borrowing than in their share in the stock of real capital, and the disparity between their financing and capital formation, Professor Copeland's monograph concentrates on the financial requirements of governments, i.e. on the draft they make upon the loanable funds in the country. In attempting to present a comparable record over a sufficiently long period, Professor

[5] Tangible assets and capital formation exclude here durable military commodities (war construction and munitions); but even their inclusion would still leave a large difference between the governments' share in capital formation and in borrowing. We can add gross war construction and munitions to both total gross capital formation and the government component of it (for 1900–1955). Although this treatment exaggerates the share of governments in the additions to *net* stock of tangible wealth, with which shares in external financing or borrowing are properly compared, the share of governments in gross capital formation becomes only 27 per cent—still well below the 45 per cent share in total borrowing.

Copeland had to deal not merely with the usual obstacles in the way of poor and discontinuous data. Two major analytical difficulties had to be resolved. The first lay in defining properly the governmental deficit that represented a draft upon the supply of loanable funds—as distinct from variant definitions of governmental deficit that have been formulated and discussed, largely in connection with budget planning and fiscal legislation. The author's decision to treat additions to assets of government corporations and trust accounts as an offset to any deficiency in nonfinancial revenues relative to nonfinancial outlays may provoke disagreement on the ground that receipt of, say, contributions to social security funds in excess of benefits paid represents implicit borrowing. And yet if governmental requirements are taken to mean the calls that the governments make upon the loan fund markets, Professor Copeland's treatment can hardly be gainsaid. The second analytical difficulty lay in the interrelation of the levels of government, with respect to the changing distribution of financing responsibility, the changing restraints imposed on the borrowing capacity of some, and a secular proliferation of types of special administrative units. While data were available for the several levels, and it appeared possible to associate the financial requirements trends at these levels with somewhat different complexes of factors, it was nevertheless necessary to emphasize that all levels are interrelated—to stress the fact that the net surpluses of local and state governments are often contingent upon the net deficits of the federal government. One may extend this point, recognizing that the same is true as between the private sector and governments: surpluses in the former are often conditioned by net deficits in the latter, and it would be misleading to view the surpluses as achievements and the deficits as failures without taking cognizance of the frequent connection between the two.

III

The findings in Professor Copeland's monograph are summarized at the end of each chapter and brought together in the last. We note here some of the broader aspects, in the hope that the wider bearing of the study will thus become patent.

(1) War expenditures have been quantitatively the major source of governmental debt. There has been a definite rise in the proportion of such expenditures financed by taxes and a corresponding decline in the proportion financed by deficits—from the War of 1812 to the Civil War, to World War I, and to World War II. But a major war in the future is likely to cause a much greater proportionate draft on the country's wealth and income than any in the past. And the fast rate at which such expenditures would be incurred, even disregarding possible war-inflicted destruction, is bound to produce a lag in the fiscal mechanism—again with

resulting large deficits and borrowing. Such deficits do not mean, of course, that nobody pays. The resources are consumed, but the burden falls on those whose uses of national product are restrained during the war and whose claims are eventually reduced by the rise in prices and the decline in the purchasing power of the dollar—if not by direct repudiation.

(2) Another important source of governmental net deficits has been countercyclical policy—the discharge of the responsibility for maintaining economic stability and reducing the impact of depressions. Here net deficits during slack times are part and parcel of the basic policy; and as Professor Copeland points out, the increased weight of cyclically sensitive revenues (such as income taxes) means the likelihood of larger deficits during the contraction phase of business cycles.

(3) Debt reductions do occur after major wars, but they are only partial and are to some extent merely consequences of the lag in the taxing mechanism. Such reductions may also occur during the expansion phase of business cycles. But the pressure for all such debt reductions is, by and large, weaker than the pressure of forces inimical to the marked scaling down of government debt, a pressure which is a combination of the pressure upon governments to assume an increasing number of functions (with consequent effects on expenditures) and resistance to high tax levels (with consequent effects on revenues). At the risk of oversimplifying, the problem can be viewed as one of conflicting pressures by producers, consumers, and asset holders (not just debt owners). While all are adversely affected by such deficit financing as results in higher prices and declining purchasing power of the dollar, the immediate interests of many groups of producers and consumers can be protected by drives for increased money incomes, or for increased contributions from governments, or for decreased taxation by governments. And such drives are likely to be far more powerful than the pressures generated by the prospective losses of the owners of fixed-value assets, or by the lagging incomes of those groups in the community whose bargaining power, for various institutional reasons, is inferior to that of other groups.

(4) The responsibility for external security and for economic stability and growth has shifted increasingly to the federal government. Partly as a consequence, the latter has had to assume also increasing responsibility for the redistributive functions within the economy. Accordingly, it was at the federal government level that the main burden of financial requirements was concentrated—to the point of taking over part of the burden originating at the state and local government levels. The very multiplication of responsibilities at the federal government level, reflecting as it does the variety of functions which by social consent the central government is expected to perform, means an increasing number of

pressures. And this makes it more, rather than less, difficult to pursue consistently any single policy objective—such as that of debt reduction once the war or depression emergency that led to the large rise in debt is over.

(5) The growth of capital formation and financing at the state and local levels is part and parcel of the technological revolution that created our cities, led to the building of our roads, called for the spread of public education, and so on. Similarly, much of the rise in the volume of federal government activities and expenditures, even including the costly wars, was a product of modern economic growth—with the increasing complexity of its institutions, larger private economic units, decreasing tolerance for economic fluctuations, and a vastly greater variety of costly tools for warfare. While there are no truly inexorable historical trends, there are patterns in the movement of society so intertwined with others that, given one set, the other is likely to follow. Thus, just as industrialization was bound up with the growth of the cities, the cities once grown demanded a wide extension of functions of municipal governments—to assure the minimum of communication, health standards, educational levels, and security—not attainable by means of the market mechanism and private enterprise. And just as the spread of industrialization to separate, sovereign national units was likely to produce international friction and war, so the increasing economic power of the nations involved was brought to bear when such friction and conflicts arose.

(6) Professor Copeland wisely minimizes discussion of whether the governmental functions that led to such large drafts upon the funds of the country, their huge financial requirements, were undertaken wisely or discharged efficiently. One can only follow his example here, except for one comment. In view of the not unexpected lag in the administrative and political mechanisms of governments in adjusting to their rapidly increasing responsibility, and the competition of governments' claims to resources with claims from other sectors in the economy, it would be surprising if there were no gaps and inadequacies in the discharge of some of the governmental functions. The point in the present connection is that the wide recourse of governments to borrowing may have, in part, contributed to some of the difficulties in the proper performance of their duties. For example, the possible effect of such borrowing on rising price levels and the consequent decline in the purchasing power of the dollar may have affected adversely the very groups within the labor force upon whom governments had to rely heavily in the important functions under their auspices; and whatever pressure federal government issues exercised upon the market for government securities may have lessened the demand for local or state issues needed for financing some badly needed capital improvements.

IV

The preceding comments are casual reflections on a broad theme and perhaps not needed to convince readers of the importance of the topic treated by Professor Copeland in his monograph. In these days it is scarcely necessary to argue the major role of governments in the country's economic life, or the value of a skillful recounting of the story of governments' financial requirements.

Since the governments are the setters of the framework, the courts of last resort, the residual legatees of economic and other problems which the private sector cannot by itself resolve, they are one complex of our institutions about which a *general* projection into the future is most easily made: in the increasingly divided and intricate world that faces us, the role of governments is bound to become greater. But despite the ease of making a general projection, there is the great difficulty of ascertaining specific aspects and magnitudes. For these require knowledge, or reasonable probings, not only of the wide range of problems that are likely to face the country, but also of the distinction between those to be assigned to the private sector and those to the public sector. To illustrate, one aspect of the projection of financial requirements of governments is linked to the country's propensity to economic instability, its proneness to depression—given the accepted, and still growing, responsibility of the government for assuring full employment of resources. Furthermore, there are bound to be shifts in functions of governments at different levels, as the apparently increasing role of the federal government in the field of education clearly illustrates. To provide a usefully specific projection of the financial requirements of governments would require a separate review of the various impending or likely changes in the factors that make for government expenditures, and of the probable responsiveness of the fiscal mechanisms.

All of this does not lessen the importance of understanding clearly what happened in the past, nor reduce the value of Professor Copeland's analysis of the financial requirements of governmental operations. As the author himself stresses, the analysis is partial; and it could hardly be otherwise, considering the scope of the subject. But it reveals clearly some of the forces at play, provides a record of wide reference value, and suggests the directions of further analysis necessary to a projection linked to some broad assumptions relating to the domestic and international scene.

Preface

This study is a part of the National Bureau's inquiry into long-term trends in capital formation and financing. Because of the special characteristics of the sector of the economy with which it is concerned and the data limitations these characteristics entail, it is largely—though not entirely—concerned with trends in financing.

While primary attention in the case of the federal government is devoted to the period since 1890, and in the case of state and local governments to the period since 1910, in various connections it has seemed advisable to delve somewhat farther into the past.

This study was begun in 1950. It would have been completed somewhat sooner if work on it had not been interrupted several times. In view of the length of time in process it has been decided in general to make 1954 the cut-off date for the figures presented. However, in a few cases it has seemed advisable to include more recent information.

There is a definite connection between government financing and government capital formation, at least in the case of state and local units. But broadly even for these units it seems necessary in considering financing requirements to deal with the government's budget as a whole. What is financed is the government deficit, or rather one kind of government deficit.

Governmental accounting and budgetary practices differ from those of private business enterprises in that a "budget" surplus is a guide to policy rather than the primary policy objective, and especially in the case of the federal government in that it is not the only kind of accounting surplus that serves as a guide to policy. Chapter II is concerned with different accounting surplus or deficit computations, and particularly with two: the budget computation and the excess of nonfinancial sources over nonfinancial uses of funds. This latter computation is pertinent in connection with a fiscal policy directed toward economic stabilization; also it is a nonfinancial deficit—not a budget deficit—that must be financed.

The course of federal nonfinancial surpluses and deficits since 1890 and the course of state and local surpluses and deficits since 1910 are sketched in Chapter I and further examined in Chapter III.

Most state and local debts have been incurred to finance capital outlays, but the extent to which such outlays have involved deficit financing has varied from time to time. The reasons for this are examined in Chapter IV. Chapter IV also undertakes several time-series explorations and cross-section explorations of financing patterns. And Section 3 of the chapter first notes that there have been somewhat recent instances of what it seems fair to call disorderly finance, and then considers the implications of a long-term trend toward greater orderliness.

Chapter V is concerned with shifts in financing responsibilities from one type of government unit to another. Disorderly state finance during the first sixty or so years of the nineteenth century led to constitutional restrictions on state borrowing, and these restrictions in turn led to a rapid growth of municipal debts. Then the sequence became: disorderly municipal finance, restrictions on municipal borrowing, and a rapid growth of school and special districts and of the indebtedness of these new kinds of government units. But this has not been the end of the process of shifting financing responsibilities. Through the development of grants-in-aid programs states have assumed an increasing part of the costs of local governments, and the federal government an increasing part of state and local costs.

Chapter VI traces the gradual assumption by the federal government of a responsibility for economic stabilization and for recovery from depressions and relief from the distress that they cause. It examines the way in which this responsibility was discharged during the 1930's and during the 1945–46, 1949, and 1953–54 recessions, and the extent of the financial requirements it entailed.

It is important to distinguish between increases in gross government debt and increases in net debt in the sense of debt minus financial assets. The latter measures the net borrowing from the sectors of the economy. A major factor in the growth of financial assets has been the development of reserve funds under social insurance programs. But the federal government has also become a large-scale lender and loan underwriter, and in recent years there has been a rapid accumulation of state and local investment and endowment funds.

Chapter VII deals with the growth of financial assets; also with a contrast between two federal legislative processes in periods of emergency. During the 1930's and during both world wars Congress in various ways in effect delegated a significant part of its appropriating power; it made no comparable concessions in the process of levying taxes. Presumably in all three emergencies this contributed to the extent of deficit financing.

Chapter VIII examines certain factors making for wartime deficit financing and notes that there has been a trend toward something a little closer to a pay-as-you-go basis. It also distinguishes the conditions under which international aid is likely to entail domestic borrowing, and it traces the gradual decrease in the disposition to retire war- and other emergency-incurred federal debts.

In Chapter IX I have attempted to draw some inferences from the findings of the earlier chapters that seem pertinent for an appraisal of the prospects for future government financial requirements.

When I was invited to undertake this study, I accepted with some hesitation because I did not feel myself entirely at home in the field of public finance. Nor do I yet. And in the course of the study I have come to recognize—no doubt I should have realized it at the outset—that there are serious difficulties in conducting a statistical inquiry of this nature from an academic post without the assistance of the controls and checks that a continuing statistical research organization can provide. Nonetheless I venture to hope that my findings in regard to trends are not in need of amendment because of any detailed errors in figures and interpretations that have crept into this study, and that the inferences I have drawn from the findings are firm.

This study has profited greatly from the constructive criticisms of an earlier draft by Moses Abramovitz, Daniel Holland, Simon Kuznets, and Lawrence Seltzer. In the case of several chapters, too, I have had helpful suggestions from Solomon Fabricant, A. Miller Hillhouse, and Harold Groves. I am indeed grateful to all these individuals.

All the authors of the monographs in this series had the benefit of the aid of the Advisory Committee on the Study of Capital Formation and Financing, which assisted in drafting plans for the over-all inquiry and reviewed the final manuscripts. The committee was composed of Leo Wolman, Chairman; Sherwin C. Badger, Donald R. Belcher, Claude L. Benner, Percival F. Brundage, Arthur F. Burns, W. Braddock Hickman, Edgar M. Hoover, DeLong H. Monohan, and Geoffrey H. Moore.

At one time I had planned to write a separate paper on federal deficit concepts. A number of people made helpful suggestions and comments on a draft of this projected paper for which I am deeply indebted: Daniel P. Brill, Roger W. Jones, J. Weldon Jones, Earl Rolph, and Carl Tiller. Although the projected paper was dropped, Chapter II has been a substantial gainer from the work that was done on it.

On the statistical documentation side I am particularly indebted to Mrs. Ester Moskowitz, who assisted in checking various portions of the manuscript during the later stages of its preparation.

Three men who were graduate students while this study was in process have helped on it: John Dawson during 1950–51, Charles D. Smith during 1953–55, and Richard Martin during 1955–56. Without their able assistance it would not have been possible. But of course—with one exception— I am solely responsible for any errors this study may contain. The one exception is the note appended to Chapter VII, of which Martin is the author.

This study, like the broad inquiry of which it is a part, was financed primarily out of a grant of funds by the Life Insurance Association of America to the National Bureau of Economic Research. During 1955–56 the study was assisted by a grant of $500 from the Eli Lilly Fund.

Ithaca, New York   MORRIS A. COPELAND

TRENDS IN GOVERNMENT FINANCING

CHAPTER I

Introduction

Government capital requirements, like the capital requirements of the various private sectors of the United States economy, are of two sorts—physical and financial. By physical requirements is here meant the actual gross capital formation demand of governments for final products of the economy. Financial requirements will be taken to be actual governmental demand for funds in the loan and security markets.

Particularly in the case of government the term "capital requirements" applied in retrospect is likely to suggest the question, Were the expenditures—and the borrowing they entailed—really necessary? The objective of this monograph is not to appraise the wisdom or necessity of government capital requirements. Rather it is to determine what borrowings and what capital outlays there actually have been and what circumstances have given rise to them, and by so doing to provide a basis for judging what they are likely to be in the future.

1. *Concepts of Capital Requirements*

While government capital requirements have much in common with private capital requirements, they also have some quite distinctive characteristics. Let us first consider, therefore, more precisely what is meant by government capital formation and government demand for funds. Because of the distinctive characteristics of government we shall be mainly concerned with the latter.

Let us take first the question, What are financial requirements? Broadly speaking we propose to mean by government financial requirements the demand for funds in the loan and security markets, or government borrowings. More specifically we propose to take as our principal measure of borrowings the increments in net debt, meaning by net debt the excess of what a government owes others over what others owe it. Although figures on gross debts outstanding still receive a good deal of attention in the press and although they are useful for some purposes, taken by themselves they can be quite misleading. As of the end of 1955 federal agencies held more than $51 billion of federal obligations. What the government borrows from its own agencies we propose to exclude from the reckoning of its financial requirements. This applies both to the

3

federal government and to other units of government. For state and local governments, Census Bureau compilations have long reported figures on outstanding debts net of sinking fund assets. Whenever such figures are available, we will prefer them to gross debt figures.

But one government unit may hold the debts of another as sinking fund assets. It may hold them for other purposes as well. All told, state and local governments have come to owe the federal government over three-quarters of a billion dollars; and the federal government has come to owe them some $14 billion.[1] In general, and unless there is some special reason for doing otherwise, we propose to exclude all inter-government debts from the reckoning of financial requirements.

Nor is this quite the end of the matter. If the financial requirements of a sector of the economy are to be measured by the increments in the sector's net indebtedness, it is desirable for many purposes that net indebtedness should be so defined that we can add the indebtedness of any two sectors of the economy together to determine the indebtedness of the two. We therefore propose to give chief attention to government net debt in the very net sense of gross debts less total portfolios and less cash balances. In the case of state and local governments this means essentially reporting debts net of cash and government securities owned.

For the federal government the situation is different. The net debt figure to which we here propose to give primary attention involves deducting a large loan and security portfolio as well as the cash balance from outstanding debts. And the cash balance is especially important in this case too. Thus it seems wise to distinguish between paying off nearly $10 billion of World War I debt out of the tax surpluses of the 1920's and paying off nearly $20 billion of World War II debt in 1946 by simply drawing down the general fund balance. While the latter operation retired government IOU's, it retired at the same stroke an equal quantity of the IOU's of the banking and monetary system held by the federal government.[2] It seems equally wise to distinguish between money the federal government borrows to relend or to invest in securities and money it borrows to finance payrolls or the purchase of munitions.

We shall, then, in measuring government financial capital requirements, give main attention to the increment in net debt, meaning by net debt the excess of gross debt outstanding over cash balances and loans and securities held. However, grosser figures are significant also, and they are often available where net figures are not. They will therefore receive attention too.

[1] The latter figure is as of December 31, 1955. See *Federal Reserve Bulletin* for March 1956. The former is as of December 31, 1954. See Board of Governors of the Federal Reserve System, *Flow of Funds in the United States, 1939–1953*, Table 78. (For bibliographical information, see Appendix B.)

[2] However, private cash balances increased by about half this amount during 1946.

4

But what about government capital requirements in the physical sense, or government capital formation? Following the analogy to private sectors of the economy we might take government capital formation to consist of (a) all new construction, (b) all new durable equipment, and (c) the increment in physical inventories. However, there is a growing consensus that military construction, equipment, and inventories should not be counted as capital formation. The life of such "fixed assets" is highly uncertain; so is the turnover rate of such inventories. And in an economic sense many would hesitate to call them productive assets, however necessary they may be for the country's national security in the present state of world affairs.

The private analogy suggests a further exclusion. Present conventions exclude consumer inventory increases from capital formation; presumably the nonenterprise inventory increases of government may well be left out by the same token. This omission seems necessary in any case because there is no satisfactory comprehensive information on the subject. We might then—in fact, present conventions suggest we should—define government capital formation as new nonmilitary construction and equipment plus physical increases in the inventories of government enterprises. This definition, however, leaves borderline cases to be classified: war housing, war industrial facilities, and additions to the stockpiles of strategic materials. In principle it is proposed to count these items as capital formation.

In application it seems advisable not to press for a rounded picture of equipment and inventory increments. The basic records are too sketchy. Further, the general objective of the study of which this monograph is only a part presumably implies for most sectors of the economy a kind of connection between physical capital formation and the demand for capital funds that in the case of governments is missing. Both because of the sketchiness of the capital formation data and because of the missing connection it has been decided to devote this monograph mainly to analyzing government financial capital requirements.

The relation between state and local government physical and financial requirements will be examined below (primarily in Chapter IV). At this juncture a brief comment contrasting it with that in the private sectors of the economy may suffice. In general gross private domestic capital formation is financed in three ways: (a) by borrowing, capital stock flotation, and the liquidation of financial assets; (b) by new noncorporate proprietorship investment; (c) by inside funds, i.e. depreciation, retained income, etc. In the case of government these lines of connection between physical and financial capital requirements are somewhat obscured. Of course there is nothing analogous to (b). Further, except in the case of government enterprises it would be practically impossible to identify anything that really corresponds to (c);[3] and even enterprise surpluses and deficits are so difficult to distinguish from indirect taxes and subsidies that the national income and product accounts currently do not attempt to draw the distinction. As for borrowings—financial capital requirements in the sense here proposed—they may be occasioned by various emergency outlays such as those connected with national defense and the depression of the 1930's, outlays that are mostly not for non-military construction and equipment or enterprise inventories. And physical capital formation can be financed out of current tax receipts.

This contrast may be put in rather different words. The established accrual accounting practices of private business draw a sharp line between capital expenditures and the means of financing them, on the one hand, and charges and credits to the income account, on the other. These practices make for a clean-cut separation of the capital from the annual budget. Through the balance sheet business financial reports tie capital requirements in the physical sense and capital requirements in the financial sense together. Government accounting practices are quite different; the development of accrual conventions has not gone very far. Only a few general government units (nonenterprise, non-trust-fund units) have anything called a capital budget, and none of these maintains a set of accrual accounts that provide a full-fledged balance sheet. The accounting tie between the two types of capital requirements is, for the most part, missing.

No doubt the wide differences between government fiscal and accounting practices and those of private business reflect a fundamental difference in policy objectives. Business accrual accounting is designed to give a measurement of profit, and profit is the central business objective. The policy objectives of government do not lend themselves to specification in financial statement terms. Nonetheless, conceivably a wider application of businesslike techniques in government fiscal procedures may bring about a closer relation between government physical and financial capital requirements in future. We will give this possibility some attention in Chapter IV.

2. An Outline of the Growth of Government Capital Requirements

Let us briefly review the growth of government debt during the past several decades. In 1890 the federal net debt was a little over $900 million, and only a little more than the total net indebtedness of all state and local governments combined. (See Table 1.) However, aggregate

[3] Raymond Goldsmith in his monograph, *Financial Intermediaries in the American Economy since 1900*, presents computations of an item he calls government "funds . . . supplied by internal sources." We doubt that this item is properly comparable to the similarly captioned items for the private sectors of the economy.

government debt reached a low point during the early 1890's. At the close of the Civil War the federal gross debt exceeded $2.75 billion; Ratchford estimates the debt of the Confederacy—which was repudiated—at $1.5 billion.[4] The census reports a state and local total (net of sinking funds) of nearly $870 million for 1870. At the end of the Civil War the total may well have exceeded a billion dollars, for the war debts of the southern states—and of some cities—were repudiated.[5] Of the $870 million about

TABLE 1

Government Gross and Net Debt, Selected Years, 1890–1950
(billions of dollars)

		1890	1913	1929	1939	1950
	GROSS AND NET DEBT					
A.	Federal gross debt	1.12	1.19	17.5	50.5	268.1
B.	Federal net debt	0.93	0.98	15.4	31.4	195.4
C.	State and local gross debt	1.34	4.78	17.8	20.1	25.6
D.	State and local net debt	0.88	3.35	10.9	11.8	4.9
E.	Total gross debt	2.46	5.97	35.3	70.6	293.7
F.	Total net debt	1.81	4.38	26.3	43.2	200.3
	INDEBTEDNESS NET OF SINKING FUNDS					
G.	States	0.23	0.35	2.48	2.95	4.44
H.	Counties	0.15	0.37	2.39	2.01	1.59
J.	Cities, villages, townships, etc.	0.72	2.95	9.18	9.01	9.67
K.	School districts	0.04	0.12	2.04	1.71	2.58
L.	Special districts	a	0.04	1.60	2.50	2.96
M.	All state and local governments	1.14	3.82	17.70	18.18	21.23

a Negligible.

NOTE: Figures for 1929, 1939, and 1950, lines A through F, refer to December 31. Other figures are fiscal-year-end figures; lines C through F, 1913–50, include territories and possessions. Other local government figures do not. Because of rounding, sums of columns may not precisely equal totals on lines E, F, and M. Terms are defined in Appendix A.

SOURCE: See Appendix A.

three-fifths were accounted for by municipalities and other local units of government. Local debts had probably more than doubled during the preceding ten years; they apparently continued to grow rapidly until 1873, a substantial amount of borrowing being undertaken to aid in financing railroad construction. (See Table 2A.) During the postwar years, too, southern state and local governments borrowed to finance reconstruction and to some extent also to finance the regime of the carpetbaggers. The severe depression which began in 1873 brought extensive defaults, and some compositions of municipal debts. And the ousting of the carpetbaggers in 1876 was followed by debt repudiations

[4] B. U. Ratchford, *American State Debts*.
[5] See Chapter IV on the amounts of war borrowing by Union and Confederate states.

and compositions totaling well over $100 million. But despite these developments total local indebtedness was larger in 1880 than in 1870 and larger still in 1890. In 1890 net of sinking funds it totaled $926 million as compared with $516 million twenty years earlier. However, state debts, net of sinking funds, declined from $353 million to $211 million during these two decades. And the federal gross debt decreased by $600 million, 1866–73, and by more than $1,300 million, 1879–93.

TABLE 2A

Bonded State and Local Government Debt Outstanding,
1880, by Purpose
(millions of dollars)

		Cities[a] (1)	Total (2)
A.	Bridges	21	25
B.	Improvement of harbors, rivers, wharves, canals, and waterpower	17	36
C.	Parks and public places	40	40
D.	Public buildings	26	48
E.	Railroad and other aid	68	185
F.	Schools and libraries	14	26
G.	Sewers	21	21
H.	Streets	82	87
J.	War expenses	29	75
K.	Water works	142	146
L.	Other (including unidentified)	222	428
M.	Total	682	1,117

[a] Cities and towns of more than 7,500 population.

NOTE: These figures are from the 1880 census. That census also cites a compilation by the comptroller of the State of New York for 1838 covering 18 of the then 26 states which shows their debt by purpose as follows:

	(millions of dollars)
Aid to banks	53
Building canals	60
Aid to railroads	43
Turnpikes and macadam roads	7
Other	8
Total	171

So far as government financing is concerned, the period from 1890 to World War I conforms in its broad outlines to a somewhat prevalent concept of "normal times." Possibly it was in a way a basis for this concept of what is normal. There were ups and downs in federal debt, of course; but for the period as a whole the federal budget was substantially in balance. The gross debt was $1.25 billion in 1889, $1.23 billion in 1916. And while state and local debts increased sharply, from $1.14 billion in 1890 to $4.5 billion in 1913, the new borrowing was mostly to finance physical capital formation. (See Tables 2B and 2C.)

Despite increased pensions in the early 1890's the budget surpluses the federal government had been enjoying in the 1880's continued until the panic year of 1893. The deficits during the ensuing depression brought debt back up to the 1889 level in 1898. Then the Spanish-American War—the war proper lasted only four months—carried it some $200 million higher. But Congress promptly passed a war revenue bill, and the continuation of most of the war emergency taxes to 1901 reduced the debt to $1.22 billion in that year. The downs and ups of federal debt during the next fifteen years reflect a variety of factors. There was a deficit in 1904 due mainly to the expenditure of $50 million for the purchase of the Panama Canal.

During the 1890's the growth of local debts was accelerated, and there was some net borrowing by states. On a per capita basis even local indebtedness had declined in the preceding decade. The financial difficulties of the 1870's had led to a substantial tightening of the legal restrictions on borrowing—we consider these restrictions in Chapter V—and the restrictions seem for a time to have been reinforced by a psychology of caution that temporarily somewhat checked recourse to borrowing. But by 1890 the factors of debt increase had again become predominant. Per capita local debt, net of sinking funds, was $14.80 in that year, $20.74 in 1902.

Broadly speaking most of the factors of increase during the latter years of the nineteenth century and the early years of the twentieth were associated with the industrial revolution. The mere growth of urban population that accompanied the process of industrialization called for substantial investments in new streets, schools, and other public improvements. But technological change also involved additional investments per capita. The more general installation of running water and inside flush toilets meant large municipal outlays on water and sewage systems. Other capital formation expenditures reflecting the new technology and rising standard of living included those for improved fire department equipment, grade crossing eliminations, better schools, city hospitals, institutions, parks and recreation facilities—not to mention municipal enterprises such as transit systems. (See Tables 2B and 2C.)

On the whole other units of government responded less promptly to the influences making for increased borrowing. Thus state capital expenditures totaled less than half a million dollars in 1890 and only $2 million in 1902. But these influences began to be felt in the early years of the twentieth century. Between 1902 and 1913 state debts (net of sinking funds) rose from $235 to $346 million, county debts from $197 to $372 million. About half the $68 million of state capital expenditures in 1917 was for highways (including the Barge Canal in New York State). The pressure of the automobile for improved roads and streets had come to be an important factor in state and county as well as in city debt increases.

But borrowing was not confined to existing units of government. Various "special districts" were established, partly as a device for getting concerted action over an area involving more than one local—or state—jurisdiction, in some cases too as a device for getting around debt and other restrictions: school districts, drainage, irrigation, and levee districts,

TABLE 2B

Functional Distribution of State Government Debt,
Selected Years, 1915–51
(millions of dollars)

		1915	1929	1941	1951
A.	Highways	207	1,181	1,524	1,974
B.	Schools	8	48	120	582
C.	Hospitals	6	25	50[a]	165[b]
D.	Veterans' aid and homes	[c]	244	[d]	1,970
E.	Housing and community development	[d]	[d]	[d]	232
F.	Welfare	11	6	460	10
G.	Parks and reservations	7	20	35	[d]
H.	Public service enterprises and investments	29	250	250	262[e]
J.	General government properties	16	29	96	[d]
K.	Other	228	369	715	779
L.	Total above	512	2,172	3,250	5,974
M.	Total gross debt	580	2,300	3,462	6,223

[a] Includes institutions for the handicapped.
[b] Health and hospitals.
[c] Less than $500,000.
[d] Included with "Other."
[e] Nonhighway transportation facilities.

NOTE: Detail covers funded and floating debt, 1915; funded, floating, and special assessment debt, 1929; long-term debt, 1941 and 1950.

SOURCE: Bureau of the Census, *State Government Finances*, annual (before 1942, called *Financial Statistics of States*).

and units of government devoted to a number of other special purposes. In part the growth of local debt, 1902–13, reflects the borrowing of new school and special districts.

The influences making for increased indebtedness of state and local governments that were prominent during the first decade of the twentieth century were even stronger during the next two decades. In 1929 the net debt of all such governmental units was $10.9 billion, or more than twelve times what it had been in 1890. The growth of school and special districts continued, too. In fact the total indebtedness of these units in 1932 was greater than that of either counties or states. We will consider the significance of special districts in Chapter V.

During the Civil War the states, particularly the Confederate states, played a considerable part in financing the war. By the time of the

Spanish-American War this financial function had been largely taken over by the federal government. Nonetheless during and after both world wars the states incurred substantial war-connected expenditures, chiefly for soldiers' and sailors' aid and homes. As Table 2B shows, such expenditures were responsible for the third largest identifiable category of state debt in 1929 and the second largest in 1951.

TABLE 2C

Functional Distribution of City Government Debt
Selected Years, 1905–51

	Year	1905	1930	1941	1951
	Number of cities	154	310	92	41
		debt in millions of dollars			
A.	Public service enterprises	446	2,799	3,353	3,529[a]
B.	Highways	208	1,416	723	893
C.	Schools and libraries	171	1,705	656	547
D.	General government properties	25	190	139	[b]
E.	Parks and playgrounds	95	341	227	227
F.	Charities, hospitals, and corrections	[c]	132	307	161
G.	Sanitation	72	792	444	512
H.	Public safety	12	101	76	78
J.	Other	494	1,875	1,107	1,262
K.	Total above	1,523	9,351	7,032	7,209
L.	Gross debt of cities of over 30,000	1,618	10,018		
M.	Gross debt of cities of over 25,000			8,355	9,975

[a] On the method of estimating this figure see Appendix A. *Large-City Finances in 1951* shows: (1) enterprises, $2,891 million; (2) nonhighway transportation facilities, $637 million; (3) housing and community development, $528 million. Portions of (2) and (3) in prior years were treated as public service enterprises.

[b] Included with "Other."

[c] $43 million, 1912.

[d] Health and hospitals only. In 1941 the figure for hospitals alone was $120 million.

NOTE: The figures for 1941 and 1951 are not exactly comparable to those for 1905 and 1930 because they exclude the computed portions of the debts of overlying counties and school and special districts. The principal effects of this exclusion are roughly indicated by the following comparison of the percentages of all debt identified by function represented by four major functions which overlying units of government perform:

	1940 (including overlying units)	1941 (excluding overlying units)
Public service enterprises	46.7%	56.5%
Schools and libraries	16.4	11.1
Parks and playgrounds	5.3	3.8
Sanitation	8.7	7.5

SOURCE: See Appendix A.

As a result of World War I the net federal debt was increased from less than $1 billion to $22 billion by June 30, 1920. During the following decade about $9 billion of war debt was paid off. Then came fifteen years of deficits. At the close of the depression decade of the 1930's the net federal debt stood at $31.4 billion; it was increased by World War II to $220 billion by December 31, 1945. In the next three years it declined by about $25 billion. Stepped-up national security and other expenditures practically eliminated the surplus in 1949–52—there was little change in net debt during these four years. It increased about $9 billion in the next two years.

Much of the time changes in state and local indebtedness have contrasted markedly with changes in federal debt. Sharp increases of the one have been accompanied by a retarded growth or even a contraction of the other. This was so in 1900–16, during World War I, and throughout the 1920's. It was so too during most of the 1930's and again during and after World War II. True, the 1929–33 recession forced state and local governments for a time to borrow—not primarily to finance capital formation but rather to make up for decreased revenues. However, by the end of 1933 the depression growth of state and local debts was checked; and during the next five years net indebtedness declined by about $1 billion. Then small increases in net debt in 1939–40 to finance capital outlays were followed by substantial decreases during the next several years. World War II brought large cash surpluses. Receipts increased, and on the whole wartime restrictions kept expenditures from increasing. As a result state and local governments, viewed collectively, got practically out of debt.

This does not mean that there were no debts outstanding on or about June 30, 1946; at that time such debts totaled some $16.5 billion. Rather it means that financial assets—cash balances and portfolios—came to about the same figure.

Nor does saying state and local governments were practically out of debt mean that each individual unit of government was in an equally favorable financial condition. For all states taken together financial assets apparently exceeded debts outstanding by more than $2 billion. And for cities of over 25,000 population net financial assets—financial assets minus total debts—were probably in excess of $1 billion. Clearly there were other units of government that had net debts.

Since the figures on state and local debt which receive most attention do not make clear the 1946 net debt situation—they are too gross—we give an approximate statement of state and local debt condition in Table 3.

After 1946 state and local governments again had recourse to net borrowing. The major purpose of the new debt issues, as Tables 2B and 2C make clear, was to finance physical capital formation. New construction, which in 1945 had totaled less than two-thirds of a billion dollars, exceeded $3 billion in 1947 and $8 billion in 1954. But, as after World War I, veterans' bonus bonds were a substantial debt item for states.

However, despite a large postwar step-up in expenditures and despite a large volume of new bond issues, the growth in net debt was moderate. It amounted to only about $6.5 billion by the end of 1954.

But gross state and local debt was about two and one-fourth times what it had been in 1929. And the major purposes of borrowing continued to be the financing of various types of capital expenditures. Still there were

TABLE 3

State and Local Government Gross and Net Debt,
December 31, 1946 and 1950
(billions of dollars)

		1946	1950
A.	Gross debt outstanding	16.5	28.2
	B. Held in sinking, trust, and investment funds	2.4	3.6
	C. Federal interest-bearing debt held in sinking, trust, and investment funds	6.8	8.9
	D. Cash balances	7.1	9.5
	E. Other securities owned	0.2	1.3
F.	Total financial assets (sum of lines B through E)	16.5	23.3
G.	Net indebtedness (line A minus line F)	0	4.9

SOURCE: See Appendix A.

significant changes among the detailed components during the period covered by Tables 2A and 2B. Highways represented 73 per cent of the state debt identified by purpose in 1915; only a little over 30 per cent in 1951. The corresponding figures for cities are: 20 per cent, 1905; 15 per cent, 1951. State school debt was relatively unimportant in 1915; in 1951 it was one-ninth of the total identified by purpose. The growth of state university debts—particularly in Texas, Michigan, Tennessee, and Oklahoma—was an important factor in this increase, although the total of such debts for all states was only three-fifths of the $582 million on line B of Table 2B. Debts incurred for welfare purposes were especially large in the post-depression year 1941. City enterprise debt accounted for some 43 per cent of all identified city debt in 1905—water supply systems alone for 26 per cent. By 1951 the percentage for enterprise debt had increased to nearly 60—transit systems alone accounted for 25 per cent of the identified total, water supply systems for 23 per cent, electric power systems for 4.5 per cent. And—to particularize further—the acquisition of the BMT and IRT subways by New York City in 1940 contributed substantially to the increase in transit system debt; it explains nearly 10 per cent of $3.4 billion on line A, 1941, in Table 2C.

No entirely satisfactory standard of comparison that would enable us to appraise the significance of the growth of government net debts from less than $2 billion in 1890 to some $200 billion sixty years later is available. Goldsmith has estimated the total investments of all types of financial intermediaries in loans and securities and their investments in government obligations at various dates. His estimates for 1900 and 1952 show:

		1900	1952
		(billions of dollars)	
A.	All government obligations	1.7	209.2
B.	Federal obligations	0.7	186.0
C.	All loans and securities	13.7	450.4
		(per cent)	
D.	All government obligations/all loans and securities	12.4	46.0
E.	Federal obligations/all loans and securities	5.1	41.1

NOTE: See Goldsmith, *op.cit.*, p. 131. Line C represents what he calls "funds made available" to domestic nonfinancial sectors and to the rest of the world.

Also, the Department of Commerce has estimated what it calls net public and net private debt, for years beginning 1916.[6] A comparison for this year and for 1950 follows:

		1916	1950
		(billions of dollars)	
A.	Government net debt	5.5	239.4
B.	Federal net debt	1.2	218.7
C.	"Net" private debt	76.5	246.4
		(per cent)	
D.	Government net debt/"net" private debt	7.3	97.0
E.	Federal net debt/"net" private debt	1.6	89.00

These two comparisons highlight the extent to which government debt, and particularly federal debt, has come to be a dominating influence in the loan and security markets.

Table 1 gives us an approximate picture of the financial capital requirements of governments, 1890–1950. The record of physical capital requirements is considerably less satisfactory. Table 4 compares physical and financial capital requirements, so far as we have somewhat acceptable measurements for the former. One would not expect to find any obvious over-all relationship in the case of the federal government, because the major factors in the growth of federal debt have been the two world wars and the depression of the 1930's. Only in a few debt issues, an issue of $125 million to help finance the purchase and construction of the Panama

[6] Public debt is gross debt less own obligations held. Private debt is gross debt of corporations other than currency and deposit liabilities of banks and policy reserves of insurance companies minus indebtedness to affiliated corporations plus gross mortgage and other debt of individuals and unincorporated enterprises. The noncorporate, nonmortgage debt component of the 1916 figures is incomplete. See *Survey of Current Business*, September 1952.

Canal and some more recent agency issues such as the TVA bond issue of 1933, is there a direct connection.

State and local governments, on the other hand, have borrowed mainly to finance new capital assets. Nonetheless, as Table 4 makes clear, the extent to which state and local governments have financed physical capital formation through recourse to the loan and security markets has varied widely from time to time.

TABLE 4

Federal and State and Local Debt Growth Compared to
Increase in Capital Assets and Construction
(billions of dollars)

		1902–12	1912–29	1929–46	1915–29	1930–40	1941–45	1946–50
		FEDERAL GOVERNMENT						
A.	Increase in capital assets[a]	0.4	1.1	21.2	c	c	c	c
B.	New nonmilitary construction	c	c	19.0[d]	1.2	6.1	12.2	5.1
C.	Increase in net debt	0.1	14.4	203.5	14.4[e]	18.4[e]	190.8[e]	−24.6[e]
		STATE AND LOCAL GOVERNMENT						
D.	Increase in capital assets[b]	3.1	12.8	8.8	c	c	c	c
E.	New construction	c	22.4	30.7[d]	21.9	23.9	5.3	18.2
F.	Increase in net debt	1.6	7.8	−10.9	7.3[e]	0.7[e]	−10.8	2.4[e]

[a] Includes corporations.

[b] Excludes roads, streets, and sewage systems.

[c] Increments for these intervals not provided in the basic figure.

[d] 1930–46.

[e] 1914–29; 1929–40; 1940–45; 1945–50.

NOTE: Federal nonmilitary new and maintenance construction totaled $0.3 billion, 1891–1902; $0.8 billion, 1903–12. (See *Historical Statistics*, H-27 and H-28.) The increment in federal net debt, 1890–1902, was $0.2 billion.

Line D in Table 4, like line A, is a measure of net capital formation. Since it omits roads, streets, and sewage systems—as well as nonconstruction items—it is seriously incomplete. It certainly understates the amount of net capital formation; probably also the percentage increase from 1902–12 to 1912–29. State highway debt outstanding increased by $52.5 million 1902–12; by $1.29 billion 1912–29.[7] Surfaced road mileage increased by 93,000 in the former period; by 431,000 in the latter.[8]

Lines B and E reflect gross capital formation other than new equipment purchases and inventory increases. Until recent years there is little comprehensive information on any components of government capital

[7] *Historical Statistics*, K-175 and K-204.

[8] *Ibid.*

15

formation except new construction. Some data on equipment purchases and on enterprise inventories are currently available. During the five years ending 1951 the inventories of federal government corporations and business-type agencies increased by some $270 million.[9] In the two years 1950 and 1951 cities of over 25,000 population made capital outlays for equipment of $193 million; construction outlays of $1,812 million.[10] These figures suggest that new construction may in recent years have accounted for perhaps as much as 84 or 90 per cent of government physical capital formation as defined above.

Judging by Table 4 net borrowing provided the funds for a substantial part of state and local government net physical capital formation, 1903–29. The dollar value of such net physical capital formation in 1930–46 including roads, streets, and sewage systems must have been larger than that in 1903–29; nonetheless in the later period net debts decreased by more than $10 billion. And during 1946–50 net borrowing was only a little over one-eighth of the dollar value of total new construction.

These comments emphasize the special nature of the problem of determining capital requirements for the government sector of our economy. We shall analyze this problem further in Chapter II in terms of government budgets and the growth of government functions.

It is tempting to conclude from Table 4 that during the initial impact of the industrial revolution there was a close relation between physical and financial capital requirements for state and local governments, a relation that more recently has largely disappeared. We shall examine this possibility more closely in Chapter IV, but it is clear from Tables 2B and 2C that even in 1951 a large part of the outstanding debt had been incurred to finance capital formation.

3. Summary

Our main concern in this monograph will be with changes in government indebtedness. It is proposed to give particular attention to changes in net debt, i.e. total debt minus holdings of cash, of government obligations, and of other financial assets.

Our brief review of the growth of government debt during the past several decades raises the question of the nature of the relation between state and local borrowing and capital formation and of recent changes in that relation. It confirms the common-sense view that the main factors in the increase in federal net debt from about $1 billion in 1913 to some $195 billion in 1950 were wars and the depression of the 1930's, rather than capital formation.

[9] *Treasury Bulletin*, April 1952, p. 67. Between June 30, 1950, and December 31, 1951, they decreased by $0.73 billion. This compilation does not include the Post Office and the Maritime Administration.

[10] *City Government Finances*. Outlays on existing assets totaled $188 million.

During the twentieth century government securities, particularly federal obligations, have had increasing influence upon the loan and security markets.

Besides the relationship between borrowing and capital formation, there are a number of questions suggested by our brief historical review to which we will need to give attention: What changes in government functions and in the governmental units responsible for financing them have taken place? What are the implications of national security programs for federal financial requirements? What are the implications of anti-recession measures for federal financial requirements? What are their implications for state and local requirements? Why has the distinction between gross and net debt become so important? What are the conditions making for retirement of large emergency-incurred debts?

We will need also to examine the history of government indebtedness and borrowing in somewhat greater detail. And we will need to give further consideration to the concept of net borrowing and to note the significance of various fiscal techniques and developments for the growth of government debts.

CHAPTER II

Capital Requirements and the Budget

Historically speaking, governments have had recourse to borrowing mainly to finance wars, and this type of borrowing is still of prime importance. Around 90 per cent of our present federal debt can be attributed to the two world wars and their aftermaths. By and large, borrowing to finance tangible asset expenditures is a relatively recent development. During the past fifty or sixty years it has accounted for the major part of state and local borrowing. (Cf. Tables 2A, 2B, and 2C.)

The purposes for which debts have been incurred are pertinent facts if we try to answer the question, Why is total public debt as big as it is today? But by themselves they do not give us the answer. They do not tell us why the investments of state and local governments in tangible assets increased by more than $8 billion between 1929 and 1946, while their net indebtedness was reduced to a negligible figure in these seventeen years. They do not tell us why wars are not financed on a pay-as-you-go basis, or why war debts seldom get paid off.

One naturally wonders whether the purposes for which debts have been incurred, or, to be more precise, the functional types of expenditure financed by the debts, do not have something in common, some common characteristic which leads to deficit financing rather than pay-as-you-go financing. It might be suggested that this common characteristic is their "bunchiness," the fact that they are, for the most part, concentrated in a relatively short period and added on top of the more usual expenditures during that period. But this is doubtless an oversimplification. Bunchiness is important, particularly for the smaller units of government. But a marked increase in the level of total expenditures that has not been adequately anticipated may entail recourse to borrowing. Also the process of finding and employing new revenue sources may prove to be slower than the process of stepping up expenditures. And during a business recession financing an expenditure increase by an increase in taxes may be deemed inadvisable.

The fact of the matter is that we cannot get much understanding of government financial capital requirements by considering solely the expenditures which are said to occasion them. Since government accounting reports do not include a comprehensive balance sheet which specifically relates (unamortized) capital expenditures—assets—to debts, we must

18

seek to understand financial capital requirements in terms of the place of the particular expenditures that are said to be the occasion for borrowing in the budget as a whole. These expenditures must be considered in relation to others and to tax and miscellaneous receipts; for it is really deficits and not particular functional categories of expenditures that have to be financed.

To say that governments borrow because they incur deficits is, in effect, to pose a whole series of questions. Some of these questions are economic in the sense that they relate to economic policies which may be forwarded by operating at a deficit for a time. Some of them are procedural; they have to do with procedures which may make it difficult or impossible, when the rate of expenditures changes rapidly, to make changes in tax receipts to match. Some of them are politico-economic; they concern the special interest groups that favor or oppose a particular debt policy.

1. *What Is a Government Deficit?*

Before going into these broader questions, indeed before attempting a more detailed review of the course of government receipts, expenditures, and deficits, we need to dispose of a very technical question: What is a deficit and what is the connection between operating at a deficit and borrowing?

We have already noted some of the ways in which the accounting and fiscal procedures of governments differ from those of private business. The necessity for dealing with this question points up a further contrast. Most private enterprises that publish financial statements of their operations offer the public a single deficit (loss) or surplus (net income) figure only. To be sure, there are still unsettled questions as to how business net income for a fiscal period ought to be defined, and different businesses define it differently. But in general each individual business adopts one definition and makes that the basis for its financial reports.[1] The federal government, on the other hand, for some years has regularly published three quite different deficit—or surplus—computations and now publishes still another. For calendar 1946 one of these showed a surplus of $5.0 billion, another a surplus of $2.2 billion, a third a surplus of $0.2 billion, and the fourth (the official "budget" computation) a deficit of $2.5 billion. Evidently when one speaks of the federal deficit, he needs to say what deficit he is talking about. And it may be added that a budget deficit does not necessarily mean "deficit financing."

Somewhat similar comments apply to state and local governments, even though for most of them only one deficit computation receives much

---

[1] A textual comment in a corporation's financial report, however, sometimes gives alternative computations of net income.

attention, the official budget computation. This computation has not always been defined in the same way, and the size of the deficit may not be a measure of the increase in government indebtedness.

In considering what sort of deficit computation does give such a measure, and how this computation differs from the budget deficit, it will be convenient to take the federal government as an illustration. Some of the special problems involved in this case have little or no parallel in the case of other branches of government, but we omit no special problems of consequence by concentrating attention on the federal government.

Further, while the federal budget deficit computation and the computation that measures net borrowing are by no means the only possible computations, we propose to concentrate attention here on these two.[2]

We pose the question, What is a federal deficit? And in so doing we assume that a federal surplus is to be regarded as a negative deficit. Equally we might have asked, What is a federal surplus? and treated deficits as negative surpluses. We do not mean to prejudice issues by the way we ask the question. Our choice of phraseology is a matter of convenience only. No value judgment in regard to fiscal policy or the relative merits of surpluses and deficits is implied. Nor is it suggested that a deficit (or surplus) has much economic significance apart from its algebraic components. For most purposes the real significance is doubtless to be found in the several receipt and expenditure items that enter into its computation. But for the sake of brevity we will speak mostly of the summary net plus or minus figure, using this as a shorthand way of designating the full financial statement of receipts and expenditures of which it is the balancing item. And we will treat deficits as pluses and surpluses as minuses, partly because in comparing various ways of computing a federal deficit or surplus during the past thirty or so years we find rather more deficits than surpluses, partly also because we take federal deficits—appropriately defined—to measure federal capital requirements.

2. *The Federal Budget Deficit*

First let us examine the budget computation. When the President submits a budget to the Congress, this is the deficit computation for the coming fiscal year that receives principal attention. Presumably Congress has intended that it should. The budget deficit computation has been developed expressly to serve as a basis of legislative fiscal control and of

---

[2] A note appended to this chapter deals with the other two federal deficit computations referred to above (net operating cash outgo and the National Income and Product Account deficit), with their relations to the two here considered, and with the evolution of the present federal budget computation.

administrative management. A good deal of careful study has gone into the various revisions that have made the budget computation what it is today.

The federal budget deficit is quite different from a business deficit, but they have some things in common. Both distinguish between those receipts and expenditures that enter into the deficit computation and those that do not. And an idea of good and bad seems to underlie both. A federal budget surplus is in some sense good; a deficit something to be avoided if circumstances permit. But here the resemblance stops. A business surplus is an end in itself; a government surplus is not. The objective in the case of government is not a surplus. Rather it is a balance between the costs of government services and the tax levies and other receipts that finance those services, a balance to be achieved as economically and efficiently as possible. This objective was set forth in the Budget and Accounting Act of 1921, and the Bureau of the Budget established by that act has been at pains to devise a deficit computation appropriate to it. It is today not the sole objective of fiscal policy, but it is still a major and a statutory objective.

Obviously a method of computing the federal deficit that has been devised to implement a particular fiscal policy will reflect the way that policy has been conceived and interpreted. The conception of the policy in turn can conveniently be indicated by noting the main categories of federal receipts and expenditures that do not enter into the budget deficit computation and the reasons for their exclusion. The main exclusions are: (a) transactions of social insurance funds, (b) certain transactions of various business-type and credit agencies of the government, and (c) certain transactions connected with the increase in the mint price of gold in 1934. In general these exclusions have been accomplished by dividing government accounts into two parts, the accounts of the general government and the accounts of trust and miscellaneous funds. The budget deficit is computed from the receipts and expenditures of the general government accounts. Except that some payments out of (and into) general government accounts may go to (or come from) the trust and miscellaneous funds, the transactions of these segregated funds do not enter into the budget deficit computation.[3]

There are a number of federal social insurance funds. Much the largest is the Old Age and Survivors Insurance Fund, the fund most people think of as *the* social security fund. But there are various others: the Railroad Retirement Fund, the Unemployment Compensation Fund, several civilian employee retirement funds (for various categories of

---

[3] The accountant thinks of the government as a collection of funds, each fund being treated as a separate transactor that enters into transactions with other funds as well as with the public.

civilian employees), and two veterans' life insurance funds (one for the veterans of World War I, the other for those of World War II).

The chief transactions of these funds are payroll tax and premium receipts, interest income, benefit payments, and portfolio investments. These funds in many years have had cash surpluses or excesses of their payroll tax, premium, interest, and other current receipts over their benefit payments and other current outgo items and have invested these surpluses in government bonds. The cash surpluses so accumulated and invested constitute a kind of policy reserve, and the Bureau of the Budget therefore considered it improper to count an annual social insurance fund cash surplus as contributing to a balancing of the general government budget. To count such surpluses in this way would be in effect to nullify the principle of maintaining a reserve. Hence it was decided that they should not be included in the budget deficit computation. Whatever one may think about the wisdom or necessity of the policy reserve principle for social insurance funds, this would appear to be a very reasonable interpretation of the intent of the Budget and Accounting Act.

The list of other government funds whose transactions have been in greater or less measure excluded from the budget deficit computation comprises a wide variety of federal government business-type and credit agencies. Among these are the Reconstruction Finance Corporation, which was originally organized to make loans to financial institutions during the crisis of 1932–33; the Commodity Credit Corporation, which has had a major role in the price parity program for farmers; the Federal Deposit Insurance Corporation, which insures bank deposits; and the Tennessee Valley Authority. The considerations which have led to exclusion in these cases are somewhat more complex than in the case of the social insurance funds, and the method of treatment of these agencies in the budget computation has gone through a number of stages. Broadly the theory in recent years appears to be that such agencies should to some extent provide the means of financing their operations for themselves and that they should affect the budget deficit insofar and only insofar as general government funds are used to finance them.

Since the mid-1940's a systematic attempt has been made to get nearly all such agencies to present business-type financial statements, income statements, and balance sheets, actual and budgeted or estimated;[4] and some special treatment of their transactions in computing the budget deficit would seem to be a logical corollary of this development. Just what treatment is most appropriate is a rather technical question. The present procedure is outlined in a note on federal surplus and deficit concepts appended to this chapter. At this point it may suffice to say it seems a reasonable conclusion from the businesslike characteristics of these agencies

---

[4] Also statements of sources and uses of funds.

that their transactions should not be simply lumped together with general government transactions in determining what constitutes a budget deficit. Rather, they appear to call for budgeting procedures more like those of business.

The increase in the mint price of gold in 1934 brought the government a paper profit of $2.8 billion. Since this was a mere bookkeeping write-up of an asset, it seemed inappropriate to count it as balancing the budget. Had it been so counted, the budget for fiscal 1934 would in fact have been almost in balance, although expenditures were—except for 1918–20—at an all-time high. But we must qualify this hypothetical statement. Part of this paper profit—$1.8 billion—was invested in the newly created Exchange Stabilization Fund, and this investment was classified as a nonbudget expenditure.

Granting the budget-balancing objective of the act of 1921 it seems wise to exclude from the budget deficit computation the cash surpluses of the social insurance funds and the paper profit on gold and to give some special treatment to the receipts and expenditures of business-type and credit agencies. However, under modern conditions the budget deficit concept so far developed is necessarily one that requires a great deal of judgment when the budget figures are used as a guide to fiscal policy. The budget cannot in general be balanced on an annual basis, only on the basis of an average for a number of years. Nonetheless the budget submitted in January of each year is an extremely valuable means of promoting the budget-balancing objective, and—short of a capital budget system—the present budget deficit concept would appear to be the appropriate one for this purpose.[5]

We say short of a capital budget system because such a system could provide a kind of moving average deficit computation that would eliminate much of the problem caused by the fact that year-to-year variations in out-of-pocket expenditures do not match year-to-year variations in receipts.[6] A small step toward a capital budget system was taken when—beginning with the 1948 budget—a table classifying civil budget expenditures into current and capital was included in the budget document.

3. *The FOF Nonfinancial Computation*

When the Budget and Accounting Act was passed, balancing the budget was widely considered the main objective of over-all fiscal policy. The depression of the 1930's stimulated interest in another objective— economic stabilization. Indeed, because of the objective of economic stabilization there is today support for the idea that a so-called cash

[5] However, it would seem advisable to treat all transactions in government credit as transactions in government debt are treated—that is, to exclude them from the definitions of budget receipts and budget expenditures.

[6] See the writer's "Capital Budget and the War Effort," pp. 38ff.

deficit computation should replace the present budget deficit computation in the budget document. However, for the purposes of this inquiry it seems best to assume that both computations are needed, and that both the budget-balancing objective and the stabilization objective will continue to receive consideration.

The deficit computation we propose to use in analyzing financial capital requirements—state and local as well as federal—may be regarded as a variant of the cash deficit computation, although strictly speaking it is not entirely on a cash basis. And the type of financial statement which defines it we consider a particularly useful one for analyzing the impacts of government fiscal operations on the rest of the economy—that is, a statement particularly appropriate to serve as an informational basis for implementing a policy of economic stabilization.[7]

The deficit computation we propose to use in analyzing government financial requirements will be referred to as the FOF nonfinancial deficit computation. It is the excess of what the Federal Reserve calls "nonfinancial uses of funds" over "nonfinancial sources."[8] This computation treats the gold account (i.e. the Treasury's monetary gold fund) as does the budget deficit computation—excludes it. But unlike the budget deficit computation it lumps together substantially all other government funds[9]—including social insurance funds and the funds of government business-type and credit agencies—and treats them as a single fund. The financial statement that defines the "nonfinancial deficit"—the flow of funds statement—is a consolidated sources and uses account for this inclusive fund.[10] It reports the results of all transactions of this fund with state, local, and foreign governments as well as with private parties. It does not reflect transactions between one federal agency and another.

One way to think of the federal nonfinancial deficit—the direct approach—is as the excess of nonfinancial expenditures or uses of funds— chiefly payrolls, procurement and construction costs, aids and benefit payments, interest, and tax refunds—over tax collections and other nonfinance-type receipts or sources of funds. It is this excess or net non-financial expenditure that has to be financed.

[7] The technical characteristics which distinguish this variant are considered in a note appended to this chapter. Considered there, too, are the two alternative types of financial statement that have been regarded as appropriate in conjunction with the economic stabilization objective. The note deals specifically with statements for the federal government, but much of what is said applies to state and local units as well.

[8] See *Flow of Funds in the United States, 1939–1953*.

[9] Strictly speaking not quite all. The funds of the District of Columbia are here classified as "state and local." Further, the "Treasury currency" account, the gold and silver accounts, the postal savings system, and the Exchange Stabilization Fund are regarded as parts of the banking and monetary system rather than as parts of the federal government.

[10] Of course the statement that defines the budget deficit is also a sources and uses account.

24

The other way to think of this deficit is in terms of the method of financing, the increase in net federal debt where net federal debt is defined as total federal direct and agency obligations held by the public (including banks and state and local governments but not including federal agencies) plus federal accounts payable minus the federal cash balance and minus federal portfolios of loans and securities.[11] A deficit can be financed by an increase in direct plus agency debt held by the public and trade debt, by a liquidation of federal portfolios, or by a decrease in cash. Financial sources of funds mean precisely increases in debts outstanding, or drawing down the cash balance, or liquidating other financial assets. And financial uses of funds mean precisely acquisitions of financial assets or retirements of debts. All other sources and uses of funds are nonfinancial. Either the excess of nonfinancial expenditures over nonfinancial receipts or the increase in net debt measures the financial capital requirement. The FOF statement details the financial sources and uses of funds as well as the nonfinancial sources and uses.

To us it seems that the proper measure of the government's financial requirement is the measure of its net borrowing from the public rather than the technical—and it might be added currently somewhat politically determined—budget deficit. It seems too that the FOF computation is a more precise and, because of the financial detail available in connection with it, a more convenient measure of net borrowing from the public than either the National Income and Product computation or the Treasury net cash operating outgo computation.

It could be argued that increases in the financial assets held by social insurance funds should not be deducted from increases in outstanding government debt in computing net government borrowing. The case for a deficit computation that does not make this deduction rests on the assumption that the persons covered by social insurance at any date have an equity in the insurance funds equal to the assets the funds hold at that date. In other words, the argument assumed that the government's future obligations to pay social insurance benefits entail a present liability to prospective social insurance beneficiaries equal to the assets of the funds. It was originally expected that the size of the Old Age and Survivors Insurance Fund would be determined by an actuarial reserve calculation. Had this plan been followed, the argument for such a liability—and so against the deduction of social insurance fund assets in computing net debt—would be a much stronger one.[12] But as things stand there appears

[11] To be precise we should note that in the Federal Reserve FOF computation a small amount of trade credit and other financial assets is also deducted.

[12] The actuarial reserve argument does apply in the case of the United States Government Life Insurance Fund (for World War I veterans). But for this fund, as for the others, the fiscal impact of financial asset accumulation seems best portrayed by the definition of net borrowing here adopted.

to be no reason for saying that a future obligation to pay benefits constitutes a present liability—and even if one grants there is such a present liability there is no agreed-upon way to determine its size.

But the main reason for defining government net borrowing as net of the increment in social insurance funds is not the question whether a future obligation to pay benefits is a present liability. Rather, it is that many economists think the fiscal impact of the social insurance system is best portrayed when we take the FOF nonfinancial deficit computation as the measure of government net borrowing. Largely because of this we have decided to define the government's financial requirement as net borrowing in this sense.

Since a concern with the fiscal impact of government operations has been such an important factor in this decision it may be well at this point to add a disclaimer relating to the nature of that impact. We do not share the concern some economists feel for the inflationary effects they assume government borrowing involves. We think there is no evidence that a government deficit in and of itself makes for rising prices. The connection between deficits and prices is an indirect one. The government can add to aggregate demand, chiefly through increased purchases and transfer payments and decreased taxes, and the addition to aggregate demand may involve a deficit and may, when the level of demand is high, exert an upward "demand pull" on prices. Our concern about fiscal impact is primarily a concern about the way government operations influence aggregate demand.

4. Summary

Two broad objectives of fiscal policy are: (a) a balance of budget receipts and expenditures, at least as an average over a period of years, and (b) promoting economic stability. The budget deficit—or surplus—is a computation that has been developed to implement the first of these objectives. The FOF nonfinancial deficit computation, the National Income and Product computation, and the Treasury net cash operating outgo computation are all more or less pertinent to the objective of economic stabilization. We have given particular attention to the FOF statement both because it provides more pertinent information for this purpose than either of the others[13] and because of the financial details it provides.

Since the budget deficit computation excludes a substantial volume of federal transactions—both sources and uses of funds—taken by itself it does not measure the net borrowing of the federal government. The FOF nonfinancial computation is precisely a measure of the net financial

[13] In 1959 the Federal Reserve revised the form of its Flow of Funds accounts. In the revised form somewhat less detail is given for the nonfinancial transactions of both the federal and the state and local government sectors.

requirement. And since the FOF statement includes both financial and nonfinancial transactions, it provides also important information on the form taken by federal financing each year, or—when there has been a surplus—on the form in which federal funds have been advanced to other sectors of the economy.

A Note on Federal Surpluses and Deficits

Prior to World War I official financial reports drew no line between budget transactions and trust and other account transactions, as they do today. The principal federal financial reports showed total receipts plus the increment in direct debt outstanding equal to total expenditures plus the increment in the general fund (cash) balance except for a small timing discrepancy. Moreover, the only difference of consequence between the receipts and expenditures reported by the Treasury and nonfinancial receipts and expenditures, as the latter terms are used in this monograph, was the netting of postal receipts against postal expenditures in the former. In the early years of the twentieth century the only government corporation was the Panama Railroad Company, and the principal trust accounts were those for the Indian tribal funds and for the District of Columbia.

The development of government corporations and business-type activities and the growth of trust funds have greatly complicated federal finances. Trust and other account receipts totaled over $9.5 billion in the year ending December 31, 1954. And we have today in addition to the budget surplus or deficit computation three other surplus or deficit computations.

The purpose of this note is twofold: first, to sketch the development of the budget surplus or deficit concept; and second, to relate the four types of concepts.

During World War I the timing discrepancy in the equation, receipts plus debt increase equals expenditures plus cash increase, became substantial. In 1927 in order to put the various reports on a uniform timing basis and to eliminate this discrepancy, expenditure reports were shifted from a warrants-issued to a checks-issued basis, with an adjustment for checks outstanding applied either to expenditures or to the general fund balance.

By 1930 the assets of the adjusted service certificate trust fund, civil service retirement funds, and government life insurance fund had grown to over $1 billion. And the total receipts of all trust funds in that year were nearly $130 million. It seemed wise, therefore, to show separately one surplus or deficit computation for general and special account (i.e. budget) transactions and another for trust accounts; and the latter computation was shortly expanded to cover the transactions of a number of government corporations and the capital gain from the 1934 increase in the value of gold. For the corporations involved this expansion of the outside-the-budget area was completed in 1938. It meant that in general capital subscriptions were reported as budget expenditures (and trust etc. account receipts), capital retirements and earnings distributions as budget receipts (and trust etc. account expenditures); that other corporate transactions and Treasury loans to corporations were only trust etc. account transactions and were reported as a single net plus or minus expenditure item entitled "Transactions in the checking accounts of government agencies (net), etc."

Distinguishing between general and special account receipts and expenditures and the receipts and expenditures of trust and other accounts was a long step forward in fiscal procedures. It was a definite recognition that the budget-balancing objective should apply to general government accounts, not to all government accounts; that a social insurance fund surplus should not be offset against a deficiency in the taxes that support general government operations; and that government business-type operations should to some extent be self-supporting. However, in the case of government corporations it went too far. It was part of the process by which government corporations came to be exempt from various fiscal controls.

The Government Corporation Control Act of 1945 had as its object the establishment of adequate budgetary, accounting, and auditing controls over such federal agencies. To help effectuate the purposes of this act the item "Transactions in the checking accounts of government agencies (net), etc." as it applied to wholly owned corporations was divided into two parts: (a) redemptions minus sales of the obligations of these government agencies in the market; and (b) "other activities (net)." Beginning with the Secretary of the Treasury's 1947 *Annual Report* and the 1949 Budget, (b) was reported for each wholly owned government corporation as a budget expenditure.

The separation of general and special accounts from trust etc. accounts developed during the 1930's had had the desirable effect of excluding from general and special account receipts and expenditures the sales and purchases by government corporations of public debt securities. The 1947 changes in corporation accounting procedures to effectuate the 1945 act had one unfortunate by-product. They brought most of these transactions in government securities by wholly owned corporations back into the budget. Accordingly, in 1951 net purchases of public debt securities by such corporations were again excluded from budget expenditures.

But there was a good deal more than this to the accounting changes in handling the transactions of government corporations that were made

28

in 1951. Quite possibly the ideal treatment of this difficult class of transactions has not yet been reached, but the 1951 changes did provide for the first time a clear-cut logical basis for drawing the line between inside-the-budget transactions and outside-the-budget transactions. The Budget for 1953 and for subsequent years gives statements of sources and uses of funds for the wholly owned corporations in which funds provided by "operations" are distinguished from funds provided by (inside) "financing," and funds applied to "operations" are distinguished from funds applied to (inside) "financing."[14] The net budget expenditure item for each corporation equals the excess of funds applied to "operations" over funds provided by "operations," i.e. net outside-the-government transactions.[15]

In February 1954 a technical change was made in budget receipts and expenditures, a shift from a daily-statement basis to a new monthly-statement basis. The result is a more accurate assignment of items by months and years.

These are the main steps in the development of the present budget surplus or deficit concept. But there have been four changes in the definitions of budget receipts and budget expenditures since 1939 that have had no effect on the surplus or deficit:

1. Exclusion of receipts appropriated to the OASI fund from both budget receipts and budget expenditures, effective July 1, 1940.

2. Exclusion of payments to the Treasury, principally by wholly owned corporations for retirement of capital stock and for distribution of earnings, from both budget receipts and budget expenditures, effective July 1, 1948.

3. Reporting amounts refunded by the government, principally for the overpayment of taxes, not as a budget expenditure but as a deduction from budget receipts, effective January 3, 1949.

4. Exclusion of receipts appropriated to the RR Retirement Fund from both budget receipts and budget expenditures, effective July 1, 1952.

The budget surplus or deficit computation is designed to serve broadly the purposes of legislative control in levying taxes and making appropriations and the purposes of administrative management. The present definition has, as the above historical sketch makes clear, evolved through

[14] The terms are not too well chosen. Many "operations" transactions are clearly financing transactions; the "financing" transactions consist of inside-the-government sources and uses of funds and market transactions in public debt securities.

[15] This is of course equal to net funds provided by (inside) "financing" (including loans as well as capital subscriptions). Of course it may be a negative quantity.

a process of experimentation. It should be added that it is the result of a great deal of careful study to devise a computation that will best serve these purposes.[16]

With the development of a federal responsibility for economic stability has come the need for another kind of surplus or deficit computation, possibly for more than one other kind. At all events there are three others today, each of them in some sense pertinent to the objective of promoting economic stability. Exhibit A compares the four computations.

The computations differ in the first place in the funds or accounts covered. The budget computation, as already noted, distinguishes receipts and expenditures of budget accounts from receipts and expenditures of trust and other accounts and is confined to the former. The cash operating income and outgo computation comes from a consolidated financial statement for all federal funds. The coverage of the FOF nonfinancial computation is only slightly less comprehensive. It comes from a consolidated statement for all federal funds except (a) District of Columbia funds (these are classed as state and local government funds), and (b) funds classed as part of the banking system.[17] The National Income and Product Account computation comes from a consolidated statement for all federal funds except (a) District of Columbia funds and (c) funds of business-type activities.[18] However, the balance in the account for business-type activities is closed into this statement; hence differences between columns 3 and 4 do not result from differences in the funds covered.

Exhibits B, C, and D give reconciliations (each for an illustrative year) between columns 1 and 2, columns 2 and 3, and columns 2 and 4, respectively. (Exhibit D treats columns 2 and 4 as net borrowing computations rather than as net nonfinancial expenditure computations.) In a general way the relations between column 1 and columns 3 and 4 can be inferred from these exhibits.

---

[16] It can be cogently argued that these purposes would be better served if capital and current expenditures were distinguished somewhat along the lines of business accounting and budgeting practice. In this connection it should be noted that recent Budgets have included a special analysis that looks in the direction of such a distinction. In Special Analysis D in the 1956 Budget actual and estimated expenditures (apart from a contingency reserve and an overlapping national security item) are classified under the following main headings: (a) additions to federal assets; (b) expenditures for developmental purposes; (c) current expenses for aids and other services; (d) other services and current operating expenses. Under (a) loans and various categories of physical assets are distinguished, and under (b) state and local physical assets, private physical assets, and several other developmental purposes. The analysis does not extend these classifications to appropriation estimates.

[17] The gold, silver, and Treasury currency accounts, the postal savings system, and the Exchange Stabilization Fund.

[18] Since financial transactions (and some others) are lumped in a single residual item it cannot be determined whether the funds listed in footnote 14 are covered or not.

The cash operating income and outgo computation has two forms. One is an accounting determination made each month by the Treasury, the other is a partly statistical annual (and sometimes semiannual) determination made by the Bureau of the Budget. The Bureau of the Budget calls the source items in this computation "receipts from the public" and the use items "payments to the public," and the Treasury has recently adopted this terminology also.[19] The Bureau of the Budget detail of receipts and expenditures is on a combined object-and-function basis that is a good deal more useful in connection with the economic stabilization objective than is the detail in the Treasury's monthly statement. There are minor technical differences between the receipts totals and the expenditures totals in these two forms of the income-outgo compilation that we will not stop to discuss.[20]

The cash income and outgo statement, unlike the others, is on a strictly cash basis. As a result there are adjustments for the excess of interest accruals over interest payments and for the excess of issues of obligations used in settlement of transactions over redemptions of these obligations in Exhibit B, and counteradjustments in Exhibits C and D.

The budget and cash operating income and outgo statements differ from the other two in three important respects: (a) The expenditures of various business-type activities, notably the Post Office, are reported net of receipts in the former two. (b) Budget expenditures and cash outgo include purchases of a substantial amount of loans and securities; budget receipts and cash income to some extent include sales of loans and securities. (c) The budget and cash income and outgo statements report procurement expenditures on an accounts-settlements basis; the National Income and Product statement and the nonfinancial transactions statement report such expenditures on a book-credit basis (i.e. in the case of merchandise at the time of delivery). Difference (a) has no effect on the surplus or deficit computations. Difference (b) results in adjustments B and C in Exhibits C and D. Difference c leads to the adjustments entitled "Decrement in net payables," when settlements exceed purchases on account, procurement outgo will be larger than the procurement expenditures in the NIP and nonfinancial transaction statements, and the surplus in column 2 will to this extent be smaller than the surpluses in columns 3 and 4.[21]

The netting of enterprise receipts against expenditures and the lumping of various financial with the nonfinancial expenditures in the cash operating income and outgo statement and in the statement of receipts

[19] After having experimented with various other captions. In what follows, to avoid confusion we will use the older, more familiar income-outgo terminology rather than the terms "receipts from the public" and "payments to the public."

[20] For reconciliations see the 1956 Budget, p. 1132.

[21] This adjustment takes account of trade receivables as well as of trade payables.

from and payments to the public both make it awkward to use the latter as an analytical tool in connection with the objective of economic stabilization.[22]

The NIP statement and the FOF nonfinancial transactions statement differ in three main respects: (a) The latter is complemented by a statement of financial transactions; in the former the surplus or deficit is a mere residual computation from the receipts and expenditures affirmatively determined, and it includes some nonfinancial transactions.[23] (b) A number of items are reported on different timing bases in the two statements—notably the NIP statement shows corporate income tax accruals, and the FOF nonfinancial transactions statement shows corporate income tax collections. (c) A single net item covers enterprise transactions and subsidy payments in the NIP statement; these transactions are on a gross basis in the FOF statement. We may note, too, that in the former corporate tax accruals are net of refunds and purchases are net of (subsequent) renegotiation receipts; also refunds are deducted from noncorporation tax receipts, interest receipts from interest payments, and sales from purchases of goods and services. In the FOF nonfinancial transactions statement netting is avoided as far as seems feasible. Again, in the NIP statement the receipt and expenditure figures exclude transactions in existing capital assets; in the nonfinancial statement they count as nonfinancial receipts and expenditures.[24]

The monthly cash operating income and outgo computation of the Treasury includes a balancing statement of financial transactions. Exhibit D relates this computation to the FOF statement. There are four principal types of steps in translating the former into the latter: (1) adjustments to take account of credit as well as debt transactions and of changes in accounts payable; (2) adjustments for differences in the timing of transactions; (3) the small adjustment to eliminate District of Columbia transactions; and (4) the grossing up of the cash income and outgo figures to get rid of the nettings.

Since the FOF statement is on a consolidated basis, the total of outstanding federal obligations it shows excludes obligations held by federal agencies like the social insurance funds. Net debt is thus computed as total liabilities of the federal government held by other sectors of the economy minus total financial assets or claims on other sectors held by the Treasury and other federal agencies. Of course net debt can also be computed when

[22] However, some effort was made to show loan transactions separately. See, for example, the (January) *1952 Economic Report of the President*, p. 160.

[23] The transactions in existing capital assets noted below. In fiscal 1951 the net effect of these on the deficit was insignificant.

[24] But the netting of various nonfinancial items in the revised FOF statement for the federal government and in that for state and local governments (see footnote 11) somewhat restricts the usefulness of these statements.

32

the claims of federal agencies on each other are counted both as assets and as liabilities.[25]

We have traced the development of the budget surplus or deficit computation. It does not seem worth while to do the same for any of the others. However, the cash operating income and outgo computation in particular has undergone a number of revisions. And it may be of interest to note that when it was started in 1937 by the Federal Reserve a separate net expenditure figure was compiled for investments in (purchases minus sales of) loans and securities. In this respect its aim was more like that of the present Federal Reserve compilations of financial and nonfinancial transactions.

Because of the advantages of a statement that avoids netting receipts from against payments to the public and that clearly distinguishes government credit transactions from nonfinancial transactions like payrolls and procurement outlays, it would seem that the usefulness of the cash income and outgo compilation would be considerably increased if it were so amended as to simplify as far as possible translations to the NIP and the FOF nonfinancial and financial transactions statements. It may be added that a shift from a monthly to a quarterly basis would not involve any great informational loss.

EXHIBIT A

A Comparison of Four Government Surplus Computations, 1943–54
(millions of dollars)

Year Ending December 31	Budget Surplus (1)	Net Cash Operating Income (2)	NIP Accounts Surplus (3)	Nonfinancial Transactions Surplus (4)
1943	−55,691	−51,068	−46,714	−52,900
1944	−53,650	−46,616	−54,577	−50,800
1945	−43,594	−36,534	−42,331	−36,800
1946	−2,512	236	2,161	5,000
1947	2,434	5,703	12,222	10,800
1948	5,241	8,076	7,957	9,900
1949	−3,592	−1,267	−2,398	500
1950	−422	482	9,229	−300
1951	−3,358	1,304	6,517	700
1952	−5,842	−1,583	−3,366	−300
1953	−9,157	−6,089	−6,214	−6,700
1954	−3,683[a]	301[a]	−6,177	−2,300

[a] On a new reporting basis. See text.

NOTE: Figures for columns 1 and 2, 1943–53, are as they appear in *Treasury Bulletin* for February 1954. Column 3, 1943–53, is from 1954 *National Income Supplement* to the *Survey of Current Business*. Column 4 is (preliminary) from the Federal Reserve study, *Flow of Funds in the United States, 1939–1953*.

[25] See Table 51 below.

EXHIBIT B

Relations between Budget Receipts and Expenditures and
Cash Income and Outgo, Fiscal Year 1953
(millions of dollars)

I. SURPLUS AND DEFICIT RELATIONSHIP

A.		Budget surplus	−9,389
B.	plus	Net surplus in trust and miscellaneous accounts[a]	3,737
C.	plus	Excess of interest accruals over interest payments	719
D.	plus	Excess of issues of armed force leave bonds over redemptions[b]	−25
E.	plus	IMF capital subscription adjustment[c]	28
F.	minus	Clearing account adjustment[d]	−312
G.	plus	Other adjustments, net[e]	25
H.	equals	Net cash operating income	−5,217

II. RECEIPT-INCOME AND EXPENDITURE-OUTGO RELATIONSHIPS

			Sources	Uses	Net Sources
J.		Budget transactions	65,218	74,607	−9,389
K.	plus	Trust and miscellaneous account transactions[a]	8,932	5,195	3,737
L.	minus	Net effect of lines C, D, E, and F	0	−410	410
M.	plus	Net effects of line G	35	10	25
N.	minus	Internal transactions[f]	−2,840	−2,840	0
P.	equals	Cash operating income and outgo	71,345	76,562	−5,217

[a] Before expenditures on investments in government securities.

[b] Includes adjusted service bonds (and in earlier years excess profits tax refund bonds).

[c] Excess of issues of special United States notes over redemptions.

[d] For outstanding checks, etc.

[e] Includes repayment of capital stock and paid-in surplus by corporations not wholly owned and net redemptions minus issues in the market of government agency securities.

[f] Interest on government obligations held in government accounts	1,275
Reimbursements of general fund for trust account administrative expenses	66
Budget expenditures for transfers to trust accounts	1,079
Payroll deductions for government employees' retirement	420
Total	2,840

SOURCE: This reconciliation is based on *Treasury Bulletin* for August 1953, pp. 12–13.

EXHIBIT C

Relations between Cash Income and Outgo and National Income and Product Accounts
Receipts and Expenditures, Fiscal Year 1951
(billions of dollars)

I. SURPLUS AND DEFICIT RELATIONSHIP

A.		Net cash operating income	−5.2
B.	plus	Net portfolio acquisitions counted as net outgo	1.0
C.	plus	Net other financial transactions counted as net outgo	−0.6
D.	minus	Excess of subsidies minus enterprise current surplus over enterprise transactions counted as net outgo	−0.3
E.	plus	Excess of tax accruals over cash income	0.3
F.	plus	Excess of social insurance contribution accruals over cash income	0.1
G.	plus	Decrement in net payables	1.0
H.	minus	Excess of interest accruals over payments	−0.7
J.	plus	Other timing difference adjustments[a]	0.1
K.	plus	Other adjustments, net	[b]
L.	equals	Net NIP Accounts surplus	−4.4

II. INCOME-RECEIPT AND OUTGO-EXPENDITURE RELATIONSHIPS

			Sources	*Uses*	*Net Sources*
M.		Cash income and outgo	71.3	76.6	−5.2
N.	plus	Positive adjustments above	0.5	1.6⎫	0.9
P.	minus	Negative adjustments above	−1.1	−3.1⎭	
Q.	minus	District of Columbia transactions	−0.1	−0.1	[b]
R.	minus	Existing asset transactions	−0.1	−0.1	[b]
S.	plus	Netting adjustment[c]	0.8	0.8	0.0
T.	equals	NIP Account receipts and expenditures	71.3	75.6	−4.4

[a] Includes redemptions minus issues of armed force leave bonds, adjusted service bonds, and excess profits tax refund bonds.

[b] Lies between ± $50 million.

[c] Government and government employees' contributions to retirement funds.

Details may not add to totals because of rounding.

Source: This reconciliation is based on Marilyn Young, "Three Federal Budgets: A Reconciliation," (Studies in Income and Wealth, Vol. 20).

EXHIBIT D

Relations between Cash Income and Outgo and Flow of Funds
Financial Transactions, Calendar Year 1947
(billions of dollars)

		I. SURPLUS AND DEFICIT RELATIONSHIP			
A.		Net cash operating income			5.7
B.	plus	Net portfolio acquisitions counted as net outgo			4.8
C.	plus	Other financial transactions counted as net outgo			0.5
D.	plus	Decrement in net payables[a]			0.7
E.	minus	Excess of interest accruals over interest payments			−0.5
F.	minus	Excess of issues of armed force leave bonds, etc. over redemptions[b]			−0.2
G.	minus	Other timing difference adjustments			−0.1
H.	equals	Net nonfinancial receipts			10.8

		II. INCOME-RECEIPT AND OUTGO-EXPENDITURE RELATIONSHIPS	Sources	Uses	Net Sources
J.		Cash income and outgo	44.3	38.6	5.7
K.	plus	Positive adjustments above	0.2	0.3	5.2
L.	minus	Negative adjustments above	−0.5	−5.8	
M.	minus	District of Columbia transactions	−0.1	−0.1	0.0
N.	plus	Netting of nonfinancial sources and uses on line J[c]	8.6	8.6	0.0
P.	equals	Nonfinancial sources and uses	52.5	41.7	10.8

[a] Is net of receipts of counterpart funds (and in earlier years reverse lend-lease).
[b] Includes adjusted service bonds and excess profits tax refund bonds.
[c] Nonfinancial receipts of government corporations and agencies netted

against expenditures	5.7
Tax refunds netted against tax receipts	2.6
Government employee contributions to retirement funds	0.2
Timing adjustment not included in I	0.1
Total	8.6

Details may not add to totals because of rounding.
SOURCE: This reconciliation is based on Tables 18 and 19 in Federal Reserve *Flow of Funds* study.

CHAPTER III

A Further Historical Review

In Chapter II we argued that the growth of government debts cannot be adequately understood by considering solely the particular expenditures which have been said to occasion particular debt issues; that it is necessary to take account of the time pattern of total nonfinancial expenditures and of the considerations which may make against matching this with a closely similar time pattern of total nonfinancial receipts.

It should contribute to an understanding of government financial requirements, therefore, to consider in somewhat greater detail the course of government expenditures, receipts, and deficits, and the growth of government functions during recent decades. But of course such a survey can be expected to turn up facts that are irrelevant to our present purpose as well as relevant ones.

Let us take first the fiscal operations of the federal government.

1. *Federal Receipts, Expenditures, and Deficits*

Table 5 shows the course of federal nonfinancial receipts, expenditures, and deficits since 1890. The low level of receipts in the mid-1890's and the 1908 decline reflect depressed business conditions. The decline in 1902 followed repeal of war emergency taxes; in that of 1915 the reduced collections of customs duties under the Underwood Tariff Act, 1913, were a major factor. The table makes clear the small effect of the Spanish-American War on expenditures and the promptness of the increase in revenues. To bring out another fiscal aspect of this war would require a more detailed table—military expenditures in subsequent years never receded to the prewar level. Capital outlays on the Panama Canal during 1904 and the succeeding decade helped to raise the level of total expenditures during these years.

During the quarter-century before World War I federal nonfinancial uses of funds showed a strongly upward trend; the annual average in 1904–13 was some 90 per cent above that for 1889–98. This increase reflected mainly a growth in federal employment; total civilian employment increased nearly 140 per cent from 1896 to 1911, the armed forces

TABLE 5

Federal Government Nonfinancial Receipts, Expenditures, and Deficits, 1890–1954
(billions of dollars)

Fiscal Year	Receipts	Expenditures	Deficit	Calendar Year	Receipts	Expenditures	Deficit
1890	.46	.38	−.08	1929	4.95	3.70	−1.25
1891	.46	.44	−.02				
1892	.42	.40	−.02	1930	4.80	3.80	−1.00
1893	.46	.46	a	1931	3.55	5.05	1.50
1894	.38	.44	.06	1932	2.70	4.10	1.40
				1933	3.05	5.05	2.00
1895	.40	.42	.02	1934	4.15	7.60	3.45
1896	.42	.44	.02				
1897	.44	.44	a	1935	4.65	7.60	2.95
1898	.50	.54	.04	1936	5.60	10.40	4.80
1899	.62	.70	.08	1937	8.20	8.20	b
				1938	8.30	9.50	1.20
1900	.66	.62	−.04	1939	7.80	10.25	2.45
1901	.70	.64	−.06				
1902	.68	.60	−.08	1940	8.60	10.80	2.20
1903	.70	.66	−.04	1941	12.50	22.20	9.70
1904	.68	.72	.04	1942	23.70	64.50	40.80
				1943	46.00	98.90	52.90
1905	.70	.72	.02	1944	58.20	109.00	50.80
1906	.76	.74	−.02				
1907	.84	.76	−.08	1945	59.00	95.80	36.80
1908	.80	.86	.06	1946	54.60	49.60	−5.00
1909	.82	.90	.08	1947	52.50	41.70	−10.80
				1948	51.30	41.40	−9.90
1910	.90	.92	.02	1949	49.00	48.50	−.50
1911	.94	.92	−.02				
1912	.94	.94	a	1950	49.10	49.40	.30
1913	.98	.98	a	1951	66.10	65.40	−.70
1914	1.02	1.02	a	1952	78.80	79.10	.30
				1953	78.40	85.10	6.70
1915	.98	1.04	.06	1954	77.60	79.90	2.30
1916	1.08	1.04	−.04				
1917	1.44	2.24	.80				
1918	4.00	12.68	8.68				
1919	5.50	18.38	12.88				
1920	7.12	6.74	−.38				
1921	6.08	5.10	−.98				
1922	4.46	3.86	−.60				
1923	4.44	3.82	−.62				
1924	4.58	3.62	−.96				
1925	4.32	3.68	−.64				
1926	4.60	3.60	−1.00				
1927	4.80	3.66	−1.14				
1928	4.68	3.80	−.88				
1929	4.72	3.88	−.84				

a Less than $10 million.
b Less than $50 million.
SOURCE: See Appendix A.

TABLE 6

A Comparison of Federal Nonfinancial Expenditures to Gross National Product

Annual Average of GNP	Ratio of Total Nonfinancial Federal Expenditures to Col. 1	Ratio of Federal GNP Expenditures to Col. 1	Ratio of Transfer-type Federal Expenditures to Col. 1	Ratio of International Aid to Col. 1	Ratio of Federal Enterprise Payrolls to Col. 1
(billions of dollars)	(per cent)	(per cent)	(per cent)	(per cent)	(per cent)
(1)	(2)	(3)	(4)	(5)	(6)
	KUZNETS ESTIMATES				
1889–98 12.73	3.4[a]				
1894–1903 15.71	3.5[a]				
1899–1908 21.58	3.3[a]				
1904–13 28.78	2.9[a]				
1909–18 40.12	5.8[a]				
1914–23 61.90	9.0[a]				
1919–28 81.20	6.8[a]				
1924–33 79.13	5.1[b]				
1929–38 69.95	9.3				
	COMMERCE DEPARTMENT				
1929–38 77.9	8.4				
1930–39 76.7	9.3	4.2	3.9	[c]	0.77
1940–45 168.8	39.2	21.6	3.2	3.6	0.53
1946–49 240.4	18.3	8.7	6.1	1.5	0.59
1950–51 306.7	18.2	10.3	5.4	1.5	0.48

[a] Average of ten fiscal years.

[b] Based on one-half fiscal year 1924 + fiscal year 1925 through 1928 + one-half fiscal year 1929 + calendar year 1929 through 1933.

[c] Negligible.

NOTE: Columns 3 and 6, and column 4 except for one component, are based upon Department of Commerce national income and product estimates. They do not include wartime subsidies. Transfer-type expenditures include grants-in-aid to state and local governments, transfer payments, interest, and farm benefits (this last from *Agricultural Statistics*). Column 5 covers aid not including loans, as shown in the balance of international payments statement.

by 260 per cent.[1] Nonetheless, while federal functions were expanded during the years 1889–1913, the rest of the economy was growing more rapidly; the ratio of federal expenditures to GNP was declining. See Table 6.

World War I had relatively little influence on federal expenditures

[1] Solomon Fabricant, *The Trend of Government Activity in the United States since 1900*, p. 182. No average figure for 1889–98 is available. Nonfinancial expenditures increased approximately 110 per cent, 1896 to 1911. It may be noted that price increases were a factor also. Albert Rees's cost of living index averaged 93.3 during 1904–13 and 87.1 during 1890–98. See Thirty-eighth Annual Report of the National Bureau of Economic Research, May 1958, p. 59.

until we entered it. But from fiscal 1916 to fiscal 1919 there was a seventeen-fold increase in expenditures.[2] Receipts were increased much more slowly—with the war debt as a result.

The war brought a sharp increase in the ratio of federal expenditures to GNP. Then something like the earlier postwar pattern repeated itself. The ratio declined. However, civilian employment reached a new high peacetime level in the decade 1924–33, some 67 per cent above that of 1904-13, reflecting mainly a substantial growth in civil functions.[3] But while the armed forces receded from their wartime level, they remained well above prewar strength; the 1924–33 average exceeded that of 1904–13 by approximately 100 per cent.[4] Further, the comparison of these two decades shows a reversal of the earlier downward trend in the ratio of federal ordinary expenditures to GNP—it was 5.1 per cent in the postwar decade, 2.9 per cent in the prewar. Still, the shorter-term movement seems to have been downward during the 1920's; the ratio was 4.4 per cent in 1923,[5] 3.6 per cent in 1929.

A lag in the adjustment of tax rates to expenditures was obvious during the war; it appeared also, though less markedly, during the 1920's. Both the idea of a "return to normalcy" and depression psychology played a part in bringing about tax cuts in 1921. A number of excises that had been levied as war emergency measures were repealed; most other tax rates were revised substantially downward. Budget surpluses encouraged milder additional downward tax revisions in 1924, in 1926, and again in 1928. But all these revisions served only to check the growth of tax yields that resulted from the expansion of business activity. Notwithstanding the revisions there were eleven years of surpluses which reduced the net debt by nearly $10 billion.

Even in calendar 1930, despite the sharp business recession in process there was a surplus; there was no marked effect of the recession on tax collections until 1931.[6] In that year in addition to the decline in receipts there was a significant countercyclical increase in expenditures, chiefly but not entirely in the form of adjusted service certificate payments. Revenues declined further in 1932 while expenditures were roughly 10 per cent above the predepression level. Somewhat larger countercyclical

[2] The table counts loans to our allies as nonfinancial expenditures. In the wisdom of hindsight it seems proper to treat these "loans" as grants-in-aid.

[3] Fabricant, *loc.cit.* The comparable increase for total defense employment including civilians was 93 per cent. *Ibid.*, pp. 186–87.

[4] *Ibid.*

[5] The average of two fiscal year figures is used in the numerator of this computation.

[6] No doubt the fact that the tax base for both the individual and the corporate income tax was the previous year's income was a major factor in the lag in the adjustment of tax collections at the start of the recession, and in the lag during World War I as well.

expenditures during the next four years—including the bonus in 1936—brought large deficits, although these increased expenditures were partially offset by several cyclically perverse tax increases. In 1937 nonfinancial receipts substantially balanced nonfinancial expenditures. Then with renewed increases in countercyclical expenditures in 1938 and 1939 there were deficits again in these two years.

With the coming of the great depression the ratio of federal expenditures to GNP had again markedly increased. The lower portion of Table 6 indicates the importance of two major components of federal nonfinancial expenditures: those for purchases of GNP and transfer-type items (interest, grants-in-aid to state and local governments, farm benefits, and what the Commerce Department calls "transfer payments").[7] A good deal of the depression increase recorded in column 2 can be attributed to transfer-type items. Interest had accounted for most such expenditures during the 1920's. Of the 3.9 per cent for 1930–39 it was only about one-fourth. Aids and benefits became important during the depression. Moreover, for some purposes work relief payrolls might well be grouped with these transfer-type items. If they were, the entry in column 4 would be increased from 3.9 per cent to 5.1 per cent.

If we take the 1939 figures in Table 5 as an approximate prewar base and subtract them from the figures for each of the immediately following years the additional expenditures attributable to World War II, 1940–45, may be roughly estimated at $335 billion, the additional revenues at $158 billion. This indicates that some 46 per cent of the war expenditures was financed out of current receipts, the rest by borrowing. We may compare these computations with similar ones for World War I, in which fiscal 1916 is taken as a base. The total step-up in expenditures in 1917–19 was $30.3 billion. In receipts it was $7.8 billion, or about 26 per cent of that in expenditures. Despite the roughness of this computation it seems fair to conclude that there was proportionately a good deal less deficit financing during World War II. The absolute increase in net debt was of course much greater. No doubt, the shifting of the individual income tax to a pay-as-you-go basis in mid-1943 had helped to speed up the increase in tax collections, but there is no reason to suppose the lag in the increase of receipts behind expenditures would have been fully eliminated had this shift been made three years earlier.

The rise in the ratio of total nonfinancial federal expenditures to GNP during World War II needs no comment. However, it may be interesting

[7] Note that the GNP base used in this portion of the table is grosser than that in the upper part. Among the components of nonfinancial expenditures, other than those indicated in columns 3 and 4, are enterprise payrolls, enterprise current procurement, and—particularly during the 1940's—cash subsidies other than farm benefits and purchases of goods offset against sales of surplus property.

to compare this ratio for 1918 and 1944. It was 18.7 per cent in the former year, 51.3 per cent in the latter.[8]

Another war comparison is suggested by Table 5. Expenditures in 1947 were nearly four times those in 1939. Expenditures in 1922 were about three and a half times those in 1916. A part of both these increases is attributable to prices, and a part to growth of the economy. But in each case much of the increase represents a higher level of expenditures after the war than before it. Bigger veterans' programs and more interest charges were factors in this higher level. But in this case the enlarged military establishment was a more important factor than after World War I. The average size of the armed forces during 1946–49 was more than 700 per cent above that during the decade 1924–33. And while average federal civilian employment during these four years was some 300 per cent above that in 1924–33, the higher level of civilian employment reflected in part the growth of the military establishment—defense agencies accounted for more than 40 per cent of civilian employment in 1949.[9]

The expenditure figures in Table 5 can be used in combination with data on the payrolls of the armed forces and on international aid to provide still another comparison, a comparison of the ratio of war costs other than aid and armed forces payroll. This provides a measure of an important sense in which the second world war was more expensive than the first. The ratio increased from 3.8 to 4.4. Presumably the increase reflects in part a general upward trend in cost; but apparently, too, war cost in the sense here measured increases with the scale of the war effort. The corresponding ratio for the Korean War was 1.8.[10]

For the last three periods covered by Table 6 the ratio of federal international aid to GNP is shown. The Commerce Department counts such aid as a federal GNP expenditure. Column 5 therefore reports a component of column 3; in all three periods it is a substantial component. Comparable figures for 1917–20 are not available, but with the still uncollected loans made during these years counted as cash grants the ratio of international aid to total nonfinancial expenditures was

[8] The figures used in the denominators of these ratios are the estimates prepared by Simon Kuznets for the series of monographs of which this is one. The denominator for 1918 is the average of two calendar year figures, the numerator is a fiscal year figure.

[9] *1950 Handbook of Labor Statistics*, p. 27.

[10] For the payroll figures see W. I. King, *The National Income and Its Purchasing Power*, p. 364, and the National Income and Product Accounts. For the figures on military grants during World War II and the Korean War see *International Transactions of the United States during the War, 1940–1945*, p. 218, and 1955 *Statistical Abstract*, p. 890. World War I grants were assumed to be $9.6 billion. See Table 49. The numerator of the ratio was taken to be the increment above the base year rate in the total expenditure during the war period other than expenditure for military payroll minus the amount of aid. The denominator was taken to be total payroll of the armed forces during the war period. The base years were 1916, 1939, and 1949; the war periods 1917–21, 1940–44, and 1950–54.

undoubtedly substantially higher in 1917–20 than in 1940–45—that is, more of our participation in World War I took this form.

In 1949 and 1950 total nonfinancial expenditures stepped up sharply, reflecting another augmentation of the military program and to a lesser extent enlarged international aid in 1949[11] and a special veterans' life insurance dividend in 1950. But in these two years taken together there was a slight nonfinancial surplus. There was also a slight surplus in 1951. Between 1950 and 1953 total nonfinancial expenditures increased more than 70 per cent, chiefly as a result of expanded national security programs (including the carrying on of the Korean War). Decreased war and other national security expenditures made possible a drop of over $5 billion in nonfinancial expenditures during the next calendar year. Indeed, the drop would have been substantially larger were it not for the fact that social insurance benefits, state withdrawals from the Unemployment Compensation Fund, and tax refunds together increased by more than $2.5 billion from 1953 to 1954.

During the four years ending with 1952 the federal net debt decreased by about $600 million despite the Korean War. But in the next two years it increased by some $9 billion.

In Chapter II we distinguished the nonfinancial deficit shown in Table 5, the budget deficit, and two other federal deficit concepts. Table 7 gives a comparison of the budget and the nonfinancial computations that covers the entire period during which the factors responsible for the differences between them—chiefly cash surpluses of social insurance funds and changes in government credit—have been important.[12] Most of the time the deficits in column 1 have been smaller (or the surpluses larger) than those in column 2.

When the government extends credit—adds to its portfolio of loans and securities—the addition often counts as a budget expenditure; when it liquidates its portfolio, the liquidation may count as a budget receipt. Column 1 treats all portfolio additions and liquidations as financial transactions; that is, they do not affect the nonfinancial deficit. In an algebraic sense column 2 was larger than column 1, 1918–21, because of portfolio additions. The bulk of these were loans to railroads and War Finance Corporation loans. But the farm credit program which got under way in 1917 was also a factor. And in 1921 the government accepted over $100 million of securities in part payment for war surplus property.

---

[11] Loans to other governments after World War II, unlike those during and after World War I, are treated as loans in Table 5; that is, they are not nonfinancial expenditures.

[12] Strictly speaking there was no budget deficit concept for the earlier years of this table. The basis used in column 2 is the same as that used in *Historical Statistics*. See the note on surplus and deficit concepts appended to Chapter I for a discussion of the development of the budget concept.

TABLE 7

Comparison of the Federal Nonfinancial Deficit with the
Budget Deficit, 1917–54
(millions of dollars)

	Nonfinancial Deficit (1)	Budget Deficit (2)
Fiscal year		
1917	800	853
1918	8,680	9,032
1919	12,880	13,363
1920	−380	−291
1921	−980	−509
1922	−600	−736
1923	−620	−713
1924	−960	−963
1925	−640	−717
1926	−1,000	−865
1927	−1,140	−1,155
1928	−880	−939
1929	−840	−734
Calendar year		
1929	−1,250	−912
1930	−1,000	−409
1931	1,500	1,632
1932	1,400	2,899
1933	2,000	2,543
1934	3,450	4,064
1935	2,950	2,854
1936	5,000	4,206
1937	a	1,888
1938	1,200	2,670
1939	2,450	4,300
1940	2,200	3,934
1941	9,700	11,762
1942	40,800	41,461
1943	52,900	55,691
1944	50,800	53,650
1945	36,800	43,594
1946	−5,000	2,512
1947	−10,800	−2,434
1948	−9,900	−5,241
1949	−500	3,592
1950	300	422
1951	−700	3,358
1952	300	5,842
1953	6,700	9,157
1954	2,300	3,683

[a] Less than $50 million.
Figures in column 2 are on the same basis as those in *Historical Statistics*.

44

Sometimes the budget deficit has been the smaller of the two computations. This was true in 1923 and 1925 when the government credit that had been extended during 1918–21 was contracted.[13]

The sharper step-up in the budget deficit figure in 1932 reflects the Treasury's subscription of $500 million to the capital stock of the Reconstruction Finance Corporation plus nearly $500 million of loans to the RFC in that year. In 1937 social insurance funds' cash surpluses began to be a substantial factor making for a lower nonfinancial deficit. Surpluses of nearly $1.5 billion in that year help to explain why during 1936–37 the decrease in column 1 gives a better indication of the fiscal impact on the economy than does that in column 2.[14]

Throughout the 1940's the cash surpluses of the social insurance funds averaged nearly $3 billion annually. Hence much of the difference between the two deficit series during these years. But the spread widened toward the end of the decade, reaching a peak of over $8 billion in 1947. The greater width of the spread, 1946–49, was largely due to the portfolio transactions counted as budget expenditures, among them subscriptions of capital to the Export-Import Bank, the International Bank for Reconstruction and Development,[15] and the International Monetary Fund,[16] the British loan, lend-lease credits, credits to finance sales of surplus property overseas,[17] and European Recovery Program credits.

2. State and Local Government Receipts, Expenditures, and Deficits

Table 8 gives nonfinancial sources and uses of state and local government funds beginning in 1910. During the first three or four years of the period covered deficits were small. Judging from Table 1 they must have averaged around $100 million per year between 1890 and 1913. But they show an upward trend from 1910 to the early 1920's. During the three years 1914–16 less than one-eleventh of the expenditures were deficit financed; during 1921–23 nearly one-seventh. The heavier deficits in the early 1920's reflect the particularly rapid increase in expenditures during these years. The growth of receipts seems not to have been much checked by the postwar business recession. Although construction expenditures were low during World War I and stepped up sharply thereafter, they

[13] An increase in federal accounts payable works in the same direction. Thus in 1942, when there was a large increase in such payables, the excess of column 2 over column 1 was substantially reduced.

[14] Column 1 gives a better indication in part also because column 2, reflecting the effect of a technical accounting procedure on the timing of expenditures, shows the payment of a part of the 1936 veterans' bonus as if it had been made in calendar 1937.

[15] A part of these two subscriptions was carried as a trust account expenditure.

[16] See footnote 14.

[17] Such sales were not counted as budget receipts when the sales were made.

TABLE 8

State and Local Government Nonfinancial Receipts,
Expenditures, and Net Deficit, 1910–54
(millions of dollars)

Year	Receipts	Expenditures	Deficit
	THREE-YEAR MOVING AVERAGES		
1910	1,950	2,000	50
1911	2,100	2,200	100
1912	2,200	2,300	100
1913	2,300	2,450	150
1914	2,350	2,600	250
1915	2,450	2,750	300
1916	2,600	2,750	150
1917	2,800	3,000	200
1918	3,000	3,250	250
1919	3,450	3,750	300
1920	4,000	4,600	600
1921	4,700	5,450	750
1922	5,250	6,100	850
1923	5,750	6,550	800
1924	6,250	7,050	800
1925	6,850	7,550	700
1926	7,500	8,100	600
1927	8,100	8,600	500
1928	8,550	8,900	350
	YEARLY FIGURES		
1929	8,850	8,950	100
1930	9,150	9,700	550
1931	9,100	9,800	700
1932	8,650	8,900	250
1933	8,550	8,700	150
1934	10,050	9,750	−300
1935	10,600	10,250	−350
1936	10,000	9,900	−100
1937	11,200	11,100	−100
1938	12,500	12,400	−100
1939	13,100	13,000	−100
1940	13,900	13,500	−400
1941	14,700	13,500	−1,200
1942	15,500	13,800	−1,700
1943	15,900	13,500	−2,400
1944	16,500	13,900	−2,600
1945	17,400	14,900	−2,500
1946	19,800	17,900	−1,900
1947	22,700	22,000	−700
1948	25,900	26,300	400
1949	29,400	30,400	1,000
1950	31,900	33,500	1,600
1951	34,700	35,600	900
1952	37,500	37,900	400
1953	40,000	40,400	400
1954	43,000	44,400	1,400

SOURCE: See Appendix A.

appear to have contributed only a small part of the total expenditure increase.

One reason for the larger recourse to borrowing during 1909–29 than in the 1890's is suggested by Table 9. State and local expenditures were growing more rapidly than gross national product. However, this explanation is subject to a possible qualification. A large part of the borrowing

TABLE 9

A Comparison of State and Local Government Nonfinancial
Expenditures to Gross National Product

	Annual Average of GNP (billions of dollars) (1)	Ratio of Total Nonfinancial State and Local Expenditures to Col. 1 (per cent) (2)	Ratio of State and Local GNP Expenditures to Col. 1 (per cent) (3)	Ratio of Transfer-type State and Local Expenditures to Col. 1 (per cent) (4)	Ratio of State and Local Enterprise Payrolls to Col. 1 (per cent) (5)
		KUZNETS ESTIMATES			
1890	12.4	4.6[a]			
1909–18	40.12	6.3			
1914–23	61.90	6.6			
1919–28	81.20	8.2			
1924–33	79.13	10.9			
1929–38	69.95	14.2			
		COMMERCE DEPARTMENT ESTIMATES			
1929–38	77.9	12.7			
1930–39	76.7	13.5	9.2	2.1	0.23
1940–45	168.8	8.2	4.6	1.1	0.18
1946–48	234.5	9.6	5.5	1.2	0.20
1949–50	270.0	11.6	7.0	1.4	0.22

[a] The state and local expenditure figure used in computing this percentage is the total shown in the Census.

NOTE: Columns 3, 4, and 5 are based on Department of Commerce income and product estimates. Transfer-type expenditures include transfer payments plus gross interest.

was by urban communities and took place during the 1920's, when the percentage of national income originating in industries other than agriculture was significantly larger than during 1890–1919.[18]

A striking feature of Table 8 is that there is no clear evidence of cyclical variation in receipts prior to 1931. This may well be due in part to inadequacies in the figures,[19] but property taxes which are somewhat

[18] See *Historical Statistics*, A-145. Martin's estimates indicate an increase from about 83.5 per cent to more than 87 per cent.

[19] This statement holds for the annual figures as well as the three-year moving averages. Especially prior to 1929—but to some extent after 1929 also—the basic compilations used in arriving at the annual figures are totals of data for individual units of government that refer to different fiscal years. See note on Table 8 in Appendix A.

inflexible cyclically accounted for more than 60 per cent of receipts in 1913 and rather more than half of them in 1932. (See Table 13 below.)

The recession years 1930–31 saw a sharp increase in expenditures; there were large deficits in these two years. But expenditures were contracted more rapidly than receipts during 1932–33. And in 1934 the increase in receipts was sufficient to produce a surplus despite additional —and in part depression connected—expenditures. A major factor in this improved financial showing was federal aid. It was $0.5 billion in 1933; over $1.6 billion in 1934.[20] Higher taxes played a relatively small part; but the ratio of property taxes to assessments in large cities did increase from 26 mills in 1933 to nearly 30 in 1934.[21] Notwithstanding year-to-year variations in expenditures there were, beginning in 1934, surpluses throughout the rest of the decade.

While the contraction in expenditures in 1932–33 exerted a cyclically perverse effect, it was not a very large one. And against this contraction might be set the fact that the level of state and local expenditures was substantially higher in the decade 1929–38 than in the preceding decade. Moreover, the ratio of these expenditures to gross national product rose substantially. It is reasonable to infer from Table 9 that this ratio during the 1930's was significantly above trend.

During the six years 1939–44 total expenditures were somewhat stable. Costs rose, employment declined slightly, and expenditures on construction and on various equipment items were sharply curtailed. The ratio of total expenditures to gross national product dropped back at least to the level it had reached in the 1920's. At the same time tax yields as well as enterprise revenues and receipts from service charges grew, while total federal aid was not greatly diminished. All nonfinancial receipts were some 26 per cent higher in 1944 than in 1939. Hence the large wartime surpluses.

The sharp step-up in expenditures after World War II, much sharper than that after World War I, began during 1945. By 1954 expenditures were nearly 3.3 times the 1939–44 average. New construction accounted for almost a quarter of this increase, but nearly every significant type of expenditure contributed to it. However, despite the size of the increase the ratio of total state and local expenditures to gross national product was lower in 1954 than it had been during the 1930's. Despite the sharpness of the increase, too, there were surpluses in 1946 and 1947, and the percentage of total expenditures that was deficit financed was markedly lower in 1949–54 than in the early 1920's. Increases in enterprise revenues and receipts from service charges as well as in tax yields contributed to a growth in total receipts that kept the deficit financing percentage below

[20] National Income and Product Account figures.
[21] *Historical Statistics*, P-251 and P-262.

3 per cent. Federal aid also contributed to the growth in receipts; it was about $1 billion in 1944, $4.9 billion in 1954.[22]

The contrast between the growth of debt during and after World War I and that during and after World War II is marked. At the end of 1929 the net indebtedness of state and local governments was approximately $11 billion; at the end of 1954 only $8 billion, despite the vastly higher level of expenditures in the years preceding this latter date. To some extent this contrast results from the surpluses during World War II. Participation of our economy in World War I was neither sufficiently extensive nor sufficiently prolonged to yield comparable surpluses. The rest of the contrast is due to the more rapid growth of net debt after World War I—by $6.5 billion in the eleven years ending 1929, by $3.5 billion in the nine years ending 1954. We think the relatively small amount of net borrowing after World War II, despite the sharpness of the expenditure step-up, reflects in part the fact that the ratio of expenditures to GNP continued even up to 1954 to be lower than it had been in the 1930's. Hence a close approach to pay-as-you-go financing was not too difficult, so far as tax and service charge increases were concerned. But the larger volume of federal aid was a factor, too. We will give this point further attention in Chapters IV and V.

3. *Trends in Receipts, Expenditures, and Employment*

Thus far we have been mainly concerned with year-to-year changes in the sources and uses of government funds, and our analysis has emphasized aggregate nonfinancial sources and uses and annual deficits. It seems advisable, too, to consider the longer-term changes that have been taking place in recent decades, giving particular attention to the composition of total nonfinancial receipts and expenditures and supplementing our expenditure analysis with an analysis of government employment.

As before let us take the federal government first.

Table 10 analyzes longer-term changes in federal nonfinancial receipts. The principal tax sources in 1890 were customs duties and liquor and tobacco excises; postal revenues accounted for a little more than an eighth of nonfinancial receipts. Customs reached a peak in 1927 that has not quite been equaled since. While liquor and tobacco taxes increased more than tenfold in 1916–50, they have grown much less rapidly than total receipts.[23] And while postal revenues kept pace with other sources of funds in 1890–1929, they have not done so since. In 1950 they were less than 4 per cent of the total.

Corporate and personal income and estate and gift taxes were relatively unimportant in 1916. The Payne-Aldrich Act (1909) had established

[22] Including Unemployment Compensation Fund withdrawals.
[23] Liquor tax collections were of course negligible in 1921–32.

TABLE 10

Federal Nonfinancial Receipts, Selected Years, 1890–1950
(millions of dollars)

		1890	1916	1929	1940	1950
A.	Customs duties	230	213	600	330	550
B.	Personal income taxes	0	68	1,240	1,040	18,500
C.	Estate and gift taxes	0	0	60	340	650
D.	Corporate income and capital stock taxes	0	57	1,250	1,400	9,900
E.	Liquor and tobacco taxes	142	335	460	1,370	3,750
F.	Taxes on petroleum products, automotive vehicles and parts	0	0	0	430	1,550
G.	Miscellaneous taxes, fees, and fines	16	70	110	320	3,025
H.	Social insurance taxes	0	0	0	880	3,425
J.	State payments into Unemployment Compensation Fund	0	0	0	860	1,225
K.	Insurance premiums	0	1	95	180	1,025
L.	Interest and dividends	a	1	300	400	525
M.	Postal revenues	61	312	695	760	1,725
N.	All other, including property sales, and miscellaneous enterprise receipts	11	23	140	290	3,250
P.	Total nonfinancial receipts	460	1,080	4,950	8,600	49,100

a Included with "All other" receipts.

NOTE: Figures for 1890 and 1916 refer to fiscal years; those for 1929, 1940, and 1950 to calendar years. They are based on Treasury *Annual Reports*. "Insurance premiums" include government life insurance premiums, federal civilian employee retirement contributions, and guaranty and insurance premium receipts of government corporations and business-type activities. The "Interest and dividends" item is net of interfund interest receipts on federal obligations.

the corporate tax; the Underwood Act, passed shortly after the ratification of the 16th Amendment in 1913, inaugurated the individual income tax; the inheritance tax did not apply until 1917.[24] But in 1929 these taxes accounted for more than 50 per cent of total nonfinancial receipts; in 1950 for nearly 60 per cent. Although personal incomes taxes decreased in 1929–40 and corporate tax collections grew by only 15 per cent, the yield of estate and gift taxes increased nearly sixfold in this period.

Social insurance premiums paid by veterans and civilian employees amounted to only $95 million in 1929. Such premiums together with payroll taxes and state contributions into the Unemployment Compensation Fund in 1940 totaled about $1.9 billion—the general federal social insurance program had gotten under way in 1937; in 1950 some $5.7 billion of nonfinancial receipts came from these sources.

Miscellaneous excise taxes were an important revenue source after the

[24] An individual income tax levied in 1894 was held unconstitutional. An inheritance tax was levied in 1898 as an emergency measure.

Spanish-American War and during World War I. This source was tapped again during the 1930's and World War II. In 1950 it (lines F and G) yielded more revenue than customs duties and liquor and tobacco taxes combined. The two largest components of the $3,025 million recorded on line G—transportation and telephone taxes—accounted for about 40 per cent of this amount.

It is difficult to present a detailed analysis of total nonfinancial federal expenditures on a comparable basis for a sixty-year span. It is offered here in two stages in Tables 11A and 11B. In 1890 apart from the Post Office the large items were veterans' programs, the military establishment, and interest. These three categories of expenditure—all three may be characterized as war-connected—accounted for 58 per cent of the total in that year. Between 1890 and 1916 their proportionate importance decreased; but World War I substantially restored it. They were responsible for 55 per cent of all nonfinancial expenditures in 1929. Table 11B shows a similar sequence, if we include international aid. The ratio of the total of lines A, B, C, and E to line P is 52 per cent in 1929, 35 per cent in 1940, and 54 per cent in 1950.

In a general way we may think of lines F, G, H, and K in Table 11A as reflecting long-established nonwar types of governmental activities. These items represented nearly 8 per cent of all expenditures in 1890; only about 3.5 per cent in 1929. The civilian nondefense payroll figures in Table 11B cover a somewhat wider range of activities; but they indicate that the declining relative importance of the older activities continued in 1929–50. The ratio of line M to line P drops from 10.5 per cent to 5 per cent. One long-established function not included in these ratio comparisons is the Post Office. The postal expenditures ratio increased from 18 per cent in 1890 to 30 per cent in 1916. But by 1950 it too had declined to less than 5 per cent.

The larger programs reflected in line D of Table 11A are: rivers and harbors, the Panama Canal (especially in 1916), public roads grants-in-aid, and aid to the merchant marine (the last two of these became important during the 1920's). Public roads grants represent five-sixths of the $0.12 billion shown on line J of Table 11B. While such grants were larger in 1940 and still larger in 1950, they were only a fraction of all grants in these years. The Social Security Act (1935) inaugurated programs that currently account for well over half of aid and transfers. The figures on line J include withdrawals from the Unemployment Compensation Fund. Grants-in-aid proper, exclusive of these withdrawals, totaled $0.86 billion in 1940—more than 40 per cent of the amount being for public assistance, public health, and employment security[25]—and $2.34 billion in 1950, over half of this

[25] Grants for administration of unemployment insurance and for employment exchanges.

for the social security programs. In 1940, too, depression emergency relief grants were still a substantial item. So were work relief wages (line F). The only social insurance benefits in 1929 were those paid out of the United States Life Insurance Fund and the civil service retirement funds. Of the $6.13 billion in 1950 over $3 billion came from the two veterans' life

TABLE 11A

Federal Nonfinancial Expenditures, Fiscal Years
1890, 1916, and 1929
(millions of dollars)

		1890	1916	1929
A.	War and Navy Departments and Coast Guard	57	294	719
B.	Interest on direct debt[a]	56	23	678
C.	Veterans' programs	110	161	742
D.	Programs for improving transportation	15	66	218
E.	Post Office	68	308	825
F.	Congress, Department of Justice, and courts	11	17	40
G.	State Department	2	6	13
H.	Collecting revenues	11	17	54
J.	Tax refunds	7	19	213
K.	Indian Affairs	7	18	34
L.	Agriculture Department	2	23	56
M.	Forestry and reclamation services and national parks	[b]	11	32
N.	Public buildings	5	18	51
P.	All other	29	59	205
Q.	Total nonfinancial expenditures	380	1,040	3,880

[a] Includes premium on purchase of bonds of $20.3 million in 1890 and $1.3 million in 1929.

[b] Less than half a million dollars.

NOTE: See last note to Table 11B.

insurance funds (mostly special dividends); $1.43 billion from the Unemployment Compensation Fund; and $1.29 billion from the Old Age and Railroad Retirement Funds.

The Department of Agriculture budget was a substantial one even in 1916. But it was a smaller percentage of the total in 1929 than in 1916, despite complaints about farm surpluses during the 1920's. It is not easy to summarize the agriculture programs since 1929. Farm benefit payments totaled some $4 billion during the eight years ending 1940. Commodity purchases were apparently a considerably smaller item during this period than such payments. But they were much larger in 1950.[26] Loan write-offs are not a nonfinancial expenditure, but they are part of the

[26] The Commodity Credit Corporation accounts for most, but not all, of such purchases. In 1950 its receipts from sales were about five-sixths of the cost of goods sold.

cost of the agriculture programs. In 1950 such write-offs by the Commodity Credit Corporation totaled only a little over half a million.

Nondefense construction and miscellaneous procurement, line N in Table 11B, includes the rivers and harbors and reclamation programs as well as public buildings. Total construction represents about 38 per cent

TABLE 11B

Federal Nonfinancial Expenditures, Calendar Years
1929, 1940, and 1950
(billions of dollars)

		1929	1940	1950
A.	International aid[a]	0.06	0.03	4.30
B.	Other national security	0.69	2.17	13.92
C.	Interest	0.69	1.09	4.37
D.	Social insurance benefits	0.04	0.84	6.13
E.	Transfer payments to veterans	0.54	0.50	4.28
F.	Work relief payrolls	0.00	1.58	0.00
G.	Farm benefits	0.00	0.72	0.28
H.	Commodity Credit Corporation, cost of goods sold	0.00	[b]	2.01
J.	State and local aid and transfers	0.12	1.38	3.50
K.	Tax refunds	0.20	0.10	2.13
L.	Post Office operating expense	0.79	0.82	2.28
M.	Civilian nondefense wages and salaries[c]	0.39	0.80	2.44
N.	All other[d]	0.24	0.77	3.76
P.	Total nonfinancial expenditures	3.70	10.80	49.40

[a] Does not include loans.
[b] Included with "All other."
[c] Does not include Post Office.
[d] Essentially procurement and construction, n.e.c.
NOTE: The reader may wish to compare this table with the rather more detailed functional classification of federal expenditures Fabricant presents for six selected years, *op.cit.*, Table 16. We have attempted to analyze total nonfinancial expenditures here. In fiscal 1949 the total of such expenditures was approximately $45 billion (average of two calendar year figures in Table 5 above); the expenditure total for that year in Fabricant's table is $35.96 billion.

of this item in 1950: conservation and development construction about 23 per cent.[27]

In 1913 federal payrolls were about 45 per cent of total nonfinancial expenditures; in 1950 they were just under 25 per cent.[28] Table 12 shows the growth of federal employment since 1900. The legislative and judicial branches of the government accounted for 1.3 per cent of all federal employees in 1900, only a little over 0.3 per cent in 1950. The military establishment represented 53 per cent of the total in the former years,

[27] New construction only.
[28] See Fabricant, *op.cit.*, for the 1913 estimate of payrolls. For 1950 see *Flow of Funds in the United States, 1939–1953*, Table 17.

67.5 per cent in the latter. The ratio of civilians in the establishment to the armed forces increased from 1:3.1 to 1:2.1 during the half-century. What may be called the executive civil service proper, line E, was about the same proportion of the total in 1950 as in 1900, 17 per cent. The enterprise employment proportion declined from 28 per cent in 1900 to 15 per cent in 1950.

TABLE 12

Federal Employment at Selected Dates, 1900–50
(thousands of persons)

		1900	1910	1920	1930	1940	1950
A.	Legislative and judicial	4	6	6	6	8	12
B.	Armed forces	126	140	344	261	549	1,694
C.	Civil national defense	40	58	237	116	276	798
D.	Enterprises	89	163	195	300	385	560
E.	Other civil	53	117	175	198	369	628
F.	Total	312	484	957	881	1,587	3,692

NOTE: These figures are on a full-time equivalent basis. They exclude work-relief employees and, beginning 1930, civil employees stationed abroad. Line D, 1900–20, covers only postal employees.

Table 13 analyzes longer-term changes in the nonfinancial receipts of state and local governments. In 1890 property taxes accounted for some 90 per cent of all local taxes and for 70 per cent of state taxes. Four-fifths of all nonfederal taxes went to local governments. None of the present main nontax sources of current receipts was of much consequence. By 1939 state taxes had become more important than local taxes. One factor that helped to bring this change about was the establishment of un-employment insurance; this meant state payroll taxes. Another factor was the growth of state aid; to some extent states collected taxes so local governments could spend. Larger state taxes do not imply larger state employment. There were somewhat more than twice as many local as state nonschool employees in 1950.

State property taxes increased gradually in 1890–1950, but the ratio of these to total state taxes has steadily declined. By 1913 this ratio was hovering around the 50 per cent mark. States were taxing various things including mortgages and securities, banks and insurance companies, railroads and utilities. And they were beginning to levy motor vehicle and operator's license taxes and income and inheritance taxes. Gasoline taxes came a few years later. In 1932 taxes on motor vehicle fuel sales were the largest single source of state tax receipts; and vehicle and operator licenses yielded more than state property taxes. In 1942 payroll taxes represented 23 per cent of the $5.03 billion total. Motor fuel taxes were the second

54

largest item. But general sales and receipts taxes had come to be a very substantial source of tax receipts. These and income taxes each accounted for about one-eighth of the $5.03 billion. The yield of taxes on alcoholic

TABLE 13

State and Local Government Nonfinancial Receipts,
Selected Years, 1890–1950
(billions of dollars)

		1890	1913	1932	1942	1950
A.	State property taxes	0.07	0.14	0.32	0.27	0.31
B.	State sales and gross receipts taxes	a	a	0.55	2.22	4.67
C.	State unemployment compensation taxes	0.00	0.00	0.00	1.16	1.23
D.	State income taxes	0.00	b	0.12	0.62	1.61
E.	Other state taxes	0.03	0.16	0.85	0.76	1.12
F.	Total state taxes	0.10	0.30	1.84	5.03	8.94
G.	Local property taxes	0.37	1.28	4.25	4.28	7.07
H.	Other local taxes	0.03	0.15	0.11	0.41	0.48
J.	Total local taxes	0.40	1.43	4.36	4.69	7.55
K.	Total tax receipts, state and local	0.50	1.73	6.20	9.72	16.49
L.	Federal aid to state and local governments plus withdrawals from Unemployment Compensation Fund	c	0.01	0.13	1.23d	3.71d
M.	State aid to local governments	c	0.09e	0.76e	1.79	4.01
N.	State alcoholic beverage monopoly receipts and enterprise receipts of cities over 100,000	e,f	0.07f	0.24f	0.87	1.64
P.	Employee contributions to retirement systems	c	c	0.06	0.12	0.38
Q.	Interest	c	c	0.19	0.20	0.33
R.	Current charges (state general governments)	c	c	0.15	0.22	0.58
S.	Other nonfinancial receipts	0.09	0.35	0.92	1.15	4.76
T.	Total nonfinancial receipts	0.59	2.25	8.65	15.30	31.90

a Included with other state taxes.

b Less than $5 million.

c Included with "Other nonfinancial receipts."

d Unemployment Compensation withdrawals were $0.34 billion in 1942 and $1.37 billion in 1950.

e Chiefly school and highway grants. Some grants during these years cannot be separated from other state operating expenditures in the tabulations.

f No alcoholic beverage monopolies.

SOURCE: See Appendix A

beverage sales and licenses—about one-sixteenth of the 1942 total—exceeded that of property taxes. Of the 1950 total of nearly $9 billion general sales taxes accounted for 19 per cent, income and estate taxes for 18 per cent, motor fuel taxes for 17 per cent, and unemployment compensation taxes for 14 per cent.

For local governments property has continued to be the main object of taxation. Indeed 1913 is the only year shown in Table 13 in which other taxes amounted to more than 10 per cent of the total. But it is significant that in recent years there has been increased resort to sales taxes and other types of taxes which are essentially new revenue sources for local governments.

TABLE 14

State and Local Government Nonfinancial Expenditures,
Selected Years, 1915–50
(billions of dollars)

		1915	1929	1939	1950
A.	Education, operation and capital outlay	0.65	2.50	2.58	7.00
B.	Highway construction and maintenance	0.46	1.99	2.29	3.64
C.	Sewer and water system construction and maintenance	0.13	0.33	0.50	0.86
D.	New construction (other than in A, B, and C)	0.10	0.43	0.87	1.35
E.	Fire departments (cities over 25,000) and police department (states plus cities over 25,000)	0.12	0.37	0.44	0.85
F.	Hospital operation (states plus cities over 25,000)	0.06	0.17	0.26	0.78
G.	General control (states plus cities over 25,000)	0.09	0.24	0.32	0.58
H.	State development and conservation of natural resources	0.01	0.06	0.10	0.32
J.	Interest	0.24	0.78	0.75	0.62
K.	Public assistance and direct and work relief	0.00	0.07	1.02[a]	2.35
L.	Social insurance benefits	0.04	0.07	0.59	1.75
M.	Payments to veterans and miscellaneous transfer payments	[b]	0.08	0.09	0.68
N.	State aid to local governments	0.11[c]	0.65[c]	1.50	4.01
P.	Payments into Unemployment Compensation Fund	0.00	0.00	0.86	1.23
Q.	Enterprise payrolls	[b]	0.18	0.20	0.61
R.	Alcoholic beverages (states, cost of goods sold)	0.00	0.00	0.19	0.61
S.	All other	0.74	1.03	0.44	6.26
T.	Total nonfinancial expenditures	2.75	8.95	13.00	33.50
U.	Total for new construction	0.65	2.25	1.67	4.98

[a] Excludes federally financed work relief.

[b] Included in "All other."

[c] Chiefly school and highway grants. Some grants during these years cannot be separated from other operating expenditures in the tabulations.

NOTE: The reader may wish to compare this table with the slightly less detailed functional classification of state and local government expenditures Fabricant presents for 1903 and 1939, *op.cit.*, Table 14. The total of nonfinancial expenditures which we have attempted to analyze here is $13 billion for 1939; the expenditure total for that year in his table is $9.11 billion.

SOURCE: See Appendix A.

56

Table 14 analyzes total nonfinancial expenditures of state and local governments somewhat along functional lines; Table 15 analyzes the general government expenditures (excluding expenditures from trust and enterprise funds) by levels of government.

TABLE 15

State and Local Government Expenditures by Level of
Government, Selected Years, 1890–1950

		1890	1902	1913	1932	1942	1950
		MILLIONS OF DOLLARS					
A.	All state and local governments	560	1,070	2,190	9,235	11,880	28,750
B.	All state and local governments excluding interunit aid	560	1,016	2,103	8,406	10,034	24,580
C.	States	72	182	378	2,734	5,558	12,907
D.	Local governments in larger communities	488	330	672	2,455	2,690	5,380
E.	Local governments in smaller communities		558	1,140	4,046	3,632	10,463
		AS A PERCENTAGE OF ALL STATE AND LOCAL GOVERNMENT EXPENDITURES					
F.	State expenditures	12.9	17.0	17.3	29.6	46.7	45.0
		PER CAPITA EXPENDITURES IN DOLLARS					
G.	Local units in larger communities	—	21.40	30.40	66.80	68.50	121.00
H.	Local units in smaller communities	—	8.75	15.55	46.00	37.70	98.30
J.	State and local units excluding interunit aid	8.90	12.80	21.60	69.50	74.30	162.00

NOTE: Lines D and G refer to cities of over 100,000 population, 1902–42. For 1902–32 the census tabulations on which these figures are based include the computed portions of the expenditures of overlying counties and school and special districts. The 1942 figure here used is that for the city corporations raised on the basis of data for 1940. The 1950 figure is based on the percentage change, 1942–50, for cities of over 25,000 population. See Appendix A.

In 1929 total state and local expenditures were somewhat more than three times what they had been in 1915. State aid increased sixfold, and expenditures on highway and miscellaneous construction (lines B and D in Table 14) quadrupled. The percentage increase in education expenditures was nearly that large. Other items showing large increases were: fire and police departments, hospital operation, transfer payments to veterans, and state development and conservation of natural resources.

In general, during the 1930's the growth of those expenditures that had previously been expanding most rapidly was somewhat checked. Particularly was this true of education. The case of highways is a less striking example; highway construction expenditures increased by some

10 per cent. But there was one expenditure program that had previously been expanding that was not checked by the depression. State grants-in-aid stepped up sharply—just how sharply cannot be precisely determined from available compilations of financial data.

On the other hand four items that were either small or zero in 1915 became of considerable importance during the 1930's: public assistance and direct and work relief, social insurance benefits, payments into the Unemployment Compensation Fund, and cost of goods sold by alcoholic beverage monopolies. By 1939 the main component of line K was special assistance to the aged, to the blind, and to dependent children, financed in part by federal aid under the Social Security Act (1935). And the main component of line L was unemployment compensation (financed by withdrawals from the Unemployment Compensation Fund). But civil service pension payments doubled during the decade 1929–39.

Presumably many expenditures that were held in check during the 1930's did not have time to expand fully before they were checked again by World War II. Hence the backlogs that help to explain the greater postwar expansion. In 1950 every expenditure category shown in Table 14 except interest was substantially above the 1939 level. The increase in expenditures on construction and at least in part those on education, fire and police departments, hospitals, and conservation and development reflect accumulated backlogs. But there were very large percentage increases in several nonbacklogs items: payments to veterans, social insurance benefits, public assistance, and enterprise operating expenses.

Between 1915 and 1950 state and local government expenditures expanded somewhat more than tenfold. But among the old established programs education is the only one identified in the table that showed such an increase. If we count state grants-in-aid and social insurance benefits (these consisted exclusively of civil service pensions in 1915) as new programs, it is the new programs that were responsible for the bulk of the increase in the total.

The expansion of functions is reflected in Table 15 as well as in Table 14. However, a substantial part of the increase in the relative importance of state expenditures indicated by line F is, as already noted, a reflection of the marked growth of state grants. In 1950 approximately 31 per cent of the $12.9 billion of state general government expenditures (i.e. expenditures other than those of state enterprises and trust funds) was for aid to local governments. Lines D and E attempt to apportion the general expenditures of local government units of all kinds between the larger urban communities—or rather the parts of such communities located inside the municipal corporate limits of larger cities—and the rest of the United States. When these local government outlays are put on a per capita basis the result is a striking one. In 1902 expenditures per person in the smaller communities were only a little more than 40 per cent of those in places of over 100,000 population. Since then, except during 1932–42, the disparity between the two groups of communities has been narrowing. The ratio of line H to line G in 1950 was 81 per cent.

State and local per capita government expenditures were small in 1890. Even with a generous allowance for the rise of prices they increased

TABLE 16

State and Local Government Employment at Selected
Dates, 1900–1950
(thousands of persons)

		1900	1930	1940	1950
A.	School	467	1,110	1,228	1,430
B.	State nonschool	68	280	456	673
C.	City, village, and town nonschool	194	706	752	959
D.	County nonschool	123	347	286	377
E.	Other nonschool			158	177
F.	Total (lines A + B + C + D + E)	852	2,443	2,880	3,616
G.	Enterprises	40	116	146	184
H.	Firemen (fire department)	15	73	78	110
J.	Law enforcement officers	48	150	152	197
K.	Other than A, G, H, and J	282	994	1,276	1,695
L.	Total nonschool (line F − line A = lines G + H + J + K)	385	1,333	1,652	2,186

NOTE: Figures are on a full-time equivalent basis. They exclude work relief. Line J includes policemen, detectives, marshals, sheriffs, and constables.

fivefold or sixfold during the following sixty years. If local government services were somewhat concentrated in the cities at the turn of the century, by 1950 they had come to be not so far from evenly distributed between larger and smaller communities.

The table does not show the general government expenditures of counties and of school and other special districts. County general expenditures were about one-fifth of the total shown on line B in 1890; about one-seventh in 1950. School and special districts were of little consequence in 1890. In 1950 the expenditures of these units that were assuming functions previously performed by counties, cities, towns, and villages were about 22 per cent of the $24.6 billion total shown on line B.

In 1913 payrolls were about 37 per cent of all state and local non-financial expenditures; in 1950 about 31 per cent.[29] Table 16 analyzes the growth of state and local government employment. A comparison of lines C and L in Table 16 confirms the decline in the relative importance of cities. They represented 50 per cent of the nonschool total in 1900,

[29] For payrolls in 1913 see Fabricant, *op.cit.*, pp. 228–34. For 1950 see *Flow of Funds in the United States*, Table 23.

45.5 per cent in 1940, and 43.7 per cent in 1950. On the other hand the relative importance of states, as measured by the ratio of line B to line L, increased from 17.5 per cent to 30.5 per cent during the half-century. School employment was nearly 55 per cent of the total (line F) in 1900, 40 per cent in 1950. The rapid growth in number of firemen in 1900–1930 suggests that paid employees were replacing volunteer workers. No doubt this was true also of other categories of employment for which we lack detailed information. During the 1930's the percentage increase in numbers of firemen and law enforcement officers appears to have been somewhat smaller than that in total nonschool employment. Between 1900 and 1950 the relative importance of enterprise employees declined from 10.4 per cent of line L to 8.4 per cent.

4. *Summary*

Our historical review of changes in the sources and uses of government funds in recent decades does not give us a complete answer to the question of why governments have engaged in deficit financing as much as they have. But it provides a good deal of significant background information for dealing with this question and it suggests several pertinent propositions.

Total nonfinancial expenditures have greatly increased during the past sixty-odd years, reflecting the expansion of government functions. Government functions have grown more rapidly than the rest of the economy. In the 1890's government nonfinancial expenditures were something like 8 per cent of gross national product; in the relatively peaceful recent years 1946–50 they were about 28 per cent of that product.[30]

During the last twenty years of the nineteenth century, government nonfinancial receipts must, on the average, have roughly matched government nonfinancial expenditures. During 1946–50 receipts were slightly larger than expenditures. It seems reasonable to say that, on the whole and apart from the major step-ups in federal expenditures during the two world wars and the depression of the 1930's, it was possible approximately to match the sharp upward trend in government expenditures in the last five or six decades with an upward trend in tax revenues and other nonfinancial receipts.

The increase in receipts meant recourse to a wide variety of new nonfinancial sources of funds. The federal and state governments have come to rely largely on types of taxes that were of little or no consequence in 1890. And local governments are currently exploring new forms of

[30] For the earlier ratio see Tables 6 and 9. The numerator of the 1946–50 ratio is total expenditures, Tables 5 and 8, minus federal and state aid and Unemployment Fund withdrawals. The denominator is from the special compilation made by Simon Kuznets for the series of monographs of which this is one.

taxation. In part, also, the expansion of functions has been financed on a *quid pro quo* basis—through service charges, enterprise revenues, and nontax (as well as tax) social insurance premiums. More and more, too, state and local governments have come to rely on grants-in-aid as a means of financing some of their expenditures.

Broadly speaking, the two world wars and the depression of the 1930's that so greatly increased the federal debt had a somewhat opposite effect on state and local debts. While there was some net state and local borrowing during World War I, the rate of borrowing seems to have been retarded. And between 1929 and 1939 state and local net debt increased by only about 6 per cent. Then during World War II net state and local debt was reduced to a negligible amount. Even in 1950 it was less than it had been before World War I.

This negative relationship is one reason for suggesting that government financial requirements are in a sense an organic whole—that there is need to consider the requirements of all the various levels of government together.

Another reason for suggesting joint consideration is that there have been changes in the allocation of functions among the different levels and in the allocation of the responsibilities for financing government functions. Thus school and special districts have taken on functions formerly performed by other local government units. And there has been a marked growth in both federal and state aid programs. We will examine these developments further in Chapter V.

The point that stands out most prominently in our analysis of year-to-year changes in nonfinancial sources and uses of funds is the impact of sharp and substantial changes in the latter on deficits. Particularly in the case of the federal government the lagging adjustment of tax rates and other means of meeting nonfinancial expenditures helps to explain not only wartime and depression deficits but also the surpluses of the 1920's. Something has been done to reduce the lag by technical improvements in tax procedures, most importantly by putting the individual income tax on a pay-as-you-go basis. But we will need to inquire into other factors making for the lag in Chapter VIII.

Lags in tax increases are explanations of deficits that run in terms of the mechanics of fiscal procedures. Sharp increases in nonfinancial expenditures may bring deficits, too, for what may be called substantive political reasons. At all events, when government expenditures grow faster than the GNP, governments are likely to have to resort to deficit financing. And contrariwise, when receipts grow with a general expansion in personal income and business volume and with but little change in tax rates, while expenditures do not grow rapidly enough to use up all of these receipts—this was the case with state and local governments during World

61

War II—government debt retirement is the result.[31] Further, when government expenditures increase sharply, even though they include a substantial volume of construction expenditures, the amount of deficit financing may be small if the ratio of the level of nonfinancial expenditures to GNP is lower than that to which the economy has become accustomed.

We have elected to mean by deficit financing the increase in a government's net debt and by its net debt the excess of its total debt outstanding over its total financial assets. In the case of the federal government the deficit that is so financed differs from the budget deficit for two main reasons: (a) It is smaller by the amount of increases in financial assets held by social insurance funds.[32] (b) It is smaller by the amount of increases in other financial assets—chiefly loans to foreign governments and to private parties in this country.[33] In Chapter VII we will consider the growth of government financial assets, state and local as well as federal.

Two lines in Table 15 reveal a very suggestive trend. Per capita expenditures in smaller communities have been increasing more rapidly than those in larger communities, and so the levels of expenditures in the smaller communities have been catching up with the levels of the larger communities. There is a somewhat parallel development in per capita debts that we will examine in Chapter IV.

The comparisons drawn between the two world wars hint at the possibility of two pertinent trends in federal finance. One is the relatively smaller recourse during World War II to deficit financing. We will see in Chapter VIII that this actually is part of a longer-term trend. The other is the increase in the ratio of costs of munitions, nonmilitary personnel, and the like to the pay of the armed forces. Despite the fact that this ratio was only 1.8 for the Korean War, it seems quite reasonable to suppose that, when allowance is made for differences in the scale of war effort, war cost as measured by such a ratio has been trending upward.

At the start of this chapter it was noted that our historical review could be expected to turn up facts not relevant to our present purpose as well as relevant ones. Perhaps it is in order to mention two not-very-relevant facts that seem to stand out: One is the growth of the military establishment; or, since this establishment exerts a pervasive influence, it seems fair to refer to its growth as a trend toward militarization. Expenditures on the military establishment were definitely less than one-half of one per cent of gross national product in 1890; almost 5 per cent in 1950.[34] The other

---

[31] And something like this sequence seems to be the explanation of various surpluses during the nineteenth century. See below, Chapter VIII, Section 3.

[32] Or larger by the amount of decreases in financial assets held.

[33] See footnote 32.

[34] The ratio of line B in Table 11B to the Department of Commerce figure for 1950 is 4.9 per cent. (The corresponding ratio for 1957 was 9.3 per cent.) The ratio of the slightly too large figure on line A of Table 11A to the slightly netter Kuznets GNP figure for 1890 is 0.46 per cent.

not-very-relevant fact is the upward trend in the number of different taxes. No doubt this trend reflects a series of concessions to political expediency. For from a strictly economic point of view the increase in the ratio of the volume of tax and other nonfinancial receipts to GNP—from something like 8 per cent in 1890 to 28 per cent in 1950[35]—is not a reason for an increase in the number of taxes, and each added tax means added collection expense and an added tax-return-making burden for taxpayers.

[35] The ratio of federal receipts (Table 5) plus the census figure for state and local receipts to the Kuznets GNP figure for 1890 is 8.25 per cent. The ratio of total government receipts (Tables 5 and 8) to the Department of Commerce figure for 1950 is 28.3 per cent. But compare also the comment on expenditures above. See the text accompanying footnote 30.

CHAPTER IV

Are There Patterns in State and Local Requirements?

Nearly all of our present federal debt is the result of national emergencies that were not, in any adequate sense, anticipated. But state and local borrowing has, for the most part, been occasioned by circumstances of a more orderly and predictable nature. It is natural to ask, therefore, how far somewhat stable state and local patterns of financial requirements can be identified so that these patterns may be of help in estimating future requirements.

Two main approaches to the question of possible patterns suggest themselves: a time series approach and a cross-section approach. The former involves the different types of circumstances which lead to borrowing, and in particular the relation between net borrowing and physical capital formation. The latter means distinguishing differences in the borrowing propensities of different types of borrower. We will take the cross-section approach first.

1. *Regional and Community Differences*

What can be done with the cross-section approach without a major statistical undertaking of a type precluded by the nature of the present inquiry is somewhat narrowly restricted. The extent of local government borrowing might be expected to reflect the volume of local government services, and since the populations of large cities in general receive more in the way of such services than do those of rural communities, one might look, for a correlation between community size and size of financial requirements. Available data permit some exploration along this line. They also permit some exploration of regional differences in financial requirements. But the explorations are limited by the fact that the main pertinent statistical compilations relate either to per capita gross debts or to the closely related measurement, per capita debts net of sinking funds. However, a little more information on city debts is available for recent years.

Table 17 analyzes municipal corporate debts and their relation to capital outlays by city size groups for 1950. The pattern revealed by column 7 is a striking one. It seems to confirm the notion that the quantity of those government services that entail financial requirements increases

64

with the size of the community. And if one computes per capita capital outlay from columns 1 and 2, he seems to get further confirmation—the resulting series exhibits a steady decline until we come to the two smallest size groups and for these two the per capita expenditure was substantially the same, $14.70. Moreover, a similar community size pattern both for per capita debts and for capital outlays seems to have been the characteristic one during the 1920's and 1930's and even before World War I.

But the relationship is not an entirely simple one. As might be expected, the per capita data for individual cities deviate somewhat from the schematic pattern of column 7. Moreover if long-term debts are mainly the result of capital outlays, we might reasonably expect the ratio of new long-term debt issues to capital outlays (Table 17, column 9) to be fairly stable. We might also expect the ratio of the debt increment to capital outlay (column 8) to be fairly stable. But on an annual basis both these ratios show a considerable dispersion. Possibly if we had analogous computations for a somewhat longer period much of the dispersion would disappear. But it seems reasonable to say that in addition to the size of the capital outlay there are other circumstances—e.g. the status of the city budget—that determine the extent of recourse to borrowing. And it may be added that, while a small city may have to borrow to finance a major construction project, a large city may adopt a capital expenditure program for such projects that spreads the outlays somewhat evenly over the years.

Table 17 does not tell us whether the pattern of column 7 continues below the 25,000 population limit. Moreover it relates to municipal corporations and the populations within municipal corporate limits. Probably it is proper to assume that the facilities of municipal corporations on the whole serve only the populations included in the table, although reimbursement arrangements and meter charge arrangements that extend such services beyond the corporate limits are more frequent than they used to be. But not all the local government services rendered the populations reported in column 1 come from the municipal corporations. Schools, parks, welfare institutions, fire protection, water supply, sewage disposal, transit systems, and utilities may or may not be provided by the municipal corporation. The inclusion of the New York subway debt in line A accounts for about a third of the $288.10 in column 7.

Column 5 does not reflect the net financial requirements of municipal corporations, nor does column 4 give net indebtedness. We noted in Chapter I that at the end of World War II the financial assets of these larger cities probably exceeded outstanding debts by something like $1 billion. For the last few years data for computing per capita net debts

TABLE 17

1950 Capital Outlays and Debt Transactions, 474 Cities, by City Size Groups

	POPULATION	CAPITAL OUTLAY	LONG-TERM DEBT (GENERAL AND ENTERPRISE)				PER CAPITA DEBT (4)/(1)	RATIOS TO OUTLAY (per cent)	
			1st of Year	End of Year	Increment	New Issues		Added Debt (5)/(2)	New Debt (6)/(2)
	(thousands)			(millions of dollars)					
	(1)	(2)	(3)	(4)	(5)	(6)	(7)	(8)	(9)
A. New York	7,892	262	2,135	2,274	139	251	$288.10	53.0	96.0
B. Other Group I	9,467	236	1,072	1,129	57	113	119.10	24.2	47.9
C. Group I	17,359	498	3,207	3,403	196	364	196.20	39.4	73.1
D. Group II	9,147	210	839	905	66	149	99.00	31.4	71.0
E. Group III	7,709	150	651	685	34	85	88.90	22.6	56.6
F. Group IV	9,944	179	773	862	89	141	86.80	49.1	78.8
G. Group V	8,855	130	531	581	50	88	65.60	38.4	67.7
H. Group VI	8,563	126	482	551	69	98	64.40	54.8	77.8
J. Total	61,577	1,294	6,483	6,987	504	926	113.40	38.9	71.5

NOTE: Data are from *City Government Finances*, 1950. Columns 3 and 4 are net of sinking funds. Column 6 excludes refunding issues. Group I cities are those with a population of over 1,000,000. Group II cities have a population of 500,000 to 1,000,000; Group III of 250,000 to 500,000; Group IV of 100,000 to 250,000; Group V of 50,000 to 100,000; Group VI of 25,000 to 50,000.

by city size groups have become available. The 1954 figures are as follows:

Per Capita Net Debt		Per Capita Net Debt	
New York City	$221.70	Group IV	$80.40
Other Group I	76.80	Group V	60.10
Group II	30.00	Group VI	64.70
Group III	52.50		

NOTE: These figures cover 481 cities. The city size groups are the same as in Table 17. Data on the financial assets of these larger cities are available beginning 1951. See *City Government Finances in 1954*. The population data used in computing the above per capita figures are from the 1950 Census.

In the absence of comparable figures for earlier years, we surmise that before the recent rapid growth of the financial assets of larger cities the community size pattern for net debt was quite similar to that in column 7. At all events financial problems were particularly serious for some of the larger cities in 1933, and there were defaults by Detroit and in the Chicago area.[1] But in 1954, while there is still a definite tendency for the per capita figure to decrease with city size, the pattern certainly is no longer a regular one. In fact even for the grosser computation the regularity is somewhat impaired.[2]

However, the tendency for per capita debt to decrease with community size apparently does continue below the 25,000 population limit. This seems clear when we add the figure $19.80 for the net small city and township per capita debt of the rest of the United States to the above list for 1954.[3]

Available data do not permit us to trace the trend of per capita net debts by community size. But it is possible to show in broad terms what has been happening to gross debts. Table 18 does this. The fact that it refers to gross debts rather than to long-term debts net of sinking funds is probably unimportant. By way of background state debts are included. The ratio of line B to line A shows an irregular downward trend. But even in 1950 local debts were three and one-half times state debts.

Table 18 differs from Table 17 in that all local government debts are included, and in that an attempt is made to include villages and rural

[1] Cook County and three special districts. See A. M. Hillhouse, *Municipal Bonds*, pp. 22–23.

[2] For long-term debts net of sinking funds the sequence runs: New York City, Other Group I, II, IV, III, VI, V.

[3] This figure is not entirely comparable to the figures for the various city size groups, because other units of government, particularly school and special districts, presumably perform a larger share of governmental functions in the smaller communities. But the drop below Group II is probably too large to be fully explained away by this fact. Moreover, there may be significant differences in the importance of these other units of government for Groups I to VI too. Possibly if we had tabulations for cities including the "computed portions" of the debts of these "overlying governments"—the Bureau of the Census used to make such compilations—the 1954 pattern of per capita net debts would be more regular.

TABLE 18

Per Capita State and Local Debt at Selected Dates, 1902–50

	1902	1922	1932	1940	1946	1950
A. State debt	$3.41	$10.53	$23.20	$26.80	$16.82	$35.60
B. Local debt	$24.30	$82.60	$133.70	$126.80	$96.40	$124.50
C. Local debt in cities of more than 100,000 population	$70.70	$161.25	$223.50	$230.50	$180.20	$203.00
D. ⎰ Two hypothetical debt computations for Hypothesis #1	$19.80	$74.80	$126.25	$112.00	$81.05	$119.75
E. ⎱ other cities, towns, and villages Hypothesis #2	$16.40	$65.00	$112.20	$100.00	$72.50	$107.75
F. Ratio of D to C	28.0%	46.3%	56.6%	48.6%	45.0%	59.0%
G. Ratio of E to C	23.2%	40.3%	50.2%	43.4%	40.1%	53.0%
H. Urban debt—rough estimate	$42.15	$122.00	$175.50	$169.50	$129.50	$157.00
J. Rural debt—rough estimate	$11.83	$46.75	$80.00	$70.90	$51.50	$76.00
K. Ratio of J to H	28.1%	38.3%	45.6%	41.8%	39.7%	48.4%

NOTE: Figures refer to gross debts per person at fiscal year-ends. The computed portions of the debts of overlying counties and school and special districts included in line C are those made by the Census Bureau for 1902–40. The estimates for 1946 and 1950 are rough. They are explained in Appendix A. Hypothesis #1 is that the ratio of per capita local debt in rural communities to that in cities, towns, and villages of less than 100,000 population is 3 : 5 in each year. Hypothesis #2 is that this rural to small urban community ratio is 3 : 4. For most years, 1905–31, infor-

mation is available on per capita debts of cities of 30,000 to 50,000 and cities of 50,000 to 100,000 population. Such information for 1923 and 1931 was analyzed, and these two hypothetical ratios were adopted on the basis of this analysis. See Appendix A. In general, per capita local debt decreases with the size of the community but appears to have been nearly as high in 1923 and 1931 for places of 2,500 to 30,000 population as for those of 30,000 to 50,000. A rural to small urban community ratio of 2 : 3 was used for computing lines H and J.

communities. Per capita debt computations are shown for cities of more than 100,000 population, for other cities and towns and villages, for all urban communities, and for rural areas. Upper and lower estimates are offered for urban communities of less than 100,000 population.[4] The figures on line J assume a constant ratio to the average of lines D and E.

Two main inferences can be drawn from this table. First, for broad community size classes, the pattern of Table 17, column 5, is confirmed as a highly stable one. Second, although it is stable, the percentage spread between large and small cities in this pattern has been gradually narrowing as the growth of debts in the smaller communities has been particularly rapid. The per capita debts of urban places of under 100,000 population were about 25 per cent of those in larger cities in 1902 and about 55 per cent in 1950. But the upward trend of this ratio was temporarily reversed during the 1930's and during World War II. The table does not enable us to say whether the percentage spread between rural areas and the smaller cities has followed a similar course. The rural-urban ratio probably did (line K).

Table 18 refers to gross debts. We think the two main inferences we have drawn from it probably apply also to debts net of sinking funds. But some qualification is necessary for debts net of all financial assets. The recent rapid growth of these assets in the case of larger cities has presumably made the community size pattern less stable as well as less regular. And while it seems reasonable to suppose that this growth has not halted the trend toward uniformity, it may quite possibly have converted the trend from a leveling-up process for the net debts of smaller communities to a leveling-down process for those of the larger ones.

It does not seem worth while to attempt directly to show that the community size per capita debt pattern applies separately in the several regions of the country. Columns 1, 2, and 3 of Table 19 are consistent with the assumption that it does so apply. But they seem to reflect also another influence. In 1942 the Middle Atlantic region had the highest per capita debts (i.e. debts net of sinking funds); the Pacific region was second; and New England was fourth. These three regions ranked highest in respect to both per capita personal incomes and per capita taxes in that year. In personal incomes the order was Pacific first, New England second, Middle Atlantic third; in taxes Middle Atlantic first, Pacific second, and New England third. At the other end of the scale was the East South Central region; it ranked ninth on all three counts.[5] The

---

[4] Including such communities when they are parts of larger metropolitan areas.

[5] For the per capita personal income figures see September 1955 *Survey of Current Business*, p. 16. The tax figures are from the census summary, *Governmental Finances in the United States: 1942*. Solomon Fabricant in his *Trend of Government Activity since 1900* finds a marked tendency for per capita government expenditure to increase with per capita income (see pp. 122ff.). His findings reflect both 1942 interstate comparisons and a comparison of 1942 with 1903.

correlations between debt and income and between debt and taxes are by no means perfect. But clearly there are significant connections here. It may be suggested that higher levels of living go with higher incomes, that higher levels of living include more extensive and more costly government services, and that higher government costs lead both to higher taxes and to more government indebtedness. The region that seems least well

TABLE 19

State and Local Debts by Census Regions, 1890, 1922, and 1942

		Per Capita Debts Net of Sinking Funds			Per Capita Indexes Designed to Eliminate Much of the Effect of Increased Urbanization		
		1890 (1)	1922 (2)	1942 (3)	1890 (4)	1922 (5)	1942 (6)
A.	New England	$31.70	$72.40	$110.25	$31.85	$72.40	$110.35
B.	Middle Atlantic	25.20	112.20	244.05	29.50	112.20	243.95
C.	E.N. Central	12.20	73.70	88.20	15.60	73.70	86.00
D.	W.N. Central	17.50	66.50	85.10	20.35	66.50	79.70
E.	S. Atlantic	18.60	51.30	98.00	22.00	51.30	90.45
F.	E.S. Central	11.70	40.50	83.20	13.50	40.50	77.20
G.	W.S. Central	12.85	65.70	106.60	15.90	65.70	94.65
H.	Mountain	19.80	108.50	128.30	21.75	108.50	120.80
J.	Pacific	11.10	134.50	154.00	13.65	134.50	152.40
K.	United States	18.02	78.90	131.20	21.50	78.90	128.90
L.	9 to 1 ratio	286%	332%	294%	236%	332%	316%
M.	8 to 2 ratio	216%	219%	181%	216%	219%	191%
N.	7 to 3 ratio	162%	165%	145%	141%	165%	140%

Data for columns 1, 2, and 3 are from the censuses of governments. Comparisons were made between 1890 and 1922 weighting the urban population 3, the rural 1, the result being adjusted to make column 5 the same as column 2 and column 4 an index number on column 5 as a base. Similar comparisons between 1922 and 1942 were made with weights of 2½ and 1 respectively to give column 6. See Appendix A. The 9 to 1 ratio on line L is the ratio of the highest to the lowest of the figures on lines A to J. The 8 to 2 ratio is the ratio of the second highest to the second lowest of these figures; the 7 to 3 ratio relates the third highest and third lowest.

to accord with this rule is the East North Central. It ranked seventh in per capita debts and fourth in per capita income and taxes in 1942.[6] Possibly legal restrictions on borrowing have been more effective in this relatively high income region than elsewhere.

The main purpose of Table 19 was to determine whether geographical differences in the propensity to borrow have been narrowing. Lines L, M, and N give measures of dispersion. In order they are (for the left-hand half of the table): the ratio of the highest regional per capita debt to the lowest; the ratio of the second highest to the second lowest; and the ratio of the third highest to the third lowest. Between 1890 and 1922 all three

[6] See footnote 5.

70

measures increase. This was a period in which there was a particularly marked impact on state and local government debt of the technological changes associated with the industrial revolution. For the country as a whole per capita debt increased nearly four and a half fold. This impact continued during the 1920's; but during the 1930's per capita debt decreased slightly (see Table 18) and during World War II it decreased sharply. The net result for the two decades ending 1942 was a narrowing of the regional percentage differences in debt; all three measures declined.

Unfortunately we do not have a satisfactory basis for carrying the table forward to 1952 to give us a firmer indication of the trend. But while line L shows a slight increase from column 1 to column 3, both the other measures of dispersion declined. We may reasonably surmise that there was a long-term tendency, 1890–1942, toward a narrowing of regional percentage differences in per capita debts, and that this tendency was overpowered by an opposite one during the years of greatest impact of modern technology.

In view of the marked relationship between debts and size of community one naturally wonders whether the trend toward a less marked regional difference is not largely a reflection of the fact that the country has been getting more evenly urbanized. Certainly it has been, as the following urban population percentages for the New England and the three least urbanized regions make clear:

	1890	1920	1940
	(percentage of urban population)		
New England[a]	75.8	75.9	76.1
South Atlantic	19.5	31.0	38.8
East South Central	12.7	22.4	29.4
West South Central	15.1	29.0	39.8

[a] New England was the most urbanized region in 1890 and 1920. In 1940 the percentage of urban population in the Middle Atlantic region was slightly higher, 76.8 per cent.

The right-hand half of Table 18 aims to answer this question. To eliminate a major part of the effect of the urbanization influence weighted per capita debt figures were computed. Since the urban-rural difference in per capita debts has been narrowing, a larger relative weight was given to urban populations in the computations for the 1890–1922 comparisons than in the set for 1922–42. The 1890 index number for each region, column 4, bears the same percentage relation to column 5 as that of the weighted regional per capita debt computation for the two dates. Similarly, the ratio of column 6 to column 5 for each region is equal to the ratio of the 1942 to the 1922 weighted regional per capita debt.

The effects of the adjustments are pretty much what one would expect. Between 1890 and 1922 the interregional differentials are widened by the elimination of the narrowing influence of the progress of urbanization in the predominantly rural regions, and between 1922 and 1942,

71

according to two of the three dispersion measures, lines L and M, the extent of the narrowing is reduced. As for the longer-term trend, it is not entirely clear that any of it remains after the adjustment. Most of the tendency toward a narrowing of regional differences in indebtedness between 1890 and 1942 seems to have been due to the fact that the country was becoming more evenly urbanized.[7]

It is tempting to conclude from this analysis of community and regional differences in per capita debts that there has been not only a trend toward higher per capita incomes and a decrease in urban-rural differences but also, as an inevitable accompaniment of these changes, a trend toward increased per capita state and local government debts.

No doubt there was a substantial upward trend in these per capita debts from 1890 to 1930. But this trend was interrupted first by the depression of the 1930's and then by World War II. Quite possibly the trend is now in process of becoming renewed. But with the recent substantial growth of state and local government financial assets the situation—at least so far as net debts are concerned—is by no means clear.

2. Different Types of Financial Requirement

The compilations of gross state and local debt by the Bureau of the Census have in general enabled us to distinguish short-term debt and to classify most long-term debt by purpose of issue. The purpose of issue classification is made essentially on the basis of government functions. The bulk of highway, school, and enterprise debts can probably be safely assumed to represent physical capital formation financing. Doubtless this is the case also with several of the other purpose categories. But debts incurred for veterans' aid and homes and for welfare combine the financing of expenditures on plant and equipment with the financing of bonuses and benefit payments. These seem to us to be two different types of financial requirement. Another difficulty with the debt by purpose classifications in the present connection is that there is commonly a substantial category of debt not identified by purpose.[8] A considerable part of this is likely to be refunding issues.

It was argued above that in the case of governments the relation between physical capital formation and financial requirements is tenuous, and that this is so in large part because governments do not follow business-like accounting procedures. Nonetheless, in distinguishing different types of net financial requirements it seems wise to push in a direction that is

---

[7] Fabricant, *loc.cit.*, finds that per capita government expenditure has tended not only to increase markedly with per capita income but also to increase significantly with urbanization (the percentage of the population living in places of 2,500 or more inhabitants) and to decrease significantly with population density.

[8] In the earlier years in Tables 2B and 2C this includes floating debt. See note on Table 2B and Appendix B.

suggestive of the distinction between balance sheet accounts and income statement accounts. We will distinguish: (a) physical capital formation financing, (b) emergency deficit financing, and (c) budget financing. This is not an exhaustive classification of net financial requirements, but these three categories should cover a very large percentage of the state and local total.

The physical capital formation type of requirement is doubtless self-explanatory. When a government incurs large capital expenditures in a given year that cannot well be met out of the year's taxes and other revenue receipts it must have recourse to financing. Usually this means a long-term debt issue. However, in 1946 some capital expenditures were financed by liquidating holdings of government securities.

There are three main types of emergency deficit requirements. A temporary government deficit may be caused by a public disaster such as a flood. Apparently the debts incurred to finance disaster deficits have not loomed very large in the aggregate figures. They cannot be identified in Tables 2A, 2B, and 2C. Again, a temporary deficit may occur during or after a war. The main occasion for this type of deficit has come to be state payments of bonuses to veterans. Over $1.75 billion of state bonus bonds were outstanding at the end of 1950.

A third type of temporary deficit results from depressions. Both state welfare debt, Table 2B, line F, and city debt for charities, hospitals, and corrections, Table 2C, line G, show marked bulges after the prolonged depression during the 1930's. But these bulges tell only part of the story, the emergency expenditures part, and this may well be less important in the future. Hereafter financing depression benefit payments is likely to come mainly from federal funds, if we count the Unemployment Compensation Fund as federal.[9] Before 1930 it is difficult to see in Table 8 any effects of depressions on state and local government receipts. Even the depression of 1921 does not show. At that time receipts came quite largely from sources that had little or no built-in flexibility, especially the general property tax. But states, and even local governments, are becoming more and more dependent on somewhat flexible sources. In the future state and local depression deficits may be due to decreased revenue receipts quite as much as to emergency expenditures.

Even though government physical capital formation expenditures are not written off in accordance with businesslike depreciation schedules, there are in general systematic annual provisions for the retirement of the debts incurred to finance them, either through sinking funds or through serial maturities. And even though government emergency deficits are not

[9] Payments into this fund are reflected in Table 8 as expenditures and in Table 5 as receipts. Payments out count as expenditures in Table 5 and as both expenditures and receipts in Table 8.

entered on the books as deferred charges and then gradually written off, here too the systematic debt retirement provisions commonly achieve a somewhat similar effect. In both cases there are effects similar to those of depreciation accounting; but as is obvious in the case of physical capital formation, there are important differences too.

The relations between financing and physical capital formation will be considered shortly. But we have not yet defined the third type of financial requirement. We have named the way of meeting this type of requirement budget financing for the expedient that it most often employs —budget borrowing. Narrowly construed, budget borrowing means temporary within-the-year borrowing to enable receipts collected in one or two annual installments to finance a somewhat continuous flow of expenditures. But it is reasonable to construe the term a little more broadly. Essentially it means short-term borrowing to modify the time pattern of receipts from other sources so that it will fit the time pattern of expenditures closely enough to avoid the necessity of a large temporary advance accumulation of cash. In its broader sense it may include short-term notes that anticipate a planned bond issue as well as short-term tax anticipation notes.

If short-term borrowing were confined to budget borrowing, even in this wider sense, we might expect that the ratio of outstanding short-term debt to total nonfinancial expenditures would—in the aggregate figures for all state and local governments—be a somewhat steady one. We might expect, too, that the ratio of cash to total nonfinancial expenditures would be fairly steady. If so, the liquidity ratio—cash to short-term debt—should also be quite stable. But Table 20 does not show much stability. Evidently in 1932 short-term borrowing was partly for depression emergency financing. And during the middle 1940's the large wartime accumulations of cash probably obviated to some extent the need for budget borrowing. The least variable ratio is that of cash to expenditures, column 8. But by 1932 cash balances had been drawn down and short-term debts had risen until the two were almost equal. Then during the war cash balances rose and debts declined. The liquidity ratio, column 5, had been 1:1 in 1932. In 1946 it was 20:1. And despite large postwar expenditures, the liquidity ratio, though down sharply from its peak, was still far higher in 1953 than the 2:1 figure of 1922. Possibly these three ratios will exhibit greater stability in the future. The record to date shows that short-term debts have varied directly and cash balances inversely with recent budget deficits; they have not mainly reflected what we have called budget financing requirements.

Sinking fund assets are commonly related to gross debt or gross long-term debt. But they do not bear a stable relation to either. The ratio to gross debt was 15.3 per cent in 1922, 9.9 per cent in 1932, and 14.5 per

74

cent in 1944. Actually they seem to reflect much the same influences as do cash and short-term debts. They have therefore been included in Table 20, column 6. The ratio of cash plus sinking fund assets[10] to short-term debt may be regarded as a second and more inclusive measure of liquidity.

One important way of thinking of cash, sinking fund portfolios, and short-term debts is to note that changes in these balances represent financial sources and uses of funds. During 1930–32 funds from these

TABLE 20

State and Local Short-Term Debt, Expenditures, and Cash
Balances at Selected Dates, 1922–53

June 30	Debt	Expenditures	Cash	Sinking Funds	(3)/(1)	(3)+(4)/1	(1)/(2)	(3)/(2)
		(billions of dollars)			(ratio)		(per cent)	
	(1)	(2)	(3)	(4)	(5)	(6)	(7)	(8)
1922	0.68	6.3	1.4	1.57	2.06	4.4	10.8	22.9
1929	1.33	9.0	2.2	3.40	1.65	4.2	14.8	24.5
1932	1.76	8.9	1.8	1.94	1.02	2.1	19.8	20.2
1942	0.97	13.8	4.6	2.02	4.53	6.8	7.0	32.0
1944	0.63	13.9	5.2	2.54	7.78	12.3	4.5	35.7
1946	0.33	17.9	6.9	2.20	20.00	27.5	1.8	34.1
1948	0.63	26.3	8.5	2.35	13.50	17.2	2.4	32.8
1950	1.05	33.5	9.5	2.96	9.15	11.9	3.1	29.8
1953	1.78	40.4	11.6	3.45	5.16	6.7	4.4	29.0

[a] Nonfinancial expenditures during the calendar year.
[b] Excludes currency prior to 1942.
SOURCE: See Appendix A.

sources exceeded the total nonfinancial deficit for the three years. During 1945–46 these balances absorbed more than a third of the nonfinancial surplus.

In Chapter I we noted that while in the earlier years of the present century a substantial part of physical capital formation by state and local governments was matched by the increase in net indebtedness, this same rule did not apply in 1930–50. Nonetheless Tables 2B and 2C show that outstanding debts have continued to be chiefly capital formation debts. It would seem therefore that there should be some pattern of relationship between borrowing and capital formation. Our present purpose is to determine whether there is, and if so, what its nature is. In view of the inadequacies of the data on other aspects of capital formation our attention will be largely confined to new construction.

The question of the capital formation financing pattern might be approached in a number of different ways. We will take first the relation between the volume of capital formation and the size of the nonfinancial

[10] Sinking fund assets include a small amount of cash, but it has not been deemed worthwhile to eliminate this double counting.

75

TABLE 21

State and Local New Construction Expenditures
and Deficits, 1916–53

	Construction (millions of dollars) (1)	Deficit (2)	(2)/(1) (per cent) (3)
	THREE-YEAR MOVING AVERAGES		
1916	637	150	23.5
1917	619	200	32.3
1918	654	250	38.2
1919	789	300	38.1
1920	1,046	600	57.3
1921	1,298	750	57.8
1922	1,436	850	59.2
1923	1,544	800	51.8
1924	1,692	800	47.3
1925	1,870	700	37.4
1926	2,050	600	29.3
1927	2,159	500	23.1
1928	2,253	350	15.5
	YEARLY FIGURES		
1929	2,254	100	4.4
1930	2,545	550	21.6
1931	2,153	700	32.5
1932	1,418	250	17.6
1933	846	150	17.7
1934	864	−300	−34.8
1935	852	−350	−41.2
1936	1,153	−100	−8.7
1937	1,203	−100	−8.3
1938	1,383	−100	−7.2
1939	1,673	300	17.9
1940	1,500	100	6.7
1941	1,303	−1,300	−100.0
1942	872	−1,700	−195.2
1943	445	−2,300	−517.0
1944	442	−2,600	−589.0
1945	562	−2,500	−445.0
1946	1,248	−1,900	−152.2
1947	2,184	−500	−22.9
1948	3,231	400	12.4
1949	4,456	1,200	26.8
1950	4,910	1,800	36.7
1951	5,957	900	15.1
1952	6,096	400	6.6
1953	6,535	200	3.1

NOTE: Column 1 excludes construction financed by federal aid.

deficit. A second relation to be considered is that between capital formation and new financing. Probably too we should examine the relation between deficits and new issues. And since debt retirement practices have effects that in some ways resemble those of depreciation accounting, it may be of interest to attempt a comparison of depreciated improvements and outstanding debts.

In general terms we considered the relation between deficits and new construction in connection with Table 4; there did not seem to be one. But certainly if we were to examine the figures for individual cities and other individual units of government, we would expect to find one. The question is, "Is there a relation in the aggregate figures?" Table 21 gives the ratio of the nonfinancial deficit to new construction expenditures by years, 1929–53, and three-year moving average computations, 1916–29. The ratio fluctuates around a third during the first ten years. It markedly declines during the late 1920's but rises above 30 per cent again in 1931. Then it drops to nearly −35 per cent in 1934 and except for 1939–40 remains negative for more than a decade, reaching a low of more than −500 per cent in the last full wartime year. With the large construction expenditures after the war it rises again to 37 per cent in 1950, then tapers off to 3 per cent in 1953. We conclude that there is a relation, but that it is obscured by another factor, the general level of nonfinancial receipts relative to nonfinancial expenditures. When this level is high, even a large volume of capital expenditures can be financed without recourse to net borrowing. When it is low, a substantial part of these expenditures must be met by an increase in net debts, or alternatively, if credit is difficult to obtain as it was during most of the 1930's, construction expenditures may be curtailed.

Net borrowing reflects emergency deficit financing as well as capital formation financial requirements. It also reflects such financial developments as increases and decreases in cash and in short-term loans and the volume of debt retired. One would expect, therefore, a somewhat closer relationship if we shift the basis of comparison from net borrowing to gross long-term borrowing exclusive of refunding issues. Column 4 of Table 22 on the whole confirms this expectation. The numerator of the ratio it reports excludes loans by federal agencies and the denominator excludes from the value of state and local construction work the amount of federal aid for such construction. The table is on a quinquennial basis. In Table 21 we used an annual basis to bring out the observed relationship. If Table 22 were on an annual basis, there would be an obvious year-to-year correlation between new issues and new construction. The fact that the quinquennial ratio in column 4 does not vary much above three-fourths or much below three-fifths except in 1940–44 and the fact that the ratio shows no clear trend are much more significant for our present long-term purpose than the year-to-year correlation. The exceptionally low ratio in 1940–44 is not surprising in view of the large surpluses during these five years. Nor are the high ratios in 1920–24 and 1945–49; construction expenditures stepped up sharply in both these instances. But the drop in the ratio to 62 per cent in 1950–53 is puzzling. However, we may note that in these four years state and local deficits were falling.

TABLE 22

State and Local New Long-Term Debt Issues and New
Construction, 1915–53

	Security Issues	New Construction (millions of dollars)	Deficit	(1)/(2) (per cent)	(3)/(1)
	(1)	(2)	(3)	(4)	(5)
1915–19	2,160	3,253	1,150	67	53
1920–24	5,371	7,022	3,700	77	69
1925–29	6,968	10,678	2,450	65	35
1930–34	4,717	7,826	1,350	60	29
1935–39	4,204	6,264	−350	67	−7½
1940–44	2,040	4,562	−7,800	45	−382
1945–49	9,060	11,681	−3,300	77	−36
1950–53	14,670	23,498	3,300	62	23

NOTE: Column 2 excludes construction financed by federal aid.

Table 22 also relates the deficit to the new issues. In general the quinquennial figures in columns 1 and 3 move in the same direction; 1925–29 is an exception. But the ratio in column 5 shows a wide variation, from −3.8 in 1940–44 to almost 0.7 in 1920–24. And if we were to compare 1949–50 with 1951–53 we would find security issues increasing and the deficit declining. We may surmise that when new construction outlays and security issues show a prolonged period of increase, as in 1915–29, a larger proportion of the outlay is likely to come out of current sources toward the latter years of the period.

In Table 23 the three main categories of state and local debts are related to *approximate* depreciated values of the types of improvement they have helped to finance that have been computed on the basis of somewhat arbitrary depreciation rates. In view of the assumptions made in computing lines B, E, and H, little significance attaches to the absolute levels of the ratios shown on lines C, F, J, and M. The purpose of the table is to give an indication of the probable movements.

The highway debt to value ratio may well have been rising for a decade or more before 1922–32. The decrease in 1932–51 is mainly a reflection of the fact that during the 1930's and 1940's federal grants-in-aid provided for a substantial part of construction cost. Had this part been excluded from line B the debt to value ratio would have been higher in 1951 than in 1932.

The arbitrariness of the depreciation rate is obviously serious in connection with the level of the ratios on line F. Forty years would be more reasonable for the life of school buildings than twenty.[11] A computation on this basis would not make the level of the debt to value ratio seem unduly high in the case of school properties.[12]

TABLE 23

State and Local Debt and Depreciated Construction, a Rough
Three-Function Comparison, Selected Years, 1922–51
(in millions of dollars)

		1922	1932	1942	1951
	HIGHWAYS				
A.	Long-term debt outstanding	1,883	4,167	3,312	4,101
B.	Depreciated construction	3,113	6,615	6,062	9,029
C.	Ratio of A to B	60.5%	62.9%	54.7%	46.3%
	EDUCATION				
D.	Long-term debt outstanding	1,747	3,798	2,662	4,728
E.	Depreciated construction	1,626	3,114	2,605	5,165
F.	Ratio of D to E	107.5%	122.0%	102.5%	91.6%
	ENTERPRISES AND SEWAGE SYSTEMS				
G.	Long-term debt outstanding	1,352	4,132	4,417	6,298
H.	Depreciated construction	1,800	3,536	4,153	5,285
J.	Ratio of G to H	75.0%	116.8%	106.0%	119.1%
K.	New York City enterprise debt outstanding	a	1,137	1,938	2,137[b]
L.	Line G minus line K	a	2,995	2,479	4,161
M.	Ratio of L to H	a	84.7%	59.7%	78.6%

a Not tabulated.
b 1950 figure.
NOTE: Figures on long-term debt outstanding cover: states, counties and cities, towns and villages, line A; states, school districts and cities, towns and villages, line D; states and cities, towns and villages, line G. Construction (including construction financed by federal aid) was depreciated at 10 per cent per year for highways and 5 per cent per year for education and enterprises and sewage systems.
SOURCE: See Appendix A.

The recent history of the school debt to value ratio seems to have been similar in several respects to that for highways. The ratio had probably been rising for a decade or more before 1922–32; total school district debt was only $46 million in 1902, $1.125 billion in 1922. School debts were retired more rapidly than school buildings depreciated in 1932–42. State

[11] But the annual construction figures used in computing line E do not go back far enough to enable us to get much notion of the movement of the debt to value ratio with a 2.5 per cent depreciation rate.
[12] For a more careful computation of the level we should add short-term debts to the numerator and the value of school sites and equipment to the denominator. In 1951 short-term school district debt was about 4.5 per cent of long-term. Probably the net effect of allowing for short-term debts, sites, and equipment would be to reduce the level of the debt to value ratios slightly, except in 1932.

grants-in-aid for education increased from about $400 million in 1932 to over $2.5 billion in 1952.

In the case of the enterprise and sewage debt to value ratio a rough check on the level is available. For 1943 the census tabulations for cities of over 250,000 population include enterprise balance sheets. These show liabilities equal to 44 per cent of the book value of the assets. Sewage systems are combined with enterprises in the third section of the table because they are not separated in the construction outlay estimates. Presumably the level of the debt to value ratio should be a little less than half that shown on line J.

Another difficulty with this ratio computation results from the acquisition of the IRT and BMT subways by New York City in 1940. Line H does not include the private construction of these properties. Consequently line M probably gives a better indication of the movement of the debt to value ratio in 1932–51 than line J. Apparently this ratio rose sharply in 1922–32, dipped in 1932–42, and then rose again in 1942–51, but was lower in 1951 than in 1932. Since many government enterprises compile annual balance sheets, we might suppose that the debt to value ratio in this case would be less sensitive to the general financial position of state and local governments than in the case of depreciated highway and school construction expenditures. Table 23 does not seem to support this supposition.

3. Orderly and Disorderly Finance

Consideration of possible patterns in state and local requirements suggests various tendencies toward patterns, tendencies which may perhaps lead to more stable relationships than those that seem to have characterized the past forty or fifty years.

Tendencies toward stability in turn suggest that state and local public finance has been somewhat orderly: this has not always been the case. In the following chapter we will comment briefly on the disorderly aspects of nineteenth-century finance that led to the establishment of various restrictions on state and local borrowing. There has been some disorderliness too in the twentieth century.

In general it has seemed wise for purposes of our present inquiry to take what governments have borrowed as the measure of their financial requirements and not to attempt to pass judgment on the adequacy of the occasions for borrowing. But at this point we must recognize that the occasions have not always been adequate. When we say finance has sometimes been disorderly, we mean that the occasions have sometimes been distinctly inadequate—indeed, that public borrowing has sometimes served primarily private purposes. On the whole the restrictions inherited from the nineteenth century have prevented such abuses, but not entirely.

Disorderly finance is especially likely to characterize periods of very rapid growth. During the 1920's Detroit was one of the most rapidly growing cities. Detroit industry was also particularly severely hit by the 1929–33 recession. It is hardly surprising that this city overdid the laying of street pavements, sidewalks, water mains, and sewers. As a result it had in 1931 a gross per capita debt for these purposes of $106; the average debt for all cities of over 500,000 population was then only $61.50.

The most striking case of disorderly finance during the past sixty years is that of the Florida land boom during the 1920's. The following figures from the 1932 census give some indication of the expansion of local government debts that accompanied this boom:

Selected Florida Counties	Per Capita Debts	
	1922	1931–32
Charlotte	$80	$827
Indian River	none	785
Martin	none	976
St. Lucie	190	1,286
Sarasota	146	947
Florida average	96	338
United States average	80	141

Note: Debt figures are net of sinking funds. The 1932 census reports include 1931 figures in the case of Florida. Indian River and Martin Counties were organized after 1922.

A community can overdo its capital outlays and overexpand its debts, and there may be nothing more sinister involved than enthusiasm and bad judgment. But the laying of street pavements and sidewalks, sewers, and water mains over a substantial area on which no dwelling units have yet been erected can, in effect, constitute a subsidy to private promoters of real estate developments. And, of course, the aid to private interests can go still further.

Hillhouse cites Coral Gables "as the outstanding example of municipal aid to bankrupt promoters."[13] Of the city's bond issues in 1925–30, some 30 per cent went for bankers' commissions, promotion, and the like. Four of the five city commissioners during 1926–27 were connected with a Coral Gables development corporation that sold properties to the city at exorbitant markups in these two years.

Against the scattered instances of disorderly state and local finance since 1890 we should set the long-term trend toward greater orderliness, if we are to have a balanced picture. We will not attempt to trace this trend in detail, but merely note some of the developments that have contributed to it.

First, there has been an increasing reliance on full-time trained and career service personnel for the management of state finances and the finances of the larger local government units. If one would fully appreciate what this means, he should have in mind that a century and a half ago few

[13] A. M. Hillhouse, *Municipal Bonds*, pp. 84–85.

units of government would have been large enough to employ this kind of financial management even if the trained personnel had been available. New York was the only city of more than 50,000 population in 1800. One should have in mind also that at that time there was a general distrust of the executive branch of government. State and city legislatures made up budgets—to the extremely limited extent that there was any budgeting— and made appointments. City councils let contracts, and various city council committees managed various municipal departments. Not only have the functions of financial management come to be vested in executive officers, but public financial administration seems today to be in process of becoming a profession, and professional competence is coming to be a requirement for appointment to the more important financial posts. This development has been aided in a general way by the spread of the civil service merit system (in 1952 some 20 states and 96 of the 105 cities of over 100,000 population had comprehensive merit systems in operation) and by changes in the direction of a greater centralization of control within the executive, as for example under the city manager plan. Much more specifically it has been aided by the organization (1906) and growth of the Municipal Finance Officers Association of the United States and Canada. In 1949 this association had over 2,000 members.

Second, in the case of local governments, orderly finance has been encouraged by state supervision. In the early nineteenth century state concern with city management was largely confined to the enactment of city charters, for the most part modeled on the federal pattern. With the growth of cities in 1820–50 came waste, mismanagement, and corruption in municipal administration. Hence the years following 1850 were characterized by state "interference." In a few cases, notably New York City, the state took over municipal functions.[14] But such abrogations of local self-government proved to be temporary. A more permanent type of state "interference" in municipal affairs consisted of restrictive provisions incorporated in state constitutions, statutes, or charters. The provisions relating to local debts are considered in Chapter V. Gradually the concept of local self-government was modified to permit supplementing such restrictions with administrative supervision. At first state supervision "was primarily concerned in overseeing local collection of taxes due the state."[15] Later the objective and nature of the supervision were broadened to include: preparing accounting manuals and standard accounting forms, classifications, and procedures; requiring financial reports on prescribed forms; requiring state or state-supervised post-audits; prescribing budget

---

[14] See E. Dana Durand, *The Finances of New York City*, Chapter IV. Central Park, the police force, fire protection, and the health service were transferred to newly created special districts, each governed by a state-appointed commission or board.

[15] Wylie Kilpatrick, *State Supervision of Local Finance*, p. 1.

forms and procedures; and determining the legality of bond issues.[16] There are instances too (principally in the case of local units that are in default) where a state has gone so far as to require the approval of a local budget and local bond issues by a state supervisory agency. It scarcely need be said that these moves in the direction of state supervision have disclosed and helped to eliminate extensive practices which had not previously been brought into accord with the law.[17]

These comments on state supervision suggest a third aspect of the trend toward more and more orderly finance—the development of new and improved techniques of financial administration and the adoption of these techniques by one unit of government after another. State supervision has helped to spread their use among local units. In the development of the techniques private research agencies played a significant role, particularly bureaus of municipal research. And individual cities seem on the whole to have taken the lead in adoptions.[18]

We will not attempt to examine the various improved techniques of financial administration. But we may note that they can fairly be expected, in the course of time, to push toward a closer connection between financial capital requirements and physical capital formation. And the growing emphasis on enterprise financial statements and the more careful long-term planning of capital formation for general governmental purposes should bring increased attention to the ratio of long-term capital improvement debts to the corresponding asset valuations.

But does this mean for general government or even for government enterprises that the relation between physical capital formation and financial capital requirements will presently be somewhere near as close as in the case of private business? For enterprises, possibly. There is good reason to expect that business accounting practices will be increasingly insisted on and no reason to doubt that regular annual compilations of debt to asset value ratios will be feasible. Of course this would leave the relation between outlay on physical capital and the raising of capital through financial channels complicated by proprietorship investments

[16] *Ibid.* See especially Tables 10–15, which summarize the extent of state supervision as of 1940. Every state did some supervising at that time. Use of state-prepared accounting systems was mandatory in Indiana and Ohio; nineteen states required comprehensive annual financial reports of all local units; nine made annual or biennial audits of all local units; ten prescribed budget systems for all local units. Kilpatrick's study does not cover state supervision of property assessments, but this phase of supervision is not pertinent here.

[17] See, for example, Don C. Powers, *The Financial History of New York State*, pp. 245ff.

[18] "The system of the executive budget, centralized accounting, and independent auditing was thus developed in both theory and practice on the municipal level before it was thought of either by states or by the national authority." Paul Studenski and Herman E. Krooss, *Financial History of the United States*, p. 351. But states have led sometimes too. An amendment to the New York State constitution gave the governor the item veto in 1872. See *ibid.*, p. 195.

and by retained earnings and other inside funds, just as it is with private noncorporate business. So far as enterprises are concerned the main limiting factor to such a development would seem to be the difficulty of defining net enterprise income so sharply and in so businesslike a way that any implicit subsidy or indirect tax can be identified. And this limiting factor does not significantly affect the possibility that a more businesslike relation between physical capital formation and financial capital requirements may presently come to prevail.

For general government the answer to our question is by no means clear. It is true that a fully developed capital budget would imply capital asset accounting in a sense that would provide up-to-date figures on depreciation reserves, and hence presumably up-to-date debt to depreciated value ratios at least on an over-all basis for each unit of government. If capital outlays were defined as expenditures on real estate and its structural improvements, on depreciable equipment, and on additions to inventories; if current budget receipts and expenditures were defined to exclude portfolio transactions as well as transactions in the public debt; if charges against current (i.e. nonfinancial) receipts were defined to include depreciation, interest, expenditures on services, and cost of nondurable goods used; and if each government unit were to pursue a policy of balancing its current budget in this sense each year, the relation between capital outlays and net borrowing might indeed become somewhat comparable to that which characterizes private business today.

But a government unit that adopted a fiscal policy of this sort would thereby be committed to confining any contribution it might make toward a fiscal countercycle to its capital expenditures on real property, on depreciable equipment, and on increased inventories. Except for these physical capital items it would have ruled out the possibility of treating recession emergency expenditures as deferred charges that could be spread over a number of years, although the term "capital budget" has sometimes been construed to cover just such a budgetary practice.[19] Moreover, if it relied on flexible revenue sources like an income tax or a sales tax, it would—apart from recession increases in federal grants-in-aid—be compelled to curtail its current expenditures during a recession or else to have recourse to additional tax levies or increased rates.

The qualification "apart from recession increases in federal grants-in-aid" is, of course, a major one. Federal aid is a part of the subject of the next chapter. And in Chapter VI we trace the gradual development of some measure of responsibility for a countercycle as a federal government function. But it is unlikely that financing recession-incurred nonfinancial deficits will, in the calculable future, cease to be a significant source of state and local government capital requirements.

[19] See the paper by the present writer referred to in Chapter II, footnote 6.

In speculating both about changes in government functions and about possible new developments in fiscal procedures such as the capital budget, it seems safe to assume a good deal of historical continuity. Surely the immediate outlook is that changes in the amount of state and local net indebtedness are likely to continue to reflect broadly the whole government budgetary position—including adverse influences on that position during recessions—and that the connection between state and local physical capital formation and financial requirements is likely to continue to be an extremely loose one.

4. *Summary*

There seems to be a somewhat definite tendency for larger communities to have larger per capita gross debts, and larger per capita debts net of sinking funds, than smaller communities. But such differences in indebtedness for communities of different sizes seem to have been diminishing, the growth of debts in the smaller communities having been in process of gradually catching up with that in the larger ones.

The pattern by community size for net debts (in the sense of fully net) is less regular and probably less stable. Also the recent rapid growth of financial assets of larger cities may have converted the trend toward diminishing differences in per capita debts from one of leveling up the debts of smaller communities to one of leveling down those of larger ones.

Regional differences in per capita state and local government debts (net of sinking funds) seem in a general way to be associated with regional differences in per capita incomes and in levels of living.

Between 1890 and 1922 such regional differences in indebtedness widened. Between 1922 and 1942 they narrowed. The longer-term trend, 1890–1942, was toward a narrowing of regional differences in indebtedness. For the most part this trend seems to have reflected the fact that the several regions have been getting more nearly alike in respect to community-size composition, the more rapid growth of urban than of rural communities having been particularly pronounced in the regions that were predominantly rural in 1890.

Consideration of the variations in per capita debts with community size and the variations between census regions seems to suggest an upward trend in the level of such debts that is likely to continue, particularly when account is taken of the strong probability that both the process of urbanization and the growth of per capita incomes will continue in the years ahead. No doubt there was an upward trend in per capita state and local debts from 1890 to 1930. But this upward movement was interrupted by the depression of the 1930's, and the interruption was prolonged by World War II. It is still too early to determine with confidence whether the trend is being resumed, especially for per capita debts net of financial assets.

Our analysis of government financial requirements by the three main

85

types of requirement reveals relatively little stability in financing patterns.

A. Barring another occasion for postwar bonuses, emergency financing will hereafter probably be chiefly depression financing. During the 1930's such financing was to a considerable extent occasioned by countercyclical expenditures. In future, revenue decreases may prove to be relatively more important than they have commonly been so far.

B. In the past, variations in short-term indebtedness—and in liquid assets—have sometimes met a substantial part of the longer-term variations in financial requirements. In future they may perhaps be used more exclusively for short-term purposes.

C. While most long-term debt has been incurred to finance physical capital formation, the relation between borrowing and construction is very much complicated by changes in the financial condition of governments. On a quinquennial basis the ratio of new (non-refunding) bond issues to new (non-federally-financed) construction has—except for 1940–44— varied between 45 and 77 per cent since 1915; but the ratio of new bonds to increase in net debt has varied widely. For the three types of capital asset for which rough debt-to-value ratio computations can readily be made, schools, highways, and even water and sewage systems, changes in the ratios appear to have been quite sensitive to changes in the financial condition of governments. They also reflect the growing importance of federal and state aid.

While in general we assume government debts are incurred to finance legitimate (though not necessarily wise) expenditures, it is well to recognize that debts have sometimes been incurred because of disorderly financial practices. There were striking instances of such borrowing in connection with the Florida land boom of the 1920's.

But the fiscal procedures of governments have been gradually improving, and this process can be expected to continue. Eventually it may quite possibly help to make the patterns in state and local financial requirements more definite and stable.

The development of more businesslike accounting and budgeting practices for government enterprises is part of this process. In the course of time it may help to give the relationship between enterprise capital assets and enterprise debts a pattern that is a good deal more like that of comparable private businesses.

The state and local government capital budget practices so far developed would not be likely to have any such effect on the relation between general government-improved real properties and durable equipment and government debts, although the further development of such practices may some day push in this direction. For the nearer future, except for public enterprises, the very loose connection between capital formation and borrowing is likely to continue.

CHAPTER V

Changing Responsibilities for Meeting Financial Requirements

If the apportionment of functions among the various levels of government were clear-cut and stable, one might safely consider the financial requirements of each level without regard to the requirements of the others. But both functions and the responsibilities for financing them overlap, and the apportionment of both functions and responsibilities has been gradually changing. Also, of course, an over-all expansion in government functions has been taking place.

There have been two main types of change in the responsibilities for meeting financial requirements, those resulting from changes in the apportionment of substantive functions and those in which one unit of government simply assumes part of the burden of financing a function performed by another. We will refer to them respectively as changes in substantive and changes in fiscal functions.

The substantive function changes we will be concerned with in this chapter are mostly on the state and local levels. But we will encounter two kinds of functions responsible for extensive state and local borrowing in the nineteenth century that have substantially ceased to involve state or local financial requirements. Although maintenance of the National Guard continues to be a state function, state borrowing to finance the raising and equipping of an army came to an end with the Spanish-American War.[1] And state and local governments have come to leave the functions of extending credit to private parties and guaranteeing private credit almost entirely to the federal government.

In connection with the substantive changes in state and local government functions we will have occasion to examine the restrictions that have developed on state and local financing.

Formerly poor relief was considered to be primarily a local community responsibility. In considering here the changes in fiscal functions brought about by federal grants-in-aid we will note the development of grants for general (i.e. unemployment) relief and special public assistance programs. But more detailed attention will be given to the change in responsibility for financing general relief in Chapter VI.

[1] Two states borrowed to help finance their parts in this brief war. See the *Census of Wealth, Debt and Taxation* for 1902, pp. 161 and 169.

1. Substantive Functional Changes and Restrictions on Financing

Table 24 sketches the growth of state and local debts since 1839. One may infer from the incompleteness of the record that local debts were relatively unimportant before 1850. And state debts were small during the early years of the nineteenth century. After the formation of the Union, Revolutionary War debts had been assumed by the new federal government, and the federal government reimbursed the states for deficits incurred during the War of 1812.[2] But New York State borrowed to finance the Erie Canal during the 1820's and the success of this canal encouraged an era of extensive state financing. We have information about state debts in 1839, because of the great volume of new issues in 1835–38— over $100 million—and because of the financial difficulties following the crisis of 1837. The totals of state indebtedness in 1839 and 1841 compare with gross federal debt of $10 million in the former year and $5 million in the latter. From 1819 until the Civil War the federal debt was less than $100 million.

Table 2A indicates that the main purposes of state borrowing in the 1830's were aid to banks, building canals, and aid to railroads. Although all three of these purposes can well be regarded as public in nature, it is clear that government borrowing was extensively used to finance privately owned enterprises. And if a major objective in such financing was encouraging the process of industrialization, this objective seems to have been combined with that of accumulating a portfolio of income-yielding investments.[3] However, the great increase in debts left several states in a definitely unsound financial condition after the 1837 crisis. Eight states defaulted and three of them repudiated bond issues.[4] The situation was complicated "by the fact that foreigners had invested liberally in the securities which were now disowned"[5] or in default or even merely selling at a substantial discount.

One result of the post-1837 financial difficulties was unsuccessful agitation, 1842–43, to have the federal government again assume state debts. A second result, which will be considered shortly, was the adoption by a number of states of constitutional restrictions on their financing. Between 1842 and 1857, nineteen states adopted such restrictions.[6]

[2] B. U. Ratchford, *American State Debts*, p. 74. New York was the principal borrower in 1800–1820 and was apparently the first state to make extensive use of the bond type of credit instrument in its financing.

[3] Cf. Ratchford, *op.cit.*, p. 78.

[4] Including Florida, then a territory. Paul Studenski and Herman E. Krooss, *Financial History of the United States*, p. 118.

[5] Davis R. Dewey, *Financial History of the United States*, p. 244.

[6] H. Secrist, *An Economic Analysis of the Constitutional Restrictions Upon Public Indebtedness in the United States*, Appendix II.

TABLE 24

The Growth of State and Local Debts since 1839
(millions of dollars)

	States (1)	Counties (2)	Cities and Other Local Units (3)	Total (4)
	GROSS DEBTS LESS SINKING FUND ASSETS			
1839	164	a	a	a
1841	190	a	a	a
1843	a	a	27.5b	a
1853	193	a	a	a
1860	257	a	a	a
1870	353	188	328	869
1880	275	124	724c	1,123
1890	211	145	781c	1,137
1902	235	197	1,433c	1,865
	GROSS DEBTS			
1902	270	205	1,720	2,195
1913	423	393	3,682	4,498
1932	2,907	2,775	13,905	19,587
1940	3,526	2,156	14,564	20,246
1950	5,361	1,707	17,123	24,191
1953	7,824	2,454	23,282	33,560

a Not available.

b This figure covers only "cities." The increase in 1843–70 is therefore somewhat overstated by column 3. However, we may compare the debt of seventeen cities in January 1843 (reported in the *United States Magazine and Democratic Review*, February 1843, cited by A. M. Hillhouse, *Municipal Bonds*, p. 33) with the bonded debt of these cities outstanding in 1880 as reported in the census. For the seventeen cities the figures are: $25.5 million, 1843; $352 million, 1880. It is estimated that between 1843 and 1880 the population of these seventeen cities nearly quadrupled, while the population in all cities of more than 10,000 inhabitants increased more than sixfold. This suggests that the urban debt increase, 1843–80, was around twentyfold rather than the twenty-six indicated in column 3.

c School district debt was $18 million in 1880, $37 million in 1890, and $46 million in 1902. It is not separately identified for 1870.

NOTE: Figures are from the 1880 census for 1839–70; from the 1902 census for 1880–1902. Column 1 includes territories and the District of Columbia. The former source indicates that the figures in column 1 are gross, but it gives $260 million for gross state debt in 1880. The figures for 1870 are apparently partly net of sinking funds. All figures for 1880–1902 are net of sinking funds.

The 1880 census reports that from the time of the assumption of state debts in 1790 by the federal government to 1820 "but a small amount of state debt was contracted." It further reports that, of the $174 million of stocks issued by eighteen states in 1820–38, $108 million was issued during 1835–38.

Figures from 1902 to 1950 are from *Governmental Debt in the United States 1946* and *Governmental Debt in 1950*. Figures for 1953 are from *Summary of Government Finances in 1953*.

During the 1850's various states—in general not the states that had defaulted after 1837—borrowed to finance public improvements. And again following the crisis of 1857 there were financial difficulties, defaults, and one repudiation.[7] Then, during the Civil War there was extensive state borrowing to finance the war, for war finance had not yet ceased to be considered at least partly a state function. War debts of the Union states totaled $112 million and known war debts of the Confederate states, 1865, $96 million.[8] But, as the victorious federal government reimbursed the northern states for army costs amounting to nearly 50 per cent of their war-connected debts and as the war debts of the southern states were repudiated, Table 24 reflects only a small part of this borrowing.

This table also fails to bring out the major developments in state and local finance in the years immediately following the war—reconstruction and alleged reconstruction borrowing mainly by states in the South, and borrowing mainly by cities and other local governments in the North and West, 1867–73, to finance new public improvements of various kinds. Per capita debts of 130 cities increased from $37.30 in 1866 to $70.50 in 1876.[9] Some indication of the nature of the improvements financed by municipal debt increases can presumably be gleaned from Table 2A, column 1. The three largest debt purposes there are identified as water works, streets, and railroads and other aid. As Hillhouse so pertinently remarks, "With state aid for internal improvements checked, municipal aid filled the gap."[10] Municipal bond issues provided, in effect, a means of detouring constitutional limitations on state borrowing, so far as aid to railroads was concerned.

We noted in Chapter I that the ousting of the carpetbaggers was followed by debt repudiations and compositions totaling more than $100 million. In view of their experiences with the carpetbaggers several southern states adopted constitutional restrictions on state borrowing. Also most of the states admitted to the Union after the Civil War included debt restrictions in their constitutions. Even before 1873 a number of states had adopted constitutional restrictions on local government financing.[11] With the extensive defaults following the 1873 crisis—it has been estimated that 20 per cent of all outstanding municipal debt was in default[12]—there came a "wave of sentiment favorable to rigid restrictions on municipal indebtedness," and during 1873–79 restrictions on local

[7] Repudiation by Minnesota, at that time a territory. See Ratchford, *op.cit.*, p. 230.

[8] See Ratchford, *op.cit.*, pp. 136 and 151. A. M. Hillhouse, *Municipal Bonds*, pp. 61ff., notes that several cities borrowed to help finance the war.

[9] Data are from *Banker's Magazine* (New York) cited by Secrist, *op.cit.* Practically all of the cities of over 25,000 population must have been included in these data. And the growth of debt was certainly concentrated in the years 1866 to 1873.

[10] *Op.cit.*, p. 34.

[11] Secrist, *op.cit.*, p. 59.

[12] This estimate is cited by Hillhouse, *op.cit.*, pp. 15–17.

government financing were incorporated in the constitutions of eighteen states.[13] Indeed during the years following 1873 restrictions on local borrowing, either constitutional or statutory, became general.

The severity and nature of the restrictions that were imposed on states and on local units varied from state to state. As of the beginning of the twentieth century about a quarter of the state constitutions vested broad borrowing powers in their respective legislatures. So far as state financing was concerned the other states were about equally divided into two groups. In one group borrowing—except borrowing in a major emergency (such as a war or an insurrection) or short-term borrowing in anticipation of tax receipts—required a constitutional amendment. In the other group most nonbudget, nonemergency borrowing required approval by a popular referendum. In some states a constitutional upper limit on most of the debt was set in terms of the ratio of specified types of debt to the assessed value of property; in a few there was an absolute upper limit. A number of constitutions prohibited borrowing for internal improvements; a number prohibited the assumption of local debts; most of them prohibited lending their credit to or becoming stockholders in private enterprises.[14] And more detailed requirements were not infrequent: these included requiring that provision be made for a sinking fund; fixing a maximum maturity period; prescribing a maximum interest rate and prohibiting sale of bonds below par; and requiring the levying of taxes to service the debt.

The restrictions imposed on local government borrowing have been of a quite similar character, except that while some of them have been written into state constitutions others have been merely statutes or municipal charter provisions. In general there are such local restrictions even in states like Massachusetts whose constitutions vest their legislatures with broad borrowing powers. The requirement of a popular referendum has been common. Frequently different quantitative restrictions have been prescribed for different types of local government units and for different classes of cities. Special limits have been set for several of the larger cities. The debt to assessed property value limit has been widely used. For a time a number of absolute limits were set.

We have noted the great increase in municipal debts, 1890–1929, and in state and local debts generally, 1902–29. At least from 1910 on, as Table 8 makes clear, this growth of debts took place despite a steady increase in nonfinancial receipts. Table 8 also shows a cyclical decline in such receipts, 1930–33, of some 6 per cent. No doubt this average figure conceals significantly sharper declines for many individual units of

[13] Secrist, op.cit., pp. 60, 70, 71.
[14] For summaries of leading provisions see ibid., Part I, Chapter 3, and Ratchford, op.cit., Chapter XVII.

government. A considerable number of units, too, had borrowed enough and had large enough current commitments to find themselves in serious financial difficulties. Several states were barely able to meet their obligations. And Arkansas, having assumed various local debts in addition to its own, defaulted on certain of its interest payments in 1932–34. But in general the particularly serious cases of financial distress were to be found among local government units. Hillhouse puts the aggregate debts of the local units defaulting during the depression of the 1930's at 10 per cent of the total outstanding.[15] According to the *Commercial and Financial Chronicle*, "Of the total bonds in default the cities of Chicago and Detroit represent by far the largest amounts, the two of them together being responsible for about 550,000,000."[16] But many smaller units were in default, over 3,000 in all up to the end of 1935.[17] About a fifth of these were in Florida.[18] Nearly 15 per cent of the reclamation, levee, irrigation, and drainage districts were involved. No satisfactory estimate of the ultimate losses of municipal bondholders during the 1930's seems to be available, but such losses were presumably a very small part of the total value of bonds in default.

The growth of state and local debt up to 1929 reflected the great pressures for highways and various local improvements, pressures that in turn reflected a combination of major technological changes and a rising level of living. Partly because of these pressures, and partly because the years from 1900 to 1929 were on the whole years of business expansion and optimism, it was inevitable that there should have been some relaxation of state and local restrictions on borrowing. Absolute local debt limits were replaced by limits permitting growth. North and South Dakota amended their constitutions to give their state legislatures broader borrowing powers; and court interpretations, particularly the special funds doctrine, had the effect, in a number of states, of exempting highway and bridge bonds and bonds of educational institutions and various special agencies from constitutional restrictions on state borrowing.[19] But relaxations also took the form of various evasions of the constitutional and statutory restrictions on local financing. The most important form of evasion—and indeed the most substantial type of relaxation—involves the growth of special districts, a development to which we will shortly give attention.

Possibly it might have been expected that the financial distress of the

---

[15] *Op.cit.*, p. 17. He compares this with the estimate of 20 per cent for the 1873 depression. Long-term local debt outstanding in 1932 totaled $14.8 billion.

[16] January 30, 1934, pp. 35ff. Presumably the reference to Chicago should read "Cook County and three special districts in the Chicago area."

[17] See the *Bond Buyer* compilation summarized by Hillhouse, *op.cit.*, p. 25.

[18] *Commercial and Financial Chronicle*, January 30, 1934, pp. 35ff.

[19] See Ratchford, *op.cit.*, p. 434.

1930's, like that following 1873, would lead to some tightening of restrictions on public borrowing. Indeed by constitutional amendments Arkansas and North Carolina did make popular referendum, instead of legislative enactment, the main procedure for authorizing state debt issues. But on the whole what was done during the 1930's did not assume the form of imposing additional or more carefully drawn inflexible statutory and constitutional limitations and requirements along the lines of those established in the nineteenth century. Instead there were steps in the direction of temporary state administrative supervision or control of the finances of defaulting local units. Thus several states adopted measures during the 1930's for the administrative supervision of distress refunding issues.[20] Several states, too, earmarked state-collected, locally shared taxes to insure the servicing of defaulting local highway 'and other debt issues.[21] A more radical procedure, the administrative receivership of municipal corporations, was experimented with in three states and authorized in a fourth, and there were a number of states that made statutory provision for court-appointed receivers for defaulting special districts and municipally owned utilities.[22] It should be added that the federal bankruptcy act was amended in 1937 and 1940 to enable federal courts to give effect to appropriately approved plans for the composition of the debts of local government units.[23]

2. *The Rise of Special Districts*

Table 25 summarizes the part played by school and special district debts in the growth of total local government debt. Such units were unimportant borrowers before 1880. Indeed special districts were of little more than negligible consequence even in 1902; this type of governmental unit was then just beginning to come into use. Between 1902 and 1932 total local debts (net of sinking funds) increased nearly $13.6 billion. Of this amount school and special districts together accounted for nearly a quarter, and school districts alone for over 14 per cent. During the next decade most local governmental units retired some of their indebtedness; school districts showed a net retirement of nearly 18 per cent. But the depression apparently did not check the increased recourse to the special district type of unit. Seven states for which the 1932 Census reported no special district debts or taxes had special district net debt amounting to

[20] See Hillhouse, *op.cit.*, pp. 330ff.

[21] *Ibid.*

[22] On the administrative receiverships see Wylie Kilpatrick, *State Supervision of Local Finance*, pp. 42 and 64. On court receiverships see Hillhouse, *op.cit.*, pp. 297–320 and 349.

[23] It may be noted that the statistical status of defaulting public corporations is somewhat anomalous. During the 1920's the Investment Bankers Association of America started and then dropped a project to establish a reporting service on defaulted liabilities comparable to the Dun and Bradstreet series for private businesses. Apparently the project was dropped because it was felt this type of market information would hamper sales. Cf. Hillhouse, *op.cit.*, p. 518.

$84 million ten years later. The total debt of all special districts more than doubled in these ten years, and in 1942 it exceeded that of school districts. During the nine years ending 1951 school and special districts together accounted for more than half of the $3.7 billion of total local debt increase. It is clear that a substantial part of local government financing during the past half-century has been financed by school and special districts.

TABLE 25

The Growth of School and Special District Debt, Selected Years, 1880–1951

	School District Debt	Special District Debt	Total Local Government Debt	School District Debt	Special District Debt
	(millions of dollars)			(per cent of total local government debt)	
	(1)	(2)	(3)	(4)	(5)
1880	18	a	849	2.1	a
1890	37	a	926	4.0	a
1902	46	5	1,630	2.8	0.3
1913	119[b]	36[b]	3,477[b]	3.4	1.0
1922	1,053	626	7,754	13.6	8.1
1932	2,034	1,369	15,216	13.3	9.0
1942	1,662	2,791	14,965	11.1	18.7
1951	3,076	3,253	18,669	16.5	17.4

[a] Negligible.

[b] Places of less than 2,500 inhabitants not enumerated.

NOTE: Dollar figures are for gross debts less sinking fund assets as reported by the Bureau of the Census.

It is convenient to use the term "special district" in a sense which excludes school districts, but the school district may be said to be the prototype. The special district is, in general, a governmental unit devoted to one particular government function, or occasionally to two or three particular functions. In most cases the operations of the unit are confined to a district which is a small part of a state. And as a rule the unit is clearly autonomous and has a separate budget of its own, but sometimes the difference between a special district and a municipal department is not very wide. Table 26 classifies the 12,000-odd special districts in existence in 1952 by functional types. An increasing number of these government units are being established to undertake the construction and operation of revenue-producing facilities such as port facilities, airports, toll roads, and bridges.

There is something of a contrast between private corporations and municipal and other public corporations in respect to the incentives that make for and against consolidation. The sacrifices entailed in the decreased number of top jobs are perhaps similar in the two cases, but the loss of local autonomy when two or more geographically adjacent units of government are combined is likely to be a more serious deterrent to combining than any corresponding loss in the case of a horizontal business combination. The nearest thing to the profit incentive making for consolidations of public corporations is the incentive to economical and efficient operation, and this incentive makes principally for the consolidation of geographically

TABLE 26

Functional Types of Special Districts in 1952

Functional Type	Number
All types	12,319
Fire	2,272
Highways	774
Health and hospitals	371
Sanitation	429
Nonhighway transportation	159
Housing	863
Natural resources	5,224
Drainage	2,174
Soil conservation	1,981
Irrigation and water conservation	641
Other	428
Cemeteries	911
Urban water supply	665
Other	651

SOURCE: Data are from Bureau of the Census, *Governments in the United States in 1952*.

adjacent like units; there is scarcely any analogue of the incentive to vertical integration. Doubtless there is some gain in prestige for those who engineer a consolidation of public corporations that promises more efficient or economical operations, but the prestige gained is probably rather smaller than that attaching to many private consolidations.

We take the weakness of the incentives to consolidate government units and the strength of the deterrents to consolidation to constitute one of the main reasons for the growth of special districts. In the first place, when there are serious obstacles to a city's annexing adjacent territory, most of the advantage in efficiency and economy that might be realized by such annexation may perhaps be obtained by establishing special school, sewage, water supply, and fire districts to serve the larger area. Again, when there are public functions that require operation over a territory larger than—or at any rate other than—a metropolitan area, such as the construction and maintenance of levees, and drainage and irrigation systems, the special district is often the answer to the jurisdictional problem. Further, the need for combining adjacent jurisdictions to make possible the performance of a function or to provide for performing it efficiently may go beyond the local level. Thus some units, like the Port of New York Authority, are interstate special districts. And the joint authority device is quite capable of handling a problem of combining jurisdictions even at the international level as in the case of the Buffalo and Fort Erie Public Bridge Authority.

But there is a second main reason for the growth of special districts. Establishing such units has proven a very convenient method of openly evading, or in effect amending, debt limits and other restrictions on local governments. If a maximum debt to assessed property value ratio has been prescribed for cities, the establishment of school and special districts with separate borrowing powers to take over some of the municipal functions means a *de facto* increase in debt limits. Similarly if maximum tax limits are prescribed and the new special districts are given taxing powers, there is a *de facto* increase in tax limits. Further, the special district device can be used to make *de facto* exceptions to civil service procedures. It is little wonder that some special districts appear to have been created merely as incidents in political manipulation.

One cannot hope to apportion responsibility for the growth of school and special district debts as between the necessity for or advantage of having a jurisdiction appropriate to the performance of a particular public function on the one hand and the desire openly to evade restrictions on borrowing, the levying of taxes, etc. on the other. But it may be noted that both these influences in some measure reflect technological change. Thus the development of improved transportation makes it possible for a school to service a larger area; the development of improved equipment (e.g. fire fighting equipment) calls for raising more money and this in turn puts pressure on debt and tax limits. And it may also be noted that there is no reason to expect the particularly rapid growth of special district debt in the past few years to slacken in the near future. It is estimated that school districts accounted for about two-thirds of total long-term school debt in 1951.[24] But, if water supply systems are indicative of special district functions, special districts apparently have plenty of room left to grow in; in 1952 they accounted for only about a sixth of total water supply system long-term debt.[25]

Most school and special districts are quite small. Nearly two-thirds of the school districts had less than fifty pupils each in 1952. More than a third of the special districts—and almost half of those devoted to fire protection—had no separate paid employees. Seventy-one per cent of the special districts had no outstanding debt. If this legal form of organization

[24] See note on Table 23 in Appendix A.

[25] On special district debt see Bureau of the Census, *Special District Governments in the United States*, 1954, p. 8. The total of other water supply system debt was estimated on the basis of Bureau of the Census data for systems of cities of over 25,000 population, the total debt of these cities, and the total debt of all cities.

seems to offer some encouragement to larger-scale combinations, it has also facilitated a great deal of very small-scale operation. Still, mainly as a result of consolidations the number of school districts was reduced 47 per cent between 1932 and 1952.

Some special districts have been established to perform new government functions such as the maintenance and operation of an airport. Others have government functions of long standing: sewage systems, fire

TABLE 27

Local Government Units in the Continental United States and Their Debts, 1951

		Number of Units	Gross Debt 1951	Gross Debt 1902	Per Cent of 1951 Debts	Debt Per Unit in 1951 (thousands of dollars)
			(millions of dollars)			
		(1)	(2)	(3)	(4)	(5)
A.	Counties	3,049	1,875	205	9.1	615
B.	Townships	17,202	411	57	2.0	24
C.	Cities of more than 25,000 population in 1950	482	9,975	1,612	48.2	20,650
D.	Other cities, towns, and villages	16,296	1,746		8.5	107
E.	School districts	67,346	3,257	46	15.7	48
F.	Special districts	12,319	3,403	5	16.5	276
G.	Total	116,694	20,667	1,925	100.0	182

SOURCE: Bureau of the Census, *Governments in the United States in 1952* and *Governmental Debt, 1951*. The number of counties reported on line A includes ten that are identified with city governments.

protection stations, highways. And of course school districts perform a long-recognized government function. Indeed a large proportion of the functions of these new forms of government have been taken over from older forms, particularly from municipalities.

It is not surprising therefore that Table 27 shows that the increase in the financing functions of school and special districts in the last half-century has been mainly at the expense of cities. Five-sixths of all local debts in 1902 were municipal; it is little wonder the term has sometimes been used to cover all state and local issues. In 1951 less than three-fifths of the total were municipal. The units here called townships are to be found in twenty-two states. They include what are locally termed "towns" in New England, New York, and Wisconsin (as well as some "plantations" in Maine). Densely populated townships in New England, New Jersey, and Pennsylvania—and to a less extent in New York and Wisconsin—may perform various functions commonly associated with municipalities. Their importance has decreased from 3 per cent to 2 per cent of the total. Counties have almost held their own.

97

3. *Grants-in-Aid and Changes in Fiscal Functions*

In 1952 there were over 113,000 local government units in the United States. But the 482 cities of over 25,000 population in 1950 and the 408 special districts having debts of over $1 million each together accounted for more than half of the total local debt in 1951. Apart from the tax-exempt privileges they enjoy, the many thousand smaller units of government are presumably not in a particularly advantageous position to borrow. Credit standing on the whole improves with increased size; so does the ability to place a loan on advantageous terms. Even the average city of over 25,000 is relatively a considerably smaller-scale borrower than the average state. The $20.7 million of debt per city compares with an average debt per state of $133 million. In 1950 the average amount of long-term debt issued by cities of 25,000 to 50,000 population was $403,000 per city; by cities of 50,000 to 100,000 population it was $723,000; by cities of 500,000 to 1,000,000 population it was $11.75 million; for the five cities of over a million it was $80 million; for the states it was $28 million per state.

Thus far we have considered mainly those cases of changes in the responsibilities for meeting financial requirements that have entailed transfers of substantive functions from one type of government unit to another. The comparisons just made suggest another kind of change, one brought about by grants-in-aid. One factor in the growth of state grant-in-aid programs is that, in respect to credit standing and ability to place loans advantageously, states are in a much better position to borrow than are the vast majority of local government units. And superior ability to borrow in combination with the huge growth of state aid helps to explain why the states have been going into debt more rapidly than local governments. In 1902 states were obligors for less than one-eighth of the total gross state and local debt outstanding; in 1953 for 23 per cent. (See Table 24.)

But in connection with the shifting of part of the financial responsibility for local government functions to the states through grant-in-aid programs there is need to consider the whole budget, both state and local. We saw in Chapter III that state employment has grown more rapidly than local, and presumably by the same token so have state expenditures on other objects than grants-in-aid. We saw, too, that state tax receipts have grown more rapidly still. The great increase in state receipts was accomplished through the development of new tax sources; state property tax receipts were slightly less in 1950 than in 1932. But local governments have continued to depend heavily on the real property tax, and even in 1950 they were only beginning to tap new tax sources.

It would seem that the states have had a superior ability to raise money through taxation as well as borrowing. In part this means that major new taxes—income, gasoline, alcoholic beverage, tobacco, and general sales taxes—can be more effectively administered on a state-wide basis; in part that even the limited recourse by local units to new tax sources that has taken place has required the states to grant them additional taxing powers. Probably it means, too, that the change in the structure of the tax system brought about by the development of the new taxes has somehow facilitated the vast expansion in tax revenues, even though the facilitation has presumably been primarily political rather than economic in nature.

To the extent that fiscal considerations have contributed to the growth of state grant-in-aid programs, we can say that this growth results from a combination of a very substantial expansion of local government functions —but a less rapid expansion than in the case of the states—and the superior ability of states to raise money by taxing and by borrowing. But nonfiscal considerations have been a factor too. In particular, states have sought to raise and maintain standards of performance of local government functions—education, welfare, and highways are the programs identified in Table 28—and to reduce interlocal inequalities in these standards of performance. No doubt these objectives involve some fiscal considerations in addition to those already noted. Interlocal differences in performance may be due to differences in ability to finance, the effects of which are diminished by the grants; also in the case of highway grants-in-aid one objective may be to make the (gasoline) tax fall on those responsible for the cost of the service. Further, the figures on state grants include state-collected, locally shared taxes; the main motive for this kind of aid is presumably improved efficiency in tax collection.

But raising, maintaining, and equalizing standards are clearly substantive rather than fiscal objectives; and to the extent that their realization requires state interference with local self-government the grant-in-aid device is a most agreeable form for the interference to take.

Table 28 outlines the growth of both federal and state grants-in-aid. State highway and welfare aid programs were apparently started a little earlier than federal programs in these fields. From the beginning aid to education has been the major type of state grants; and to date there have been only peripheral federal programs in this area such as the vocational training of veterans and school lunch programs.

Federal aid increased from less than one per cent of federal non-financial receipts and about 2.5 per cent of state receipts in 1913 to 17.2 per cent of state receipts and nearly 5 per cent of federal in 1950. State aid seems to have been a consistently larger total than federal. Even in 1913 (when the full amount cannot be identified) it must have been nearly

99

TABLE 28

Intergovernmental Aid Compared to Nonfinancial Receipts,
Selected Years, 1913–50

		1913	1929	1942	1950
		Millions of dollars			
A.	Federal nonfinancial receipts	980	4,950	23,700	49,100
B.	Federal aid	9	117	888	2,339
C.	State nonfinancial receipts	368	2,375	6,870	13,600
D.	State aid	87[a]	647[b]	1,791	4,011
E.	Local nonfinancial receipts	1,882	6,325	8,630	18,000
F.	Aid received by larger cities	26[c]	116	394[d]	744[e]
G.	Nonfinancial receipts of larger cities	700[c]	2,597	2,516[d]	4,512[e]
		Per cent			
H.	B/A	0.9	2.4	3.8	4.8
J.	B/C	2.4	4.9	12.9	17.2
K.	D/C	23.6	27.3	26.1	29.5
L.	D/E	4.6	10.2	20.7	22.3
M.	F/G	3.7	4.5	15.6	16.5
	THE LARGER FEDERAL AID PROGRAMS				
		Millions of dollars			
N.	Highways	0	84	164	455
P.	Public assistance and relief	0	0	412[f]	1,123
Q.	Employment security	0	0	72	215[g]
R.	Public health and maternal and child welfare	0	1	31	214[h]
S.	Vocational training and rehabilitation	0	8	134	55
T.	Agriculture and forestry[j]	2[c]	12	29	61
U.	Total above	2[c]	105	842	2,123
	THE LARGER STATE PROGRAMS				
		Millions of dollars			
V.	Highways	12[k]	194	338	576
W.	Welfare	m	m	389	733
X.	Schools	98[k]	336	766	1,982
Y.	Total above	110[k]	530	1,493	3,291

NOTE: Figures on lines A and B, 1929 through 1950, are on a calendar year basis; other dollar amounts are on a fiscal year basis. Lines F and G are for cities of more than 100,000 population; but see note d. Some grants-in-aid are paid by local governments; in 1942 such payments totaled $48 million. Cities of over 250,000 population received $3 million in local grants in 1942; $22 million in 1950. There are major types of intergovernment payments not treated as grants-in-aid in this table; see accompanying text.

a Incomplete total. Only highway and education grants were fully identified for these years.

b By interpolation on data for 1927 and 1932.

c 1912 figure.

d This figure is for 1940. It covers only city corporations; figures for 1912 and 1929 include computed portions of receipts of overlying counties and school and special districts. On this more comprehensive basis the figure for line F is $540 million; for line G, $3,156 million.

e This figure covers only city corporations.

f The total was $975 million in 1936.

g Includes reimbursements for administering veterans' readjustment allowances.

h Includes school lunch program.

j Excludes colleges of agriculture.

k 1915 figure.

m Not available.

SOURCE: See Appendix A.

a quarter of state nonfinancial receipts and nearly 5 per cent of local receipts. By 1950 these ratios had risen to about 29 per cent and 22 per cent respectively. But again it should be noted that the figures on line D include state-collected, locally shared taxes.

It can be argued that for 1942 and 1950 the ratios on line J understate the importance of federal aid, because the figures for total state non-financial receipts include withdrawals from the Unemployment Compensation Fund while the figures on line B do not. Excluding such withdrawals from their denominators the ratios become respectively 15.5 and 19.2 per cent.

Aid seems to have represented a smaller proportion of nonfinancial receipts for the larger cities than for other local units from the very start.

The considerations which have led to the growth of federal aid are somewhat similar to those already noted in the case of the states. The federal government has fiscal advantages over the states; and it has sought to promote standards for the performance of various state functions and to decrease interstate inequalities in performance. Some of the substantive objectives of federal aid programs might have involved both political and constitutional difficulties had a less agreeable method than offering grants on the condition of meeting the standards been employed. In general the substantive considerations seem to have been more important in federal than in state aid programs. The public assistance and relief grants were intended to provide a national system of benefits to relieve general unemployment and aid the blind, the aged, mothers of dependent children, and the totally disabled in a way that would complement the national unemployment and old age insurance programs. The employment security grants—for state unemployment compensation administrations and employment exchanges—have constituted integral parts of the un-employment insurance system. The highway grants have provided a national system of rural roads which, among other things, serves the interests of national defense. Both the grants for veterans' education and rehabilitation and those for agriculture are small parts of broad federal programs. And one may suspect that the present health and education grants are parts of incipient more ambitious programs.

Table 29 analyzes by regions ratios for 1952 which are approximately equivalent to those shown on lines J and K of Table 28. All but 7 per cent of the intergovernmental revenue is federal aid; the intergovernmental expenditure includes in addition to state aid only a small unidentified amount of reimbursements for the cost of services performed by other units; total revenue is a slightly less inclusive concept than total non-financial receipts. Aid received is in general a larger proportion of state revenue in those states where per capita income payments to individuals are relatively low. The proportion of state revenue paid out in local aid

101

follows no clear pattern. Presumably the ratios in column 5 reflect both the extent of the need to supplement local fiscal capacity and the degree to which the various states have sought to influence the standards of performance of local government functions.

Not quite all grants-in-aid are paid by federal and state governments; but no comprehensive recent compilation of total local grants is available. In 1942 local grants amounted to $48 million, or about 2 per cent of the

TABLE 29

1952 Intergovernmental Revenue and Expenditure and Total Revenue of
State Governments in Relation to Per Capita Income, by Regions

		$(2)/(3)$ (per cent) (1)	Inter- governmental Revenue (2)	Total Revenue (millions of dollars) (3)	Inter- governmental Expenditures (4)	$(4)/(3)$ (per cent) (5)	Per Capita Income Payments to Individuals (6)
A.	New England	13.8	146	1,061	244	23.0	1,763
B.	Middle East	10.0	370	3,698	1,035	28.0	1,892
C.	S. East	18.3	578	3,157	871	27.6	1,127
D.	S. West	21.0	253	1,205	334	27.7	1,422
E.	Central	13.8	582	4,201	1,299	30.9	1,782
F.	N. West	21.5	213	990	276	27.9	1,541
G.	Far West	13.5	347	2,507	980	38.1	1,928
H.	Total	14.8	2,485	16,815	5,044	30.0	1,644

Data for the Middle Eastern region (Del., D.C., Md., N.J., N.Y., Pa., and W. Va.) in columns 2, 3, and 4 do not include the District of Columbia. Other regions and the states they include are Southeast: Ala., Ark., Fla., Ga., Ky., La., Miss., N.C., S.C., Tenn., and Va.; Southwest: Ariz., N. Mex., Okla., and Tex.; Central: Ill., Ind., Iowa, Mich., Minn., Mo., Ohio, and Wisc.; Northwest: Colo., Ida., Kan., Mont., Nebr., N.D., S.D., Utah, and Wyo.; Far West: Calif., Nev., Ore., and Wash.

SOURCES: Columns 2, 3, and 4, *State Government Finances in 1952*; Column 6, *Survey of Current Business*, August 1954, p. 15. Note: Details may not add to totals because of rounding.

grants by all levels of government in that year. Three-quarters of the 1942 local grants were made by counties.

At least in respect to fiscal considerations cash grants by one nation to others, either directly or through United Nation channels, should be classed with grants to state and local governments. But we will defer comment on international grants to Chapter VIII.

4. Summary

Because of the changes that have taken place in the apportionment of substantive government functions among the various levels of government and because of the growth of federal and state aid programs, it is advisable to consider the financial requirements of all the levels of government together.

Formerly states shared with the federal government the responsibility for expanding and equipping the army in time of war; what remains of state responsibility for the National Guard is unlikely again to involve state governments in war finance. And although state and local governments formerly engaged in extending credit to and guaranteeing the credit of privately owned undertakings, such activities are today almost exclusively federal functions.

Past financial difficulties have led to the imposition of various restrictions on the borrowing powers first of state and later of local governments.

With restrictions on state borrowing and on state aid to railroads and other enterprises incorporated in the constitutions of many states between the crisis of 1837 and the end of the Civil War, municipal aid programs and municipal borrowing expanded rapidly, 1866–73. Then the financial difficulties following the 1873 crisis led to a wave of restrictions on local borrowing.

In 1902 school and special district debts were less than 3 per cent of all local debts. By 1951 this ratio had increased to nearly one-third. These districts have important advantages from the point of view of the horizontal integration of local government functions. They are also means of getting around debt and tax limits and other legal restrictions on local governments. Some of the functions of these units are new; most of them have been taken over from other forms of local government, particularly municipalities, and from the states.

The relative importance of the financial requirements of school and special districts is likely to continue to increase. Consolidations decreased the number of school districts between 1932 and 1952, and this process too is likely to continue. In the course of time it may embrace special districts as well.

States have been assuming responsibility for providing a larger and larger share of the costs of local government, and the federal government has been doing so for both states and local units. In 1950 federal aid was 17.2 per cent of state nonfinancial receipts. Fiscal considerations have played an important part in aid programs—particularly the advantages of the federal government and the states over other units both as tax collectors and as borrowers. Another major set of considerations, more important in the case of federal than of state programs, relates to substantive policies: the promotion of standards of performance and uniform performance on the part of the units of government receiving the aid. The grant-in-aid device is an agreeable form for such supervision of local and of state performance to take, and in the case of federal aid a form that sometimes avoids the possibility of constitutional questions.

In general, federal aid is a larger proportion of state revenues in those parts of the country in which personal income per capita is low.

CHAPTER VI

Fiscal Flexibility and Countercyclical Financial Requirements

Since World War I and more especially since the 1929–33 recession there has been an increasing tendency to think that the federal government has some measure of responsibility for seeing that the employment of our manpower and material resources is kept at a high and fairly stable level.

We have noted that practically all of the net federal debt that is not war debt is attributable to efforts to discharge this responsibility during the 1930's. From 1929 to 1939 net federal debt increased by $16 billion, and we may take this amount as a rough measure of depression-connected debt.

In this chapter we will first review federal fiscal policy during the years when the full-employment responsibility was emerging as a new government function, then examine the experiences of the 1930's and of three recessions that have occurred since that decade as they bear on the financial requirements which this function may entail.

Past experience seems to make it advisable to distinguish two sets of circumstances under which measures designed to maintain or raise the level of employment may occasion financial requirements. On the one hand there have been short, relatively minor recessions from high level employment that have commonly been followed without great delay by periods of substantial prosperity. On the other hand there have been periods of far more severe unemployment. We propose therefore to treat separately the experience of the 1930's and the recessions of 1945, 1949, and 1953–54. Whatever the future may have in store in the way of business recessions, we deem it advisable to deal separately with the experience of the 1930's and, despite the minor cyclical peak in 1937, to treat 1929–40 as a single period.

1. On the Evolution of Fiscal Policy

Before World War I federal fiscal policy reflected business cycles in a passive sense only. Table 30 shows average annual general receipts and surpluses by alternate periods of relatively good and relatively poor business. In the absence of a countercyclical policy we might expect both column 1 and column 2 to increase or decrease with general business activity. In seven out of the thirteen cases shown they do. And the other

TABLE 30

Federal General Receipts and Surpluses by Selected Business Cycle
Periods, 1867–1915

(annual averages for fiscal years in millions of dollars)

Years of Relatively Good and Relatively Poor Business	Receipts (1)	Surpluses (2)	NBER Contraction Periods (3)
1867–73	395.6	77.5	June 1869–Dec. 1870
1874–79	283.3	18.8	Oct. 1873–Mar. 1879
1880–82	365.9	103.8	
1883–85	356.8	100.2	Mar. 1882–May 1885
1886–92	374.9	74.0	⎰ Mar. 1887–Apr. 1888
			⎱ July 1890–May 1891
1893–97	340.6	−25.4	⎰ Jan. 1893–June 1894
			⎱ Dec. 1895–June 1897
1898–1902	527.7	11.9	June 1899–Dec. 1900
1903–04	551.5	1.2	Sept. 1902–Aug. 1904
1905–07	601.7	32.8	
1908	601.8	−57.3	May 1907–June 1908
1909–10	639.9	−53.8	
1911	701.8	10.6	Jan. 1910–Jan. 1912
1912–13	708.4	1.2	
1914–15	716.3	−31.5	Jan. 1913–Dec. 1914

Source: Columns 1 and 2 are from *Historical Statistics*, pp. 89, 97. Column 2 reports the excess of nonfinancial receipts over nonfinancial expenditures. General receipts in column 1 are less than total nonfinancial receipts by the amount of postal revenues. The left-hand dates in column 3 are upper cyclical turning points, the right-hand dates are the immediately following lower turning points. The dates are from A. F. Burns and W. C. Mitchell, *Measuring Business Cycles*, pp. 510–511. Thus three of the periods here classified as periods of relatively good business include minor recessions: 1867–73, 1886–92, and 1898–1902; and the period of relatively poor business, 1893–97, includes a minor upswing.

six can hardly be considered exceptions to the rule of a cyclically passive fiscal policy.

There was a persistent surplus in 1866–92, resulting in large part from the retention of customs duties at not far from the levels they had reached during the Civil War. The contracyclical drop in the average surplus from $100 million in 1883–85 to $74 million during the next seven years was mainly the result of steps taken to eliminate this surplus, particularly various increases in veterans' pensions in 1886–90 and the substitution in the McKinley Tariff Act (1890) of a subsidy on domestic sugar for the previous import duty.

In three of the cases shown the surplus declines when business activity declines, but not as a result of decreased receipts: 1903–04, 1908, and 1914–15. However, there is no reason to regard the expenditure increases in these three cases as reflecting a countercyclical policy. The chief factor in 1903–04 was the $50 million purchase cost of the Panama Canal. And while in 1908 there were various increases in expenditures, particularly

105

those on the War and Navy Departments, on the Panama Canal and rivers and harbors, and on veterans' pensions, these must have been authorized by Congress by the midsummer of 1907. Again, the 1914–15 deficit reflected mainly a resumption in the marked upward trend in expenditures following a temporary check in 1909–12. But in this instance the revenue increase was small too, owing in part to a cut in customs receipts following the Underwood Tariff Act (1913).

While the cases of positive cyclical correlation help to support the proposition that before 1916 federal fiscal policy reflected business cycles in a passive sense only, the decrease in receipts from 1886–92 to 1893–97 by no means fully explains the $100 million surplus drop. Increased pensions and other expenditures were factors here too. And while the average surplus increased simultaneously with an improvement in business conditions from 1893–97 to 1898–1902, dropped during the 1902–04 business contraction, and rose again with improved business in 1905–07, the 1898–1902 surplus increase reflects in large measure the prompt enactment of war taxes during the brief Spanish-American War and the continuation of most of these emergency levies until 1901. On the other hand if the relationship between surpluses and cycles seems to be negative, 1909–12, this appearance results at least in part from the failure of fiscal year-ends to coincide with cyclical turning points.

On the whole the attitude of the federal government toward the cycle throughout this period was one of *laissez faire* both with respect to the possibility of controlling or influencing the level of gross national product and with respect to measures for relieving or diminishing the suffering caused by business recessions and depressions. Indeed, in accord with this philosophy it was in general considered that provision of relief beyond what could come from private charity was the responsibility of local governments, and that relief should be given only to persons incapable of self-support and should be provided through poorhouses and orphan asylums rather than in the form of an "out-relief" dole. However, the Homestead Act, the veterans' programs, the Indian reservation policy since the Dawes Act (1887), and the extension of relief to victims of various major disasters might be cited as exceptions to this view of government functions.

Though the *laissez faire* philosophy dominated the attitudes of the federal government toward business cycles, the main components of the tax system were, paradoxically, of a regulatory nature. Thus the protective tariff together with the excises on alcoholic beverages and tobacco manufactures yielded almost nine-tenths of total general receipts in 1880 and were still yielding about this proportion in 1910.[1] But despite their regulatory character these revenue sources were quite compatible with one

[1] That is, nine-tenths of total nonfinancial receipts other than postal revenues.

basic tenet of *laissez faire* fiscal policy—a balanced budget. And from 1890 to 1916 the gross federal debt was approximately stabilized at a little over $1 billion.

During the period following the Civil War the idea of federal responsibility for taking steps to end bad times or assure good ones was injected into political campaigns in various ways. Both Greenback and Populist parties were concerned to remedy the hard times for farmers and urban wage earners that followed deflationary financial crises.[2] And it can be cogently argued that the real issue in the campaign of 1896 was whether the free coinage of silver in the ratio of 16 to 1 or retention of "sound money" together with a tariff that protected "the full dinner pail" was the more effective countercyclical policy.

With the somewhat buoyant business that characterized the early years of the twentieth century, agitation for countercyclical measures concentrated for a time on revising the banking and monetary system so that it would not be a cyclically disturbing influence. Then, a decade after the establishment of the Federal Reserve System, the Reserve Board in its Tenth Annual Report proposed, in part because "central bank practices associated with an effective international gold standard are now inoperative," to substitute "current surveys of business conditions" for "the reserve ratio" as a guide to its credit policy.[3] Thus it adopted a countercyclical credit policy as a major objective.

During the 1920's the federal government took one other step that could be characterized as a move in the direction of a countercycle—it accepted some responsibility for helping farmers to dispose of agricultural surpluses. Thus when the 1929–33 recession began there were several more or less established policies that could be brought to bear on it: Federal Reserve policy, the veterans' benefits program, and Federal Farm Board loans on commodities to cooperatives and stabilization corporations. To these were quite promptly added an acceleration of work on federal construction projects and increased grants-in-aid of road construction to the states. Table 31 relates the countercyclical expenditure programs undertaken during the early 1930's to the gross national product. If the increases in federal expenditures in 1929–31 seem extremely small in relation to the

---

[2] "Two of the three Presidential candidates (1876–1884) nominated by the Greenback party represented labor rather than agriculture." Earl D. Ross, "The Emergence of Agricultural Regionalism," in *The Growth of the American Economy*, edited by Harold F. Williamson, pp. 385–86. According to Studenski and Krooss, *Financial History of the United States*, p. 221, the legislation for which Coxey's army pleaded in 1893 included bills to authorize the issue of "$500 million of noninterest-bearing legal-tender notes by the federal government to finance construction of roads," and by state and local governments of "noninterest-bearing bonds against the credit of the United States up to one-half of the assessed valuation of property, the proceeds to be spent for the relief of the unemployed."

[3] Pp. 29–39.

drop in gross national product, and if expenditures were contracted in 1932,[4] it must be remembered that belief in balancing the budget was still prevalent. Both major parties had balance-the-budget planks in their 1932 platforms. Probably it should be added, too, that three times during

TABLE 31

Various Federal Expenditure Programs and Federal Credit, 1929–33
(millions of dollars, calendar years)

		1929	1930	1931	1932	1933
A.	Benefit payments to veterans[a]	562	603	1,577	781	554
B.	Direct new construction expenditures	155	209	271	333	346
C.	Construction grants-in-aid to states	80	104	235	111	286
D.	Work relief payrolls	0	0	0	0	356
E.	Total nonfinancial expenditures	3,700	3,800	5,050	4,100	5,050
F.	Federal Farm Board cumulative advances less repayments, December 31	41	232[b]	436[b]	480[c]	334[d]
G.	Other Farm Credit Administration loans outstanding, December 31	1,282	1,328	1,349	1,335	1,633
H.	Reconstruction Finance Corporation portfolio of non-agricultural loans and securities	0	0	0	1,187	1,993
J.	Gross national product	104,436	91,105	76,271	58,466	55,964

[a] Includes loans on the security of adjusted service certificates. Loans made on such security by the United States Government Life Insurance Fund are not included in line E.

[b] Includes a small amount of delinquent loans.

[c] As of May 26, 1933, when the Board and other agricultural credit agencies were consolidated into the Farm Credit Administration. Includes $13.5 million of foreclosed loans on wheat, collateral for which had been donated to the Red Cross, and $5 million of delinquent loans.

[d] A part of the decrease from May 26 (footnote c above) reflects losses. Total losses in 1935 were estimated at $345 million (see Appendix A).

SOURCE: See Appendix A.

1930–32 temporary reversals of the downward trend of industrial production seem to give some ground for thinking "prosperity is just around the corner."

The federal countercyclical expenditure programs identified in Table 31 undoubtedly set a new precedent regarding federal responsibilities. But they did very little to provide unemployment relief. And as the recession continued and incomes and employment declined further and further, the need for relief and assistance grew far beyond what local and private agencies could provide. Indeed, with the decline in personal and national income the ability of such agencies to finance relief and assistance programs

[4] Federal payrolls other than work relief payrolls decreased from $1,353 million in 1932 to $1,232 million in 1933.

was seriously curtailed. In September 1931 New York State established a Temporary Emergency Relief Administration and appropriated $20 million[5] for state aid to localities for unemployment relief. Other states followed New York's example. But the problem had become too large even for the states, and in July 1932 Congress, after more than six months of consideration, passed a $322 million appropriation bill (the Emergency Relief and Construction Act of 1932), which authorized the newly organized Reconstruction Finance Corporation to make $300 million of loans to states and local governments for unemployment relief. Originally it had been expected that the RFC would extend financial assistance to agriculture, commerce, and industry by making loans to banks and other financial institutions; and it had been intended that the corporation should confine its operations to "fully and adequately secured" loans.[6] But the nearly $300 million of loans extended to states under the enlarged RFC authority of the July 1932 act were later made forgiven debts. And in May 1933 Congress passed another Federal Emergency Relief Act which made unemployment relief definitely a federal function. Moreover, 1933 saw the inauguration of what turned out to be a $12 billion work relief program.[7]

Other steps taken during 1933–39—they are considered in Section 2 below—broadened federal responsibilities both for promoting an increase in business activity when business is poor and for relieving the distress caused by a depression. But the objective of a balanced budget had not been entirely dropped. In March 1933, pursuant to a recommendation by President Roosevelt, Congress had passed an Economy Act providing for a 15 per cent cut in federal salaries and for restricting the payments of veterans' pensions.[8] Also the years 1931–36 were characterized by a general upward trend in tax rates and a resort to additional tax revenue sources. As a result the ratio of federal taxes to gross national product increased from 3.5 per cent in 1929 to 7.5 per cent in 1937.[9] And in 1935, despite

[5] Intended to last eight months. Another $20 million was appropriated five months later.

[6] Cf. the first Quarterly Report, March 31, 1932, p. 2.

[7] The Civilian Conservation Corps was organized in April, the Civil Works Administration in November 1933. The Works Progress Administration was organized in May, the National Youth Administration in June 1935.

[8] Cf. footnote 4 above on federal payrolls. The cut proved to be temporary. See Table 31 on veterans' benefits. Veterans' benefits were reduced again in 1934. They were $554 million in 1933; $452 million in 1934.

[9] The numerators of these ratios are net tax accruals and miscellaneous receipts computed from Tables 8, 34, and 35 of the 1954 *National Income Supplement* to the *Survey of Current Business*. They equal total federal receipts minus contributions for social insurance on account of federal civilian employee retirement systems and government life insurance. The comparison presumably understates the increase, because of the "built-in flexibility" of the individual and corporation income taxes. In 1937, 14.3 per cent of the labor force was unemployed; in 1929, only 3.2 per cent.

the fact that there were over ten million unemployed, work relief payrolls were cut 20 per cent below their 1934 level to $611 million. But in January 1936 Congress passed a veterans' bonus bill over a presidential veto.

Although the deficit in nonfinancial transactions showed a decrease of about $500 million in 1935,[10] on the whole federal fiscal policy for 1933–36 pushed in the direction of an increase in gross national product. But from 1936 to 1937 the push was markedly in the other direction. The nonfinancial transactions deficit dropped from a little under $5 billion to less than $50 million.[11] In substantial part this drop resulted from what the veterans' bonus added to the 1936 deficit. But tax increases were quite as important. Individual income, estate, and gift tax collections in 1937 were up some $840 million over 1936; corporation income and related tax collections were up some $680 million; and the receipts of social security taxes—which began in 1937—were about $660 million.[12] Moreover, the Revenue Act of 1936 imposed an undistributed earnings tax on corporations. And whatever the theoretical merits of undistributed earnings as a tax base, the 1936 tax seems to have proven administratively to be very irritating.

In the third quarter of 1937 private domestic demand for gross national product was at an annual rate of $86.1 billion. By the second quarter of 1938 it had shrunk to $64.2 billion. Of this $21.9 billion decline, the inventory increment accounted for $8.1 billion, consumer expenditures for $10.0 billion, and construction and producers' durables for $4.8 billion.[13] In view of the large part played by inventories in the 1937–38 business contraction, and the fact that wholesale price increases in late 1936 and early 1937 contributed to profits reckoned on a FIFO basis, wholesale price decreases in late 1937 and early 1938 to FIFO basis losses, it is reasonable to suppose that the immediate cause of the contraction was a change in business psychology. And the magnitude of the adverse

[10] For this deficit see Table 5.

[11] In the national income and product accounts the drop is from $3.5 billion to $186 million. On this basis veterans' benefits, other than life insurance policy benefits, were $1.9 billion in 1936; on the basis used in Table 5 (which includes the taking up of adjusted service certificates used as collateral for prior year loans by the United States Government Life Insurance Fund) they were $2.5 billion. Also 1936 corporation income and profits tax collections in the Table 5 computation were slightly larger than the corresponding accruals in the national income and product account computations. Other factors common to 1935 and 1936 tend to make the Table 5 deficit larger than that shown in the national income and product accounts in both years.

[12] The Revenue Act of 1935 increased tax rates particularly for the upper brackets, although it did not go as far in taxing large incomes as President Roosevelt had recommended.

[13] See Harold Barger, *Outlay and Income in the United States 1921–38*, Table 11. The annual rate figures are seasonally adjusted. The inventory increment fell from plus $5.95 billion to minus $2.13 billion.

impulse from federal fiscal policy makes it seem probable that this adverse impulse touched off the change in psychology.[14]

The 1937–38 contraction made many converts to the view that economic stabilization should be a major—if not the main—objective of fiscal policy. And the widespread concern about a possible sharp postwar recession that prevailed immediately before V-J Day helped the passage of the Employment Act of 1946. But in February 1946, when the act was passed, it was clear that the recession was less sharp than the Office of War Mobilization and Reconversion had predicted, and the language used was qualified accordingly. Section 2 of the act declares it to be a federal policy to create and maintain "conditions under which there will be afforded useful employment opportunities . . . for those able, willing, and seeking to work, and to promote maximum employment, production, and purchasing power," this policy to be carried out in a manner consistent with the federal government's "needs and obligations and other considerations of national policy" and "in a manner calculated to foster free competitive enterprise and the general welfare," and to be carried out "with the assistance of industry, agriculture, labor, and state and local governments." In effect, the act, having declared this policy, left its implementation largely to subsequent acts of Congress.

If one may draw a firm conclusion from this review of the process by which a government responsibility for economic stability has been developing, it would appear to be that a prolonged period of high employment would be likely to weaken the responsibility, a period of severe unemployment to push in the other direction. But the trend is toward broadening the responsibility and making it more categorical.

---

[14] It can be argued that Federal Reserve policy (and Treasury policy in "sterilizing" gold) helped to start the contraction; cf. Kenneth D. Roose, *The Economics of Recession and Revival*, p. 239; "The Federal Reserve action on excess reserves caused short-term governments to weaken and . . . thereby . . . the weakening of the securities markets to which business expectations are very sensitive."
This seems an overstatement of the contractive influence of central banking and monetary policy. There were still $750 million of excess member bank reserves in August 1937 ($108 million of these in New York City); and the New York Federal Reserve Bank reduced its rediscount rate from one and one-half to one per cent on August 27. It is true that member bank borrowings increased during the first nine months of 1937, particularly in New York City, and that member bank holdings of governments were reduced from $13.5 billion on December 31, 1936, to $12.7 billion on June 30, 1937, and to $12.4 billion on December 31 of that year. But member bank loan portfolios were increased from $13.4 to $14.3 billion during the first six months of 1937 and reporting member bank loans continued at the June 30 level until the last week in October. Also, while the open market rate on four to six months commercial paper in New York rose from the 1936 level of three-fourths per cent to one per cent in March 1937 and continued at that figure for nearly a year, the rates on ninety day loans and call loans on the Stock Exchange remained steady from June 1936 to the end of 1938. The tightness in the money market does not seem to have become serious enough to have been a major recession-precipitating factor.

2. *The Experience of the 1930's*

Since the idea of countering the cycle as a major federal policy objective was a new one developed in response to the severe and prolonged depression of the 1930's and one not yet wholeheartedly accepted, there was naturally a wide variety of measures adopted and programs undertaken to implement this objective, some more, some less apropos, some experimented with only to be dropped. Some of the measures and programs, too, entailed a substantial increase in the federal net debt, others meant an increase in the gross volume of federal obligations held by the public but had little or no effect on the net debt, and still others affected neither the net nor the gross debt significantly.

It will be convenient to consider the measures adopted and programs undertaken under the four following heads: (a) those which, though motivated in some way by the depression, were primarily of a noncyclical character; (b) those allegedly apropos measures and programs whose cyclical relevance or effectiveness is open to some question; (c) countercyclical nonfinancial expenditure programs; and (d) apropos measures and programs primarily of a financial nature.

Let us first simply note the primarily noncyclical measures and programs. Among these were the Norris-LaGuardia Act; the National Labor Relations Act; the Chandler amendments to the bankruptcy act; the holding-company death sentence; most of the provisions of the Securities Exchange Act of 1934; the Fair Labor Standards Act (which can be regarded as about all that survived of the NRA codes); several of the provisions of the Banking Acts of 1933 and 1935;[15] the Merchant Marine Act of 1936; the Old Age and Survivors Insurance system; and the special public assistance programs (old age assistance, aid to the blind, and aid to dependent children). Each of these was in some sense a product of the depression. And no doubt the inauguration of several of them made contributions to recovery and relief. But they do not constitute significant continuing measures against a major depression;[16] and, although four of them—the OASI system and the three public assistance programs—entail substantial additions to federal nonfinancial expenditures, no part of the $16 billion debt increase can be attributed to this group of primarily noncyclical measures and programs. Indeed, were it not for the OASI system, the net debt increase might have been larger.

Next let us briefly consider three types of measures and programs

[15] Notably the prohibition of interest on demand deposits; vesting the control of interest on time deposits in the Board of Governors of the Federal Reserve System; requiring the separation of security affiliates from commercial and savings banks; permitting national banks to engage in branch banking to a limited extent; and a cumulative voting requirement for national banks.

[16] It can be argued that the OASI system slightly increases the built-in flexibility of federal fiscal operations.

112

whose cyclical relevance or effectiveness is open to some question. None of these entailed any significant financial requirement.

In our résumé of the development of the view that the federal government has a responsibility for promoting full and stable employment and for relieving the distress caused by business depressions, we noted several proposed monetary measures that were advocated as means of increasing prices and employment. Since the effectiveness of these devices is open to some question, we venture to call them monetary nostrums. More than one monetary nostrum was tried during the 1930's. The most important was the devaluation of the dollar, which began with the national bank holiday of March 6, 1933.[17] The Swiss franc rate,[18] which had been 19.4 cents in February and March 1933, rose until in February 1934, after the United States Treasury had fixed the mint price of gold at $35 an ounce,[19] it was 31.7 cents. The major part of this increase took place before the Warren plan to raise the commodity price level by raising the price of gold went into operation on October 25, 1933; in September the franc rate had been 28.7 cents. And while the Bureau of Labor Statistics wholesale price index rose from 59.8 in February to 71.2 in October, it dipped slightly in November and December despite increasing the gold price to $35, and in January when the Warren plan was terminated it had risen only to 72.2.

We will not stop to comment on the other monetary nostrums that were tried during the 1930's.[20] Devaluation was not only a monetary device, but a part of a quite general reaction to the severe prolonged depression, a reaction in the direction of autarchy and economic nationalism.[21] The other main steps taken in this direction by the United States were the Fordney-McCumber Tariff Act (1930), and the authorizations to the President under the National Industrial Recovery Act and the Agricultural Adjustment Act to impose quotas and additional duties. Because autarchic moves were quite general they were not very effective countercyclically. Two major steps that contributed to a reversal of the direction of the external economic policies of the United States were the Trade Agreements Act (1934), and the Tripartite Accord (September 25, 1936) entered into by Great Britain, France, and the United States to stabilize exchange rates.

[17] Most of the commercial banks in the country had already been closed at this date through state "holidays."

[18] The Swiss franc is used here since it was one of the currencies that was not devalued until after 1934.

[19] Under the provisions of the Gold Reserve Act, January 31, 1934. This represented almost a 70 per cent increase over the preholiday price.

[20] The silver purchase program and several attempts to legislate an increase in the quantity of paper money.

[21] So was the silver purchase program, for it discriminated in favor of domestic production.

Another type of measure that it seems fair to characterize as allegedly but not clearly a very effective part of an antidepression program was the competition-restricting industry code. Such codes were adopted under the provisions of the National Industrial Recovery Act (1933), and, in the case of some industries, under the Agricultural Adjustment Act (1933). Possibly they had some part in checking the downward price and wage spiral, and it has been suggested that efforts to make purchases before the codes took effect, many of them in the late summer and the fall of 1933, contributed to business revival.[22] But their contribution to recovery does not seem to have been a major one, and they were terminated by a decision of the Supreme Court.[23]

So much for the measures of questionable cyclical relevance. Next as to the nonfinancial countercyclical expenditure programs. This type of policy during the 1930's was a distinctly vacillating one. Even under the Democratic administration there continued to be two strongly opposed schools of thought, the budget-balancing school and the fiscal countercycle school. As a result the countercyclical stimulus was interrupted in 1935 and again more markedly in 1937. Further, much of the time while an expanded expenditure stimulus was being applied with one hand, the other hand was simultaneously effecting expenditure cuts. This inevitably made it necessary to draw a sharp legal line between expenditures on functions subject to the cuts (the "normal functions") and emergency expenditures for recovery and relief, so that no made-work project could be approved and allocated funds to perform a normal function.[24]

Despite their vacillating nature such emergency expenditures were undoubtedly of substantial importance. They served both to provide relief by contributing to disposable personal income and to aid recovery by augmenting aggregate demand. Table 32 summarizes the program expenditures that helped to provide relief. Since the level of such expenditures was substantially higher during the second half of the decade of the 1930's a separate column is devoted to the averages for these five years. But even in the 1935–39 column the ratio of line F to the $16.8 decrease shown on line G is only about 1 to 5; the corresponding ratio for the decade is 1 to 10.3. However, the purchasing power of the consumer's dollar averaged nearly 20 per cent above the 1929 level during the 1930's,

[22] The declines in prices, wages, and production were checked before any code went into effect. The Federal Reserve index of industrial production (seasonally adjusted) rose from 59 in March to 100 in July, then fluctuated between 71 and 91 for more than a year. The Bureau of Labor Statistics index of wholesale prices of nonfarm, nonfood commodities started a sharp upward movement in May; average hourly earnings of manufacturing employees did likewise in July.

[23] Schechter v. United States, 295 U.S. 495 (June 1935).

[24] But there is a presumption that the normal functions subject to the expenditure cuts were socially more important than the functions performed by the made-work projects.

TABLE 32

Federal Countercyclical Programs Related to Personal Income and
Farm Income, 1929–39
(millions of dollars per year)

		1929	1930–39 Average	1935–39 Average
A.	Federal direct relief	0	10	21
B.	Public assistance grants-in-aid	8	412[a]	617
C.	Unemployment compensation benefits	0	83	166
D.	Work relief payrolls	0	953	1,682
E.	Veterans' pensions, etc.[b]	536	766	776
F.	Total above	544	2,224	3,262
G.	Disposable personal income	83,120	61,628	66,336
H.	Government payments to farmers	0	309	573
J.	Federal Farm Board loan losses	0	35	0
K.	Net cash income to persons on farms from farming	4,304	2,711	3,293

[a] Includes $280 million of RFC loans to states, 1923–33, which were later forgiven, grants for vocational education and rehabilitation, for maternal and child health and welfare, for old age assistance, for aid to dependent children, and for aid to the blind, and FERA grants for general relief.

[b] Pension, disability, and retirement payments and adjusted compensation benefits.

SOURCE: See Appendix A.

and a fair comparison of relief expenditure to income decline should take account of this fact. A fair comparison, too, should take account of the growth of population. The following computation makes a rough allowance both for price changes and for population growth:

		1930–39 Average	1935–39 Average
a.	Consumer expenditure price index[a]	80.4	79.7
b.	Population (in millions)[b]	126.9	129.0
c.	Line G/(line a × line b)	$603[c]	$644[c]
d.	(Line G — line F)/(line a × line b)	$581[c]	$612[c]

[a] Index in Table 41, *1954 National Income Supplement* to the *Survey of Current Business*, converted to a 1929 base.

[b] Continental United States.

[c] 1929 dollars.

Per capita disposable income in 1929 was $682. Line c indicates that for the following decade it averaged the equivalent of 603 1929 dollars, and that during 1935–39 it averaged the equivalent of 644 of these dollars, or about 5.6 per cent below the 1929 level. Without the transfer payment (and work relief) items summarized on line F of Table 32, per capita disposable income would have been $677 in 1929, 581 1929 dollars per year during 1930–39; and 612 1929 dollars per year during 1935–39 or 9.6 per cent below the 1929 level. The transfer (and work relief) items

115

seem to have been large enough in 1935–39 to offset about half the average per capita income decline.[25] The 1935–39 level of per capita farm income, corrected for price changes, was about 4 per cent below that of 1929. Without government transfer payments it might have been something like 20 per cent down from the 1929 level.

TABLE 33

Federal Countercyclical Programs Related to Aggregate Demand, 1929–39
(millions of dollars)

		1929	1930–39 Average	1935–39 Average
A.	Work relief payrolls	0	953	1,682
B.	New construction[a]	155	414	511
C.	Purchases of silver[b]	0	28	43
D.	Other federal GNP expenditures	1,156	1,823	2,312
E.	Non-public-assistance grants-in-aid	109	355	375
F.	Total above	1,420	3,575	4,923
G.	Total GNP expenditures	104,436	76,913	84,469

[a] Excludes relief work construction.
[b] Domestic only.
SOURCE: See Appendix A.

The WPA and other work relief programs—Civilian Conservation Corps, Civil Works Administration, and National Youth Administration —accounted for a very substantial part of the relief expenditures shown in Table 32. They also accounted for a substantial part of federal demand for GNP. Table 33 relates the components of this demand, and federal grants-in-aid that added to state and local demand for GNP in 1930–39, to 1929 levels. Line F in Table 33 may be taken as a rough measure of the total direct federal contribution to aggregate demand. There is no very satisfactory way of appraising quantitatively the significance of line F for recovery. However, we may note that the average annual contribution to aggregate demand in 1930–34 was $2.2 billion; average GNP was $69.4

[25] This comparison of declines with and without the expenditure programs takes no account of any possible "multiplier effect." Nor does the farm incomes comparison that follows.

Corresponding computations for farm income are as follows:

	1929	1930–39 Average	1935–39 Average
a. Price index[a]	100	77.5	77.5
b. Population (in millions)	30.2	31.1	30.9
c. Line K/(line a × line b)	$142.5	$112[b]	$137[b]
d. (Line K − line H − line J)/(line a × line b)	$142.5	$98.2[b]	$113[b]

[a] Prices paid by farmers for family living expense items. *Historical Statistics*, E-99, converted to a 1929 base.
[b] 1929 dollars.

116

billion. Thus from 1930–34 to 1935–39 the annual level of the GNP increased by $15.1 billion, and the increment in the direct federal contribution accounted for $2.7 billion or roughly 18 per cent of this increase.

It remains to consider recovery, relief, and economic stabilization measures and programs of a financial nature. Three general types may be distinguished: (a) central banking measures, (b) private credit underwriting measures, and (c) direct federal lending. Only in the case of the third type is a substantial financial requirement involved, and this requirement relates to gross rather than net debt. During the decade of the 1930's the federal loan portfolio increased by $9 billion.[26]

The principal central banking measures adopted during the 1930's were as follows: giving the Board of Governors of the Federal Reserve System limited discretionary power to vary member bank reserve requirements; giving this Board discretionary power to vary margin requirements for margin trading on the stock exchanges; and giving the System's Open Market Committee power to regulate Federal Reserve Bank open market operations. There is no reason to suppose these measures contributed anything significant to the objective of recovery, still less to that of relief. Rather what they did provide was the basis for a strengthened countercyclical central bank credit policy whose effectiveness was mainly pertinent to other stages of the cycle.

The principal federal credit underwriting programs inaugurated during the 1930's were: insurance of demand and time deposits in most commercial banks and mutual savings banks; insurance of most of the purchasable shares (and credited earnings) of savings and loan associations; insurance of important types of home mortgage loans and loans to finance home repairs and improvements. If in this connection we stretch the subject of the chapter, we may add to the list the more recent programs of the Veterans' Administration for guaranteeing loans to veterans for purchase or construction of homes and purchase of farms or business property.

Since 1950 deposit insurance has covered deposits up to $10,000. As of the end of 1954 there were $212 billion demand and time deposits in banks in the United States; 53 per cent of these were insured by the Federal Deposit Insurance Corporation. At this time also the private savings capital of all savings and loan associations in the United States totaled $27.3 billion; of this amount practically 90 per cent was invested in institutions insured by the Federal Savings and Loan Insurance Corporation. The extent of other government underwriting programs for private credit is shown in Table 34.

[26] See Table 35. The spread between gross and net debt is affected by other factors as well as the loan portfolio, particularly the balance in the general fund and federal obligations held by federal agencies.

The FDIC began operating in 1934, probably not soon enough to have contributed significantly to the restoration of confidence in the nation's banking system that followed the bank holiday. The Federal Housing Administration loan insurance programs may well have done something to augment the volume of residential construction in the later 1930's.[27] Also, in the future FHA terms may be adjusted from time to

TABLE 34

Loans Guaranteed or Insured by Federal Agencies, 1939 and 1954

		December 31, 1939	June 30, 1954
	UNDERWRITTEN LOANS OUTSTANDING		
		(billions of dollars)	
A.	Housing and home loans	2.14	37.6
B.	Farm credit	0.0	2.2
C.	Other loans	0.5	0.9
D.	Total federally underwritten loans	2.6	40.7
	RATIO OF UNDERWRITTEN LOANS TO ALL OUTSTANDINGS		
		(per cent)	
E.	Mortgages on 1- to 4-family nonfarm residential properties	11	42
F.	Farm credit	0	13

SOURCE: See Appendix A.

time so as to provide a countercyclical credit policy.[28] But the principal countercyclical significance of all these credit underwriting programs surely is not in providing relief from a depression or in promoting recovery. Rather it is that they serve to strengthen important parts of the economy's financial structure, so that these parts will not again accelerate a downswing as they did during 1929–33.

In discussing federal lending programs it will be convenient to stretch the subject of this chapter somewhat further, considering not only those inaugurated during the 1930's but also those started earlier and those started since.

Although with negligible exceptions state and local governments had long before that ceased to engage in credit operations, prior to World War I there had been no direct federal activities in the credit field since the Second Bank of the United States. A major credit program was initiated

[27] Cf. Leo Grebler, David Blank, and Louis Winnick, *Capital Formation in Residential Real Estate*, pp. 148–49.

[28] The home mortgage insurance system established under the National Housing Act (1934), was designed to operate with countercyclical variations in insurance premium rates. And provisions for varying down payments and amortization periods have since been added. But there is no real provision for the cyclical coordination of FHA policies with those of the Federal Reserve, or of Veterans' Administration policies with either.

by the Federal Farm Loan Act (1916), which provided for the organization of federal and joint-stock land banks. Then when the United States entered the war it promptly began to help finance the war activities of its allies by extending them loans, though viewed in retrospect these loans are better

TABLE 35

Federal Credit at Selected Dates, 1920–53
(millions of dollars)

		June 30, 1920	December 31, 1929	December 31, 1939	December 31, 1953
A.	Farm credit	350[a]	1,296	3,620	6,811
B.	Housing loans	0	0	2,540	2,930
C.	Obligations of financial institutions	0[b]	0	1,185	985
D.	State and local government obligations	0	0	455	645
E.	Railroad obligations	445[b]	60	500	79
F.	Life insurance funds loans to veterans	0	270	152	208[c]
G.	Investments in IMF, IBRD, and Exchange Stabilization Fund	0	0	2,000	3,585
H.	Recent loans to foreign governments	0	0	0	11,883[d]
J.	Other loans and securities	119[b]	80	248	1,070
K.	Total above	914	1,706	10,700	28,196
L.	World War I obligations of foreign governments	10,092	11,532[e]	12,661[e]	12,553[f]

[a] December 31.

[b] Line J reports War Finance Corporation loans as of November 15, 1920. About one-half of the $119 million were loans to railroads, and about one-third were loans to banks and exporters to finance agricultural and other exports. By June 30, 1921, railroad obligations as reported in line E had increased to $680 million.

[c] Life insurance policy loans only.

[d] Includes loans made by the Export-Import Bank and RFC prior to V-J Day.

[e] Excludes accrued interest.

[f] As of June 30, 1954, excludes accrued interest, but includes $91.5 million debt of Federal Republic of Germany under agreement of February 27, 1953.

Source: See Appendix A.

called grants. And by the Act of April 5, 1918, the War Finance Corporation was established. While it was initially expected the WFC would lend chiefly to banks, the corporation made direct industrial loans, and after the war and before the establishment of federal intermediate credit banks under the Agricultural Credits Act (1923), it was for a time primarily an agricultural credit agency.

On June 30, 1920, the loans and securities held by the federal government and its agencies included the foreign government obligations, the portfolios of the WFC and the land banks, loans extended to railroads during federal control and in connection with their return to private operation, and securities acquired in exchange for war surplus properties (see Table 35). During the 1920's farm credit increased by some 270 per cent, and a new type of credit appeared, loans to veterans by the United States Life Insurance Fund. The other portfolio items, being war-connected, declined.

If we do not count Federal Farm Board loans, the expansion of federal credit activities during the 1930's began with the establishment of the Reconstruction Finance Corporation by the Act of January 22, 1932, of twelve Regional Agricultural Credit Corporations under the Emergency Relief and Construction Act (1932), and of twelve federal home loan banks under the Act of July 22, 1932. We have noted that the original idea that the RFC should make only fully and adequately secured loans was shortly modified. What could be done at the time to promote business recovery by extending loans on a strictly commercial basis was extremely limited. At the end of February 1933 the home loan banks (which were still operating on this basis) held only $9 million of home mortgages. However, during the three years ending December 31, 1932, federal credit more than doubled. Then during 1933 it increased by $1.2 billion and during 1934 by $4.1 billion.[29] A major part of this expansion reflected the temporary substitution of federal for private credit at strategic points in order to bolster up the whole credit structure of the economy. And striking as these figures are, they do not include what was by far the largest and most important operation of this sort, the very temporary substitution of the

---

[29] Credit figures for these three year-ends are as follows:

		12/31/32	12/31/33	12/31/34
A.	Loans and preferred stock held by government corporations and credit agencies, n.e.c.	3,192	4,174	8,202
B.	Loans held by U.S. Life Insurance Fund	477	529	561
C.	State and local government securities held by federal agencies	14	90	250
D.	Total credit above	3,683	4,793	9,013

On line A see R. J. Saulnier, Harold G. Halcrow, and Neil H. Jacoby, *Federal Lending and Loan Insurance*, Tables A-1, A-4, A-5, A-6, A-8, and A-10. Line A of the above table includes loans by Federal Land Banks, banks for cooperatives, intermediate credit banks, and Federal Home Loan Banks. It excludes Veterans' Administration loans and loans to state and local governments that are components of the Table A-1 total and loans by Federal Reserve Banks shown in Table A-5. On line B of the above table, see Administrator of Veterans' Affairs, 1935 *Annual Report*, p. 90. On line C see Secretary of the Treasury, 1945 *Annual Report*, p. 697 (average of two June 30 figures).

Lines B and C have the effect of adjusting the definition of total federal credit (line D) to suit our present purpose. The line B adjustment makes it inclusive of Adjusted Service Certificate loans; the line C adjustment excludes the $300 million RFC loans to states that subsequently became grants-in-aid.

government's credit for that of all the banks of the country in 1933 during the brief interval following the holiday in which they were in process of being reopened. But the figures do include two large-scale credit substitutions, the taking over of distress home and farm mortgages at a loss by two corporations organized especially for the purpose, the Home Owners Loan Corporation and the Federal Farm Mortgage Corporation. Smaller in volume but at least of equal strategic importance were the loans to banks by the RFC and the Federal Deposit Insurance Corporation and the acquisitions of bank preferred stock and the loans to other financial institutions by the RFC.

In addition to this temporary distress refinancing, federal credit was expanded during the 1930's to finance purchases of new national product. Thus there were emergency loans by the Public Works Administration and, especially after 1937, loans by a number of corporations and agencies organized to promote particular programs.[30]

During World War II federal credit at first increased, then markedly declined. Other sectors of our economy, having substantial cash surpluses after 1941, paid off debts and added to their holdings of cash, governments, and private securities. Also, after the passage of the Lend-Lease Act, March 11, 1941, financial assistance was extended to allied governments by purchasing goods for them—the nature of the obligations involved not being definitely fixed at the time—rather than through loans as in World War I.

By June 30, 1945, federal loans to foreign governments, other than the World War I obligations on line L of Table 35, totaled only about $800 million. Thus there has been an expansion of over $11 billion in such loans since that date and up to the end of 1953.[31] Most of the rest of the increase in external federal credit after V-J Day reflects capital subscriptions to two international financial institutions, the International Monetary Fund and the International Bank for Reconstruction and Development. However, a substantial part of the IMF subscription, $1.8 billion, was provided by reducing investment in the Exchange Stabilization Fund, the main function of which—to discharge American obligations under the Tripartite Accord of 1936—in effect passed on to the IMF.

The increases in internal credit from V-J Day to the end of 1953 were small by comparison. The chief expansions were in loans to finance farms and homes (including veterans' homes and farms) and in other loans to veterans.

[30] The following list of lending agencies will serve to indicate the variety of programs so promoted: Rural Electrification Administration, Federal National Mortgage Association, United States Housing Authority, Electric Home and Farm Authority, Farm Security Administration, Commodity Credit Corporation, Export-Import Bank, RFC Mortgage Corporation, United States Maritime Commission.

[31] See Chapter VIII for a comparison between loans and grants during this period.

On the basis of the above examination of the experience of the 1930's it may be in order to speculate briefly on some of the developments that might take place if perchance our economy were again to undergo a severe recession and depression lasting, say, as long as three years.

If the depression were sufficiently severe, it might well be the occasion for adopting various measures and programs that were not cyclically particularly relevant. And there would probably be allegedly pertinent measures and programs whose actual effectiveness was small, among them one or more monetary nostrums. Again the process of recession would be likely to disclose additional weak parts of our economy's credit structure, with the result that measures would be adopted to strengthen these parts. Also steps might be taken toward a stronger, better coordinated counter-cyclical credit policy, and other countercyclical measures of a regulatory nature might be adopted. Quite possibly none of these developments would involve any extra net financial requirement; none would be likely to except perhaps some cyclically irrelevant measure or program.

If the process of recession disclosed additional weak spots in our credit structure, there might again be need for large-scale substitutions of federal for private credit. And in any case large federal lending programs might be inaugurated to finance and to encourage expanded purchases of our national product. It would be strange indeed, with the growth of our economy since the 1930's, the extent to which the federal government has come to be involved in making loans, and the higher level of prices pre-vailing in recent years,[32] if depression lending did not lead to a step-up of gross in relation to net debt of a number of times $9 billion.

In general the measures that contribute most to dealing with a severe depression, once there has been a sufficient business contraction to involve one, are measures that require to be financed either in the grosser sense of borrowing to finance lending or in the net sense of financing increased GNP expenditures, state and local grants-in-aid, and transfer payments to individuals.[33] Should there be another severe depression, it is reasonable to suppose that there would be a fuller and more general recognition of federal responsibility for promoting recovery and providing relief and that the balance-the-budget-during-depression school of thought would have somewhat less of a following, so that expenditure programs would get under way less tardily and be maintained more consistently, and so that they would be larger relative to the size of the economy and to the degree of business contraction. One might expect too, that federal taxes would

[32] The implicit deflator of the GNP for 1954 is 71 per cent above that for 1929.

[33] It could be argued that it would theoretically be possible to stimulate recovery and relieve distress without incurring a deficit, provided there is a sufficiently large expansion of nonfinancial expenditures and receipts. But it will probably be conceded that the expansion would have to be so large as to make such a government budget most unlikely.

not be stepped up as they were during the 1930's; rather yields would decrease and rates might be reduced. Possibly too there would be experimentation with incentive tax concessions or subsidies to encourage increases in private components of aggregate demand. These considerations —and the higher level of prices—suggest that, if our economy were again to undergo a marked recession and depression, even though it were shorter and far less severe than was the case in the 1930's, net borrowing to the extent of quite a number of times $16 billion might easily be entailed.

These speculations regarding possible developments in the event of another marked business contraction imply a premise that should be made explicit. We assume that the changes in the economy of the United States and of the world that have come about since 1929—both planned and unplanned—do not preclude such a contraction. It would mean somewhat of a digression to argue that this is so; hence it is merely stated as a premise. One who rejects the premise will of course reject the speculations too.

3. *More Recent Minor Recession Experiences*

Of the four main types of measures and programs distinguished in the preceding section there is one we certainly need not consider in connection with minor recessions: new programs that are primarily of a noncyclical character. Nor is there much reason to expect a minor recession in the United States to stimulate recourse to monetary nostrums, general competition-restricting arrangements, or autarchic measures under present conditions.[34] But what is often called monetary policy—accurately speaking, what is usually meant is mostly central bank credit policy—was an important part of federal policy toward the 1953–54 recession. And if definite countercyclical movements in Federal Reserve rediscount rates, the volume of Federal Reserve credit outstanding, member bank reserve requirements, and margin requirements did not characterize the twelve months following V-J Day, and if rediscount rates were maintained and Federal Reserve credit was contracted during the 1949 recession, there were special postwar circumstances to explain these facts.[35]

Table 36 summarizes the main other phases of federal policy and federal operations pertinent to recent recessions, except for policies and operations relating to agriculture. During 1945–46, despite the drop in distributive share receipts, disposable income was maintained chiefly as a result of increases in veterans' and unemployment compensation benefit payments. And with the decrease in corporate profits tax accruals, profits after tax averaged about the same in the first half of 1946 as in the second

[34] Of course the 1949 recession did precipitate devaluation of the pound sterling and various other currencies.

[35] Rediscount rates were raised in April–May 1946. There were reductions in member bank reserve requirements and in margin requirements during 1949.

TABLE 36

Countercyclical Fiscal Influences in Recent Minor Recessions, 1945–54

(QUARTERLY TOTALS AT ANNUAL RATES IN BILLIONS OF DOLLARS)

	II 1945	I 1946	II 1946	III 1948	IV 1948	III 1949	IV 1949	I 1953	II 1953	II 1954	III 1954
A. Personal receipts of distributive shares[a]	165.2	153.7	159.4	196.7	197.6	188.2	188.1	263.2	265.9	264.6	265.1
B. Unemployment compensation benefits	.1	2.9	3.1	1.2	1.1	2.3	2.1	1.3	1.1	2.6	2.3
C. Other government transfer payments	4.1	9.1	8.0	9.2	8.8	9.6	9.7	11.3	11.5	12.2	12.4
D. Federal personal taxes	19.8	16.2	17.0	18.0	18.2	16.2	16.1	32.3	32.8	29.2	29.2
E. Fiscal influences identified above = B + C − D	−15.6	−4.2	−5.9	−7.6	−8.3	−4.3	−4.3	−19.7	−20.2	−14.4	−14.5
F. Disposable personal income	152.2	152.8	157.0	192.1	192.4	186.9	186.7	245.4	247.7	252.9	253.2
G. Corporate profits tax liability	13.0	6.0	7.8	13.1	12.0	10.5	9.9	24.4	25.0	17.0	16.8
H. Corporate profits after tax	10.1	8.8	11.5	21.2	19.5	15.9	15.0	20.3	20.8	17.5	17.4
J. Net effect on federal financial requirements above[b]	−28.6	−10.2	−13.7	−20.7	−20.3	−14.8	−14.2	−44.1	−45.2	−31.4	−31.3
K. Loans outstanding, government corporations and credit agencies	5.8	5.3	5.4	10.6	11.7	11.7	12.7	18.1	17.6	18.5	18.6
L. Government underwritten housing loans outstanding[c]	4.2	4.7	4.8	11.9	12.5	13.3	15.0	26.1	26.7	29.7	30.5

[a] Distributive shares included in personal income.

[b] Line E minus line G.

[c] Mortgage loans on nonfarm 1- to 4-family properties.

NOTE: Line A and lines D through J are adjusted for seasonal variation; lines B, K, and L are not. Line C was computed by subtracting line B from the seasonally adjusted total of all government transfer payments. Line H includes a relatively small amount of state taxes, about 5 per cent of the total.

SOURCE: See Appendix A.

quarter of 1945. Government credit and government underwritten credit were not important cyclical influences in this period.

During the 1949 recession the annual rate of distributive share receipts decreased by about $9 billion. Roughly half of this decrease was offset by the three fiscal influences identified on lines B, C, and D. And of the cyclical decrease of over $9 billion in the annual rate of corporate profits (before tax) the tax accrual decrease absorbed about one-third. There were minor increases during this recession in government credit and government underwritten credit. The nonfinancial surplus of the federal government dropped from $9.9 billion in 1948 to $0.5 billion in 1949.

Between the second quarter of 1953 and the second quarter of 1954 distributive share receipts declined only slightly. The decrease in personal taxes during this interval and the increases in unemployment compensation benefits and miscellaneous federal transfer payments were sufficient to boost the annual rate of disposable income by some $5 billion. The annual rate for corporate profits after tax declined nearly 16 per cent despite the sharp cut in profits tax accruals. There was a small increase in federal credit, a significant increase in government underwritten loans.

Line J indicates a substantial increase in federal financial requirements between the second quarter of 1953 and that of 1954. But there must have been other developments that helped to offset those shown in the table. The federal nonfinancial deficit for the year ending June 30, 1954, was only $1.5 billion; the deficit for the third quarter of 1954 was only $0.5 billion above that a year earlier.[36]

It is convenient to deal separately with the federal policies and operations affecting agriculture because it seems desirable to use annual data to portray them and because the year-to-year changes are not purely cyclical (see Table 37). Net income of farm operators dropped sharply from the 1948 level during 1949, recovered somewhat during 1950–51, and then contracted during the three years 1952–54. Three fiscal influences on net operator income are identified in the table: government payments, the increment in inventories and the loan portfolio of the Commodity Credit Corporation, and property taxes. Although these taxes are levied by state and local governments, especially the latter, it seems wise to

[36] These figures are derived from the quarterly federal sources and uses statement, 1953–55, compiled as a part of the National Bureau's study of Postwar Capital Markets. An annual figure and a year-ago comparison are given here because there is a marked seasonal variation in the federal nonfinancial deficit for which no seasonal adjustment is yet available.

Quite possibly some part of the $2 billion financial requirement indicated by these figures is due to factors other than the 1953–54 recession. While the nonfinancial transactions account was in balance for calendar 1952, if due allowance could be made for seasonal variation, it might show a deficit even before the recession began. The adjusted National Income and Product Account for the federal government does show one for the first half of 1953.

TABLE 37

Fiscal Influences on Net Income of Farm Operators since World War II
(billions of dollars)

	1945	1946	1947	1948	1949	1950	1951	1952	1953	1954
A. Gross cash income from marketings[a]	22.1	25.3	30.0	30.5	28.1	28.6	33.1	33.0	31.6	30.2
B. Government payments	0.74	0.77	0.31	0.26	0.19	0.28	0.29	0.28	0.21	0.26
C. CCC net contribution[b]	−0.67	−0.55	0.15	1.00	1.38	−0.57	−0.57	0.44	2.76	1.12
D. Federal fiscal influence identified above[c]	0.07	0.22	0.46	1.26	1.57	−0.29	−0.28	0.72	2.97	2.38
E. Property taxes	0.55	0.62	0.71	0.77	0.82	0.92	0.99	1.05	1.08	1.11
F. Net fiscal influence identified above[d]	−0.48	−0.40	−0.25	0.49	0.75	−1.21	−1.27	−0.33	1.89	0.25
G. Net income of farm operators	11.8	13.9	14.5	16.7	12.7	13.3	15.8	14.3	12.5	12.3

a Includes government payments and CCC contribution.
b Increment in inventories plus increment in loans outstanding.
c B plus C.
d D minus E.

NOTE: All figures refer to calendar years. Data for lines A, B, E, and G are from the Agricultural Marketing Service Farm Income Situation. Data for line C are from CCC balance sheets filed with the Treasury.

include them in the table, because they have often been cyclically perverse. The combined fiscal influence reflected in line F made some contribution to net operator income in 1949, and a substantial one in 1953.

The significance of the fiscal operations covered by the two tables for federal capital requirements can perhaps be best appraised in terms of the increments shown. The maximum cyclical increments in the annual rates on line J of Table 36 are: for 1945–46, $18.4 billion; for 1948–49, $6.5 billion; for 1953–54, $13.9 billion. In Table 37 line D increases by $1.11 billion from 1947 to 1949 and by $3.25 billion from 1951 to 1953.

These figures suggest that even a minor recession might easily entail net borrowing of the order of magnitude of $16 billion, if at the outset nonfinancial receipts did not exceed nonfinancial expenditures. Particularly is this so in view of the possibility that federal fiscal operations in time may well become somewhat more markedly flexible countercyclically not only in a built-in but also in a managed sense than in the three postwar recessions we have been considering. And while conceivably the federal government might at the outset of a recession be enjoying a substantial nonfinancial surplus, as in 1948 (see Table 5), we should note also that the cash surpluses of the social insurance funds may be smaller in the future than they were during the 1940's.

Assuming net borrowing during a business contraction, either major or minor, the question arises, Is the resulting additional net debt likely to be paid off when the depression is over? Some attention is given to this question in Chapter VIII.

4. Summary

Responsibility for seeing that the economy operates at a somewhat stable, high employment level seems to have been becoming a recognized function of the federal government. Recognition of this function has tended to grow during periods of depressed business; interest in it to weaken during periods of prolonged prosperity.

The great depression of the 1930's stimulated the federal government to take a wide variety of steps. Among these were measures and programs that, though in some sense motivated by the depression, were definitely not primarily countercyclical in nature, e.g. the National Labor Relations Act and the Old Age and Survivors Insurance System. There were also measures of alleged but questionable pertinence or effectiveness, monetary nostrums, autarchic measures, and the NRA and AAA competition-restricting codes. And there were measures and programs that clearly served the objective of recovery and relief: expenditure programs to bolster personal and farm income and aggregate demand and lending and loan underwriting programs, some aimed at relieving financial distress, others at increasing the private components of aggregate demand, still others like deposit and savings insurance at strengthening the economy's financial structure.

Before the 1930's relief programs were quite generally regarded as functions of private charity and of local government; and federal counter-cyclical responsibilities were for the most part confined to those exercised by the Federal Reserve System. During the 1930's the Federal Reserve's countercyclical powers were strengthened through new controls of margin trading requirements and member bank reserve requirements and through statutory recognition of the Open Market Committeee. The great 1929–33 recession also brought recognition of a new federal function, responsibility for recovery and relief. And the 1937–38 recession pushed this function in a more forward-looking direction, a responsibility for maintaining a high and stable level of employment.

Were we to experience another severe, long-continued business depression, a number of the developments of the 1930's might be more or less closely paralleled. The response might well include various measures and the inauguration of various programs of essentially an irrelevant nature as well as allegedly relevant ones that did not contribute much to recovery and relief. Of course it would encourage relevant measures and programs too. We might expect a strengthening of central bank countercyclical influences and development of other forms of counter-cyclical influence. Also we might expect new weak spots in our credit structure to be revealed, and anticipate that measures would be adopted to remedy them. And there might easily be federal credit extension programs both to relieve financial distress and to promote recovery—programs that would entail an increase in the federal loan portfolio of far more than $9 billion. Likewise there might easily be expenditure programs —for purchases of GNP, for grants-in-aid, for subsidies, and for transfer payments to individuals—which, together with tax decreases, would mean an increase in net federal debt of many times more than $16 billion.

In the minor recessions since World War II there have been substantial countercyclical variations in federal nonfinancial receipts and expenditures—to a considerable extent built-in variations. And while there were special postwar circumstances that precluded this development in the 1945 and 1949 recessions, during 1953–54 countercyclical Federal Reserve policy—along with other credit measures—was a principal reliance. In future, countercyclical fiscal operations may well be on a larger scale than they were during the postwar decade. In any case from that experience it is clear that even a minor recession could easily entail a net debt increase as large as the increase incurred during the 1930's, particularly if at the start of the recession federal nonfinancial expenditures were as large as nonfinancial receipts.

CHAPTER VII

Some Fiscal Developments That Affect the Growth of Public Debts

Chapter VI was in large part concerned with a major depression emergency, and in Chapter VIII we will take up the world war emergencies. Some of the fiscal procedures that developed during these two very different kinds of emergencies were quite similar. Emergency procedures constitute a part of the subject of the present chapter.

But there are fiscal developments to be considered here too that are not of an emergency character or that reflect nonemergency as well as emergency influences. In particular, the net indebtedness of the federal government and also the net indebtedness of state and local governments have increased less than they otherwise might have because of the growth of financial assets. Let us take up this development first.

1. *The Growth of Financial Assets*

In the case of the federal government there are two main types of financial asset other than cash: federal credit, which we have already considered, and federal obligations held by federal agencies.

Most of the federal obligations so held are held by the social insurance funds. And federal obligations are the main asset of these funds; in fact with two exceptions they are the only asset other than the cash balance on deposit with the Treasury. The two exceptions are the two veterans' life insurance funds; their assets include loans to veterans, but as of December 31, 1953, government obligations made up over 94 per cent of their assets.

Table 38 summarizes the growth of federal social insurance funds. Between 1939 and 1945, while the first three funds listed were quite new, total assets were increasing at the rate of nearly $3 billion per year. Between 1951 and 1954 the average annual increase was $2.3 billion. Federal nonfinancial surpluses in recent years (see Table 5) can fairly be said to be mainly the result of the growth of the social insurance funds.

If one adds to the balance in the general fund total federal credit and the federal obligation held by federal social insurance funds, the result will represent most, but not quite all, of the difference between gross and net federal debt. In Chapter VIII we will consider the components of this difference further.

TABLE 38

Assets in Federal Social Insurance Funds at Selected Dates, 1929–54
(as of December 31, millions of dollars)

		1929	1939	1945	1951	1954
A.	Old Age and Survivors Insurance Fund	0	1,724	7,121	15,540	20,576
B.	Railroad Retirement Account	0	148	644	2,695	3,441
C.	Unemployment Trust Fund	0	1,525	7,537	8,526	8,744
D.	Veterans' life insurance funds[a]	424	1,015	5,180	6,694	6,533[d]
E.	Government employees retirement funds[b]	116[c]	553[d]	2,195[d]	4,820[d]	5,997[d]
F.	Total	540	4,965	22,677	38,275	45,291

[a] National Service Life Insurance Fund and Government Life Insurance Fund. Excludes non-ledger assets of latter.

[b] Civil Service Retirement and Disability Fund and Foreign Service Retirement and Disability Fund.

[c] June 30.

[d] Estimated.

SOURCE: See Appendix A.

TABLE 39

Cash and Securities in Various State and Local Government
Funds at Selected Dates, 1915–50
(fiscal year-ends, billions of dollars)

		1915	1929	1937	1942	1950
A.	General funds (cash only)	0.4	1.9	2.7	3.3	7.7
B.	Sinking funds	0.8	2.9	2.2	2.0	3.0
C.	Retirement funds	0.2	0.4	1.1	1.9	4.6
D.	Investment and miscellaneous trust funds	0.4	1.8	1.4	1.8	7.5
E.	Total cash and securities	1.8	7.0	7.4	9.0	22.8

NOTE: These figures do not include the balance in the Unemployment Compensation Fund. Nor do they include real estate. This latter item is negligible except for investment and miscellaneous trust funds. Of the $1.8 billion on line D, 1942, school trust funds accounted for nearly $0.75 billion, workmen's compensation funds for $0.26 billion.

SOURCE: See Appendix A.

Most social insurance funds are federal. But state and local government retirement funds amounted to more than $4.5 billion in 1950 and state-administered workmen's compensation funds to more than $600 million. Also, although there is little that could be called state or local credit, there have come to be substantial investment and endowment funds (including the endowment funds of libraries and educational and other institutions). The growth of the cash and security holdings of various types of state and local funds, 1915–50, is summarized in Table 39.[1]

As in the case of the federal government, because the volume of transactions of such special funds—trust, investment, and endowment funds—and of business-type government enterprises has become large, it is necessary to distinguish between budget or general government surpluses and deficits and total nonfinancial transaction surpluses and deficits.

2. *Emergency Fiscal Developments*

Somewhat tardily the federal government followed the example of many states and cities when the Budget and Accounting Act was approved on June 10, 1921. In a sense this act meant a strengthening of the executive, for it established in the executive a central agency for fiscal planning and administrative management, an agency which by Reorganization Plan I under the Reorganization Act of April 3, 1939, became the main organization unit in the Executive Office of the President. But if the executive was strengthened it was not at the expense of the legislative branch. The Bureau of the Budget performs functions which could not be effectively performed by congressional committees. So does the General Accounting Office, though by the terms of the 1921 act this agency is "independent of the executive departments and under the control and direction of the Comptroller General of the United States."[2]

Both before and after the 1921 act Congress controlled the way government money was spent through the exercise of its appropriating power. Each executive department and independent office prepared its estimates. In the appropriation act Congress specified the amount of money made available—it might be more or less than the estimated amount—and specified the agency to which it was made available, the period during which it was to be available (ordinarily a particular fiscal year), the purpose or purposes for which it could be used, and the objects on which it could be spent (personal services, purchase of equipment, printing and binding, etc.). Preaudits or postaudits determined that the money was spent in accordance with the provisions of the appropriation act.

But these appropriation procedures take a considerable amount of time. And since the 1921 act rather more time is required than was required previously—time for Bureau of the Budget hearings on the estimates before they are transmitted to Congress. Hence an agency that

[1] Since 1950 such holdings have increased markedly. At the close of the 1956 fiscal year the total had grown to $38 billion, $12.6 billion of this being in retirement and other social insurance funds. See Bureau of the Census, *Summary of Government Finances in 1956*, Table 19.

[2] The act transferred to the newly established GAO the auditing functions and certain accounting functions previously vested in the Treasury.

TABLE 40

Federal Recovery and Relief Funds and Expenditures, 1934–38

	Allocations of Emergency Appropriations (1)	RFC Funds (2)	Specific Appropriations (3)	Total Source to 6/30/38 (4)	Budget Expenditures to June 30, 1938 Out of These Funds (5)	Budget Expenditures to June 30, 1938 Out of Other Funds (6)
A. Federal Emergency Relief Administration[a]	2,172	911	0	3,083	3,078[b]	0
B. Civil Works Administration	732	89	0	821	817	0
C. Civilian Conservation Corps	1,232	0	773	2,005	1,975[c]	0
D. Works Progress Administration[d]	4,680	0	0	4,680	4,480	0
E. National Youth Administration[e]	155	0	0	155	153	0
F. Public Works Administration[f]	1,147	0[g]	0	1,147	857	88[h]
G. Agricultural Adjustment Administration	37	186	161	198	198	1,563
H. Farm Credit Administration[j]	167	367	58	411	359	64[k]
J. Commodity Credit Corporation	3	0	94	464	217	0[h]
K. Farm Security Administration[m]	586	0	0	586	536	0
L. Rural Electrification Administration	15	47	0	62	50	0[h]
M. Department of Agriculture n.e.c.[j]	84	0	0	84	84	199[j]
N. Bureau of Public Roads[j]	945	0	255	1,200	1,146	0[j]
P. Corps of Engineers, War Department[j]	513	0	0	513	501	0[j]
Q. Puerto Rico Reconstruction Administration	50	0	0	50	40	0[h]
R. Tennessee Valley Authority	75	0	0	75	75	0[h]
S. National Recovery Administration	24	0	0	24	24	0
T. Other agencies	1,489[m]	107	83	1,679	1,553	0[n]
U. Total	14,106	1,707	1,424	17,237	16,163	1,914

a Expenditures include expenditures by Federal Surplus Commodities Corporation from funds provided by FERA.
b Includes $38 million spent in 1933.
c Includes $9 million spent in 1933.
d Subsequently called Works Projects Administration.
e NYA administrative expenses are included with WPA.
f Includes United States Housing Authority.
g Includes $1 million unallocated.
h Agency operated as a revolving fund. Expenditures are reported net of receipts. Apparently a not fully identified part of the excess of expenditures over receipts shown in column 5 for TVA, CCC, and REA was not, as of 1938, classified as general and special account (or budget) expenditures.
j Emergency expenditure programs only.

k Excludes emergency expenditures of $136 million during 1932–33. FCA operated as a revolving fund.
m Originally called Resettlement Administration. Includes allocations and expenditures a/c subsistence homesteads.
n There were $2,260 millions of emergency expenditures in 1934–38 other than those listed in column 5.
NOTE: Column 1 covers the following appropriation acts: Fourth Deficiency Appropriation Act (June 16, 1933); Emergency Appropriation Act (June 19, 1934); Emergency Relief Appropriation Act (April 8, 1935); Emergency Relief Appropriation Act (June 22, 1936); First Deficiency Appropriation Act (February 9, 1937); Emergency Relief Appropriation Act (June 29, 1937); and Supplemental Appropriation (March 2, 1938).
SOURCE: See Appendix A.

operates with only a regular annual appropriation may prepare its estimates in August for the entire year beginning on the following July 1. In either a war emergency or an emergency like that of the 1930's this is likely to be considered too slow a process, and strong pressure toward short cuts is the inevitable result. The short cuts adopted have taken various forms, but in general they mean a strengthening of the executive that does take place at the expense of the legislative branch; they mean that *de facto* Congress delegates some of its control of government expenditures to the executive.

One form of short cut may be called the blank-check appropriation, although what is left blank is not the amount but the payee and the precise purpose. The Fourth Deficiency Appropriation Act (1933), is a good example. It made available until June 30, 1935, $3.3 billion "to be expended in the discretion and under the direction of the President" mainly to implement the National Industrial Recovery Act (1933), but not to exceed $50 million for the TVA. This act created something of a palace politics problem in the executive branch to determine who was to spend the money. Part of it went to agencies not in existence at the time the act was passed.

In theory the executive is restrained from establishing new agencies without specific statutory authorization. But during the 1930's a good many agencies were created by executive order under the broad provisions of emergency legislation and were financed at first by allocations out of blank-check appropriations. In subsequent years, if the agencies were continued, there were specific congressional authorizations and appropriations for them. Among the agencies created under executive discretion during the 1930's and financed for a time by executive allocations[3] are: the Civil Works Administration, the National Youth Administration, the Civilian Conservation Corps,[4] the Farm Security Administration,[5] the Commodity Credit Corporation,[6] the Works Progress Administration,[7] the Rural Electrification Administration, the Electric Home and Farm Authority,[8] the (first) Export-Import Bank, the RFC Mortgage Company,[9] and the Federal National Mortgage Association.

In addition to the $3.3 billion act in 1933 there were six large blank-check appropriations during the five following years that made available for the somewhat elastic purposes of recovery and relief (but not for the normal functions of government) a total of nearly $11 billion. Table 40

---

[3] Including the RFC stock subscriptions discussed below.
[4] At first called Emergency Conservation Work.
[5] Originally called the Resettlement Administration.
[6] This corporation originally had a Delaware charter.
[7] Later renamed Works Projects Administration.
[8] This authority originally had a Delaware charter.
[9] A national mortgage association under Title III of the National Housing Act.

shows how, under the discretion of the President, these funds were allocated.[10] Specific emergency appropriations during 1934–38 to the agencies identified are included, also certain allocations of funds by the RFC. If one were to infer on the basis of this table that for five years the control retained by Congress over the emergency recovery and relief funds was confined for the most part to fixing the total amount, he would not be far wrong. But it should be noted that there was a tendency to bring the emergency agencies under regular fiscal procedures, realized earlier in the case of the AAA, FCA, and Civilian Conservation Corps than in that of the other emergency agencies in Table 40. It should be noted, too, that Congress did not in any effective sense fix the total of the RFC funds shown in column 2.

The blank-check device clearly involved a *de facto* delegation of a part of the appropriating power to the executive. Another device to the same effect may be called developing emergency activities outside the budget. We propose to use this language first to describe certain developments during World War I, even though there was at that time no formal, executive budget. In general, control of an agency's expenditures through the appropriating power requires that the agency shall be dependent on appropriations for the money it spends. To the extent that it has non-financial receipts of its own, or power to borrow on its own (or float an issue of stock), it is outside the control of the appropriating power and may fairly be said to be outside the budget. During World War I a number of corporations and agencies were established that had sources of funds other than appropriations. Their expenditures were not reported as federal expenditures, or were incompletely so reported. In the case of the War Finance Corporation and other corporations subscriptions to capital stock were reported as federal expenditures, retirements as federal receipts. In the case of the Railroad Administration the excess of expenditures over receipts was reported as a federal expenditure. However, these wartime agencies and the Russian Bureau of the War Trade Board maintained checking accounts with the Treasurer of the United States. The amounts of checks drawn on these accounts up to the end of October 1920 are shown in Table 41. Except for the Railroad Administration they probably give a reasonable indication of the volume of business transacted.

It did not seem appropriate to include the federal land banks and joint-stock land banks in Table 41, since these "government corporations" had many of the attributes of a private enterprise. Certainly they were outside the budget at the time, particularly the joint-stock land banks, which were technically government corporations mainly in the sense that

[10] But there were some suballocations. Thus, although most WPA projects were operated by nonfederal agencies, there were also federal projects. Up to June 30, 1938, $130 million was spent on federal projects.

they could issue tax-exempt obligations. Beginning in 1933 these banks were gradually liquidated. The connection of the federal land banks with the government was closer, but still rather indirect. Among the connecting links may be mentioned the fact that the distress refinancing of the 1930's included substantial subsidies to these banks. However, after the depression

TABLE 41

World War I Government Corporations and Business-Type Agencies
(millions of dollars)

		Checks on Account with Treasurer of U.S. Prior to October 31, 1920 (1)	Authorized Capital and Debt (2)	Stock Held by U.S. June 30, 1920 (3)
A.	Emergency Fleet Corporation	5,965	50	50
B.	U.S. Housing Corporation	135	70a	66.5b
C.	War Finance Corporation	2,998	700c	119b
D.	U.S. Grain Corporation	902	500	150b
E.	Sugar Equilization Board	d	5	5
F.	Russian Bureau of War Trade Board	13	e	e
G.	Railroad Administration	1,812	f	f
H.	Total	11,825	1,325	390.5

a Total issued.

b Amount retired equals excess of column 2 over column 3.

c Authorized capital $500 million, authorized debt $200 million.

d The Sugar Equalization Board did not maintain a deposit account with the Treasurer.

e Not a corporation. No securities issued.

f Not a corporation. No stock issued. But in 1919 the Administration borrowed from the WFC to tide over a temporary emergency due to delay in congressional action on its appropriation.

NOTE: The data for this table are from Secretary of the Treasury, 1920 *Annual Report*, pp. 237 and 320, except for the borrowing power of the War Finance Corporation. On this see the Corporation's 1919 *Annual Report*.

emergency there appeared to be no reason for continuing their connection with the government; the federal proprietary interest in them ended June 26, 1947.

A number of the agencies created during the 1930's—both those that were creatures of Congress and those originating in the executive branch— were to some extent outside the budget. All the corporations and credit agencies shown in Table 42 had operating incomes of their own. And it will be observed that the initial capital of many of them was subscribed either by the RFC or through an allocation out of a blank-check appropriation. However, a zero entry in column 11 does not necessarily imply absence of specific action by Congress. In the case of the federal home

TABLE 42

Government Corporations and Credit Agencies—1940 Balance Sheets and Operating Incomes[a]
(millions of dollars)

	Net Loaned to Other Government Agencies (1)	Other Loans and Securities (2)	Tangible Assets (3)	Bank Deposits, Current Receivables, and Other Assets (4)	Total Assets = Total Claims (5)	Securities Held by Public (6)	Accounted Interest Payable and Other liabilities (7)	Net Borrowed from Other Government Agencies (8)	Capital Subscribed by Government — by RFC (9)	Capital Subscribed by Government — by Relief Allocation (10)	Capital Subscribed by Government — by Specific Appropriations (11)	Surplus Reserves (12)	Operating Income (13)
A. Federal Deposit Insurance Corporation	364	24	23[c]	60	471	139	2	0	0	0	150	180[b]	54
B. Export-Import Bank of Washington	0	52	[c]	28	80	0	2	0	74	1	0	5	2
C. Tennessee Valley Authority	0	0	319	6	325	0	4	52	0	75	194	0	17
D. United States Maritime Commission	1	48	21[c]	128	198	0	34	0	0	0	164	−1	5
E. Disaster Loan Corporation	0	22		1	23	0	[c]	0	24[d]	0	0	0	[c]
F. Federal Housing Administration	35		7	19	61	9	2	0	81[d]	0	0	−31[e]	18
G. Federal National Mortgage Association	0	163	1	4	168	85	4	63	11	0	0	5	7
H. RFC Mortgage Corporation	0	58	[c]	2	60	0	[c]	35	25	0	0	[c]	3
J. Home Owners' Loan Corporation	0	2,169	426	9	2,604	2,524	31	25	100[f]	0	0	−76	124
K. Federal Savings and Loan Insurance Corporation	123	0	0	2	125	0	1	0	100[f]	0	0	24	6
L. Federal home loan banks	90	157	0	13	260	91	34	0	125[d]	0	0	10	5
M. United States Housing Authority	40	83	128		252	113	1	0	0	142	0	−4	7
N. Commodity Credit Corporation	0	133	380	21	534	406	3	25	97[d]	3	0	0[g]	6
P. Farm Credit Administration	12	74	0		92	0	[c]	0	64[d]	3	130	−102[e]	12
Q. Federal Farm Mortgage Corporation	747	669	12	44	1,472	1,258	14	0	200[d]	0	0	0	62
R. Federal land banks	0	1,857	90	233	2,180	1,062	31	676	0	0	313	98[h]	75
S. Federal intermediate credit banks	69	231	[c]	20	320	197	2	0	40[d]	0	60	21	3
T. Production credit corporations	46	75		1	122	0	[c]	0	45[d]	0	75	2[c]	3
U. Regional agricultural credit corporations	13	6	[c]	1	20	0	[c]	0	25[j]	0	0	−5[k]	[c]
V. Banks for cooperatives	103	60	[c]	6	169	3	[c]	0	0	0	150[m]	16	3
W. Rural Electrification Administration	0	220	0	2	222	0	0	127	0	15	80	0	4
X. Total above	1,643	6,101	1,407	607	9,758	5,887	163	1,003	1,011	236	1,316	142	416

aBalance sheet as of June 30; income during year ending June 30.

bOperating reserve.

cLess than $500 thousand.

dIn accordance with the act approved February 24, 1938, the Treasury subsequently canceled the indebtedness incurred by the RFC to finance this expenditure and the RFC (in the case of the corporations) transferred the stock to the Treasury.

eResidual figure. Balance sheet shows no deficit.

fRFC subscribed $200 million to HOLC; HOLC $100 million to FSLIC. Note 4 applies to the $200 million.

g$170 million had been appropriated to CCC for restoration of capital impairment (net after deducting surplus distributions of $44 million to the Treasury).

h$173 million had been appropriated to those banks for reduction of interest rates on mortgages.

jIncludes $17.4 million for expenses. Note 4 applies to the $25 million.

kResidual figure. Balance sheet shows a deficit of $1.4 million.

mBy Agricultural Marketing Act revolving fund.

SOURCE: See Appendix A.

loan banks, for example, an amendment to the RFC's organic act authorized the $125 million subscription.[11] But most of the zero entries signify
outside-the-budget capital funds. And the table shows two other major
sources of funds that are outside the budget: net borrowing from other
agencies and net sales of securities to the public. Of course, when an
agency has been specifically authorized by Congress, its borrowing power
will in general have a statutory upper limit, or, as in the case of the RFC
during most of the 1930's, various upper limits for various specified purposes. But the limits may be wide. As of June 30, 1940, the HOLC,
FFMC, and CCC together had authorized borrowing power of more than
$8 billion. This may be compared with the statutory limit of $45 billion
imposed on direct federal debt during the late 1930's.

The RFC was left out of Table 42; a fuller treatment of this corporation seemed advisable. Table 43 is a rough statement of sources and uses
of RFC funds during two periods, from its inception to June 30, 1940, and
from June 30, 1940, to June 30, 1946. During the earlier period total
sources exceeded $4.5 billion. Half this total was net borrowings from the
Treasury.[12] Although established to make loans on essentially a commercial basis, nearly 40 per cent of its funds during the period went into relief
and subsidies (the subsidies were to regional agricultural credit corporations).

The table covers operations of subsidiary corporations to the extent
that these are revealed in the 1946 financial statement. The wartime
subsidiaries were particularly important. Under an amendment to its
organic act, approved June 25, 1940, the RFC organized the Metals
Reserve Corporation, Rubber Reserve Corporation, Defense Plant
Corporation, Defense Supplies Corporation, War Damage Corporation,
U.S. Commercial Company, and Petroleum Reserves Corporation.[13]
Thus provision was made for a $7 billion munitions plant construction
program; for investing nearly $1 billion in stockpiles of strategic materials;
for spending some $200 million on a preclusive buying program; and for
practically $3 billion in direct subsidy payments, all essentially outside
the budget.[14] Because of the special interest attaching to the delegation of
(negative) taxing power involved in this last program a note on the subject,
prepared by Richard S. Martin, is appended to this chapter.

[11] The form of the action taken by Congress here means the appropriation committees
held no hearings on the item.

[12] Net of the increase in most government and government agency obligations held
by the RFC.

[13] The two last named were transferred in 1943 to the Office of Economic Warfare,
which office was shortly consolidated into the Foreign Economic Administration. In
1945 these two corporations and the Rubber Development Corporation (originally
chartered by the RFC in Delaware) were transferred back to the RFC for liquidation.

[14] The RFC kept Congress informed of its operations except to the extent that information concerning them was classified for national security reasons.

But if Congress did not authorize these huge expenditure programs by appropriating the money for them before they could be carried out, it was called upon to approve them after the fact. Under acts of February 24,

TABLE 43

Total RFC Sources and Uses of Funds, from
Inception to June 30, 1946
(millions of dollars)

		2/20/32 to 6/30/40	6/30/40 to 6/30/46
	SOURCES OF FUNDS		
A.	Net borrowing from other federal agencies	2,334	9,443
B.	Reimbursements by other federal agencies a/c "defense" plants	0	1,365
C.	Net borrowing in the market	1,093	−1,093
D.	Net operating receipts	471	1,437
E.	Initial capital subscription	500	−175
F.	Other sources	240	276
G.	Total above	4,638	11,253
	USES OF FUNDS		
H.	Net increase in cash and receivables	30	168
J.	Invested in capital assets	a	8
K.	Invested in miscellaneous property	42	−42
L.	Net increase in loans and preferred stock held	1,791	−507
M.	Subscriptions to capital of other government corporations	619	14
N.	Relief expenditures	1,782	0
P.	"Direct" subsidies	17	2,981[b]
Q.	Invested in defense plants	0	6,868
R.	Invested in strategic materials, etc.[c]	0	1,135
S.	Interest expense	265	383
T.	Administrative expense	74	174
U.	Other uses	16	72
		4,636	11,254
		1938 and 1941 acts	*1947 and 1948 acts*
V.	RFC notes canceled	2,786	10,063
W.	Cash recoveries and assets transferred to other agencies	1,491[d]	995

[a] Less than $500,000.
[b] Chiefly food subsidies.
[c] Includes preclusive procurement.
[d] Includes some assets transferred under later acts.
SOURCE: See Appendix A.

1938, and March 28, 1941, nearly $2.8 billion of RFC notes issued to finance expenditures during the earlier period and held by the Treasury were canceled. At the same time the securities and other assets acquired by the RFC through these expenditures were transferred to the Treasury or other federal agencies. During 1947 and 1948 a number of acts were passed authorizing additional RFC note cancellations totaling over $10 billion and directing the RFC to make the additional property transfers appropriate thereto. Transferred securities and other properties valued at $744 million were retained; most of these had been transferred under the 1938 and 1941 acts. Other properties were liquidated; about three-quarters of a billion was realized under the 1938 and 1941 act transfers, nearly a billion from the later transfers.

A sources and uses of funds statement for the Commodity Credit Corporation would be of considerable interest; for the CCC is the principal other agency that has operated on an appropriation-after-the-fact basis. But it would be extremely difficult to piece such a statement together. As a substitute, Table 44 gives a record of the after-the-fact acts of Congress[15] to restore the corporation's capital impairment. Before World War II it engaged principally in making loans on agricultural commodities to promote orderly marketing and iron out year-to-year variations in prices and supplies. During the war its activities were expanded to include purchases for use by the United States and by foreign governments, purchases for surplus disposal, price support purchases and nonrecourse price support loans. An act approved March 8, 1938, provided for maintaining the corporation's capital unimpaired at $100 million through an appraisal by the Secretary of the Treasury as of March 31 of each year of its assets and liabilities (in 1945 the appraisal date was changed to June 30). Under the 1938 act as amended, if what the CCC spends during the year results in the appraisal's showing a deficit in the corporation's net worth, an estimate in the amount of the deficit is incorporated in the budget for the second following year.[16] If, however, the appraisal shows a surplus, the surplus is returned to the Treasury. As the table indicates, in addition to the regular annual provisions for the restoration of capital impairment (during 1938–54 there were only four surplus years), Congress has recently made after-the-fact provisions of funds in connection with several special programs. And besides the reimbursements covered by the table, there was a somewhat larger total of executive reimbursements for operations by the corporation as a procurement agent.

This review of the short cuts in fiscal procedures resorted to during the two world wars and the 1930's has focused on the development of outside-the-budget activities in all three periods and on blank-check appropriations in the 1930's. There were indeed blank-check appropriations during both wars, though as here defined they played a smaller role

---

[15] Technically some of these are called cancellations of obligations, some of them appropriations.

[16] The lag of appropriation behind appraisal was less than five months in the case of the 1938, 1939, and 1941 appraisals.

than in the depression emergency. And there were other short cuts in fiscal procedures. Among them were very large appropriations without very precise specifications passed with anything but detailed hearings.[17]

TABLE 44

CCC Capital Reimbursements and Surplus Distributions, 1938–54
(millions of dollars)

Restorations of capital impairment	
1938	94
1940	120
1942	2
1945	257
1947	1,563
1951	67
1952	421
1953	109
1954	646
Total restorations	3,279
Less surpluses returned to the Treasury	
1940	44
1942	28
1948	18
1949	49
Total returned	138
Plus other capital reimbursements	
Losses on commodities, Foreign Aid Act of 1947	56
Foot and mouth disease eradication program	53
Costs of operations under International Wheat Agreement Act of 1949	483
Total other capital reimbursements	593
Net capital reimbursements	3,702

NOTE: This table is derived from information in Secretary of the Treasury, 1954 *Annual Report*, p. 652. Annual figures refer to fiscal years. Table excludes a larger total of reimbursements for procurement of commodities for government use under lend-lease, etc. Details may not add to totals because of rounding.

We may note, too, that funds appropriated for a particular fiscal year or other period will lapse if not legally obligated by a contract or other definite expenditure commitment made during the period; in general

[17] The Third Supplemental National Defense Appropriation Act of 1942 (December 17, 1941), was for $9.1 billion; the Fourth Supplemental (January 30, 1942), for $12.5 billion; the Fifth Supplemental (March 5, 1942), for $30.4 billion; the Sixth Supplemental (April 28, 1942), for $18.9 billion. There were also seven very large regular appropriation acts during 1942–45: the Military Appropriation Act (1942), $10.4 billion; the Military Appropriation Act (1943), $42.8 billion; the Naval Appropriation Act (1943), $23.7 billion; the Military Appropriation Act (1944), $59 billion; the Naval Appropriation Act (1944), $27.6 billion; the Military Appropriation Act (1945), $15.4 billion; and the Naval Appropriation Act (1945), $27.6 billion.

the commitment when not a formal contract must bind the two parties much as a formal contract would.[18] But very indefinite expenditure commitments by the War and Navy Departments were taken to obligate appropriated funds during World War II.

This is certainly not an exhaustive list of the fiscal procedure short cuts; but what has been said should suffice to show that expenditure controls were significantly relaxed during the three emergencies, and that in effect important aspects of the appropriating power were delegated to the executive.

The outside-the-budget device, like that of the blank-check appropriation, was an emergency expedient of a temporary nature. In both cases there was the tendency to revert to normal fiscal procedures. Under the definitions of budget receipts and expenditures that prevailed from 1938 until 1945 (then called general and special account receipts and expenditures) the principal expenditures included in connection with government corporations were those for capital stock subscriptions and capital reimbursements. It is true the Budget included certain estimates for trust, etc. accounts as well as estimates for the general and special accounts and that among these were some estimates for corporation administrative expenses and for limitations on lending power.[19] But in accordance with the Government Corporations Control Act (1945), the definitions were revised to bring corporations back under the budget and under audit by the General Accounting Office.[20] And the Public Debt Act (1945), in setting a new statutory limit of $300 billion, brought those agency obligations fully guaranteed by the United States under this limit.

Indeed, even before these 1945 acts there were steps taken in this direction. Between 1930 and 1941 the obligations of government agencies held by the public had increased from $2 billion to $8 billion.[21] During

[18] *Budget-Treasury Regulation No. 1* (June 1952) provides in regard to letters of intent, "Where such letters constitute binding agreements under which the contractor is authorized to proceed, obligations will cover the amount indicated in the letters. If the letters merely indicate an intention on the part of the Government to enter into a contractual relation at a later date the amounts involved will not be treated as obligations."

[19] The estimates in the 1945 Budget for the RFC and CCC were for administrative expenses only and totaled less than $18 million.

[20] See the note on surplus and deficit concepts at the end of this chapter.

[21] Figures for 1945, 1950, and 1954 are computed as follows:

A. Securities of federal instrumentalities not guaranteed by U.S. (Table 48)
minus B. Such securities held by U.S. government in investment accounts (Table 48)
plus C. Guaranteed agency obligations held outside the Treasury (Table 16)
plus D. Private proprietary interest in government corporations (Table 76)
equals E. Total federal agency bonds, notes, debentures, and capital stock held by the public.

All figures are as of June 30. Table number references are to Secretary of the Treasury, 1954 *Annual Report*. Of the $1.5 billion held by the public as of June 30, 1954, only $81 million were included in the general statutory debt limit.

the war a policy of contracting these then outside-the-debt-limit obligations was put into operation. On June 30, 1945, the volume held by the public was down to $1.9 billion; five years later it was below $1 billion.[22] It is true that more recently this volume has increased again. On June 30, 1954, there were public holdings of $1.5 billion. However, this total consisted of: (a) debentures of the FHA fully guaranteed by the United States, (b) obligations and private proprietary interests of banks for cooperatives and federal home loan banks, (c) obligations of federal intermediate credit banks, and (d) a small amount of matured HOLC and FFMC obligations. It seems fair to say that financing the activities of federal agencies by sales of securities to the public, 1945–54, was essentially confined to the financing of portfolio additions by government financial institutions.

3. Summary

The growth of social insurance funds in recent years has made non-financial deficits significantly smaller than budget deficits for state and local governments as well as for the federal government.

The growth of endowment and investment funds has had a like effect in the case of state and local governments.

Various fiscal devices resorted to during the two world wars emergencies and the depression emergency of the 1930's have amounted to *de facto* temporary delegation of a substantial part of the appropriating power of Congress to the federal executive branch. Such devices include: (a) appropriations that permitted the President to determine the purposes for which the funds were to be spent and the agencies that were to spend them, and (b) granting agencies powers that meant outside-the-budget sources and uses of funds. During World War II *de facto* delegation also took the form of appropriating very large sums for war purposes with the ordinary peacetime controls somewhat relaxed.

Had the emergency developments in respect to appropriation procedures been paralleled by analogous emergency developments in the levying of taxes, this chapter would have included another section. But the fact of the matter is that Congress has been far less ready to concede emergency short cuts in the legislative process of levying taxes than in that of making appropriations. We will follow one important implication of this fact in Chapter VIII.

4. A Note on RFC Subsidy Payments, 1940–46, by
Richard S. Martin

This note concerns the approximately $3 billion paid in direct subsidies by the Reconstruction Finance Corporation as a result of World War II (see Table 43). Interest in these payments arises particularly from the

[22] See footnote 21.

142

delegation by Congress of control over the subsidy program. This delegation of what is essentially negative taxing power is in contrast to the historical reluctance of Congress to delegate positive taxing power.

THE DEFENSE PERIOD

During the defense period the RFC became involved in the government's program to ease shortages of strategic and critical materials. In June 1940 the organic RFC Act was amended to authorize the creation of one or more subsidiary corporations whose powers would include authority to "... produce, acquire, and carry ..." these materials.[23] In June 1941 these powers were broadened to allow the corporations to "... produce, acquire, carry, sell, or otherwise deal in strategic and critical materials ...."[24] The grant of these broader powers occurred after the passage of the Lend-Lease Act in March and the declaration by the President on May 27 of an unlimited national emergency. Despite the broad powers of the June 1941 amendment, however, the RFC prior to Pearl Harbor refused to engage in even indirect subsidies for strategic and critical materials.[25]

THE WAR PERIOD

Direct subsidy payments were explicitly authorized by Congress in the Emergency Price Control Act of 1942.[26] According to section 2(e):

"Whenever the [Price] Administrator determines that the maximum necessary production of any commodity is not being obtained or may not be obtained during the ensuing year, he may, on behalf of the United States, without regard to the provisions of law requiring competitive bidding, buy or sell at public or private sale, ... or make subsidy payments to domestic producers of such commodity in such amounts and in such manner and upon such terms and conditions as he determines to be necessary to obtain the maximum necessary production thereof: *Provided,* That in the case of any commodity which has heretofore or may hereafter be defined as a strategic or critical material ... such determinations shall be made by the Federal Loan Administrator, with the approval of the President, and, ... such commodity may be bought or sold, or stored or used, and

---

[23] Act approved June 25, 1940 (54 Stat. chap. 427, pp. 573–74).

[24] Act approved June 10, 1941 (55 Stat. chap. 190, pp. 249–50).

[25] Thus the RFC would not purchase copper from marginal producers at premium prices until arrangements had been made, in this case under the lend-lease program, to dispose of the copper at a gain rather than a loss. See testimony of Leon Henderson before the Senate Committee on Banking and Currency during hearings on the Emergency Price Control Act of 1942.

[26] Act approved January 30, 1942 (56 Stat. chap. 26, pp. 26–27).

143

such subsidy payments to domestic producers thereof may be paid, only by corporations created or organized pursuant to section 5d [of the RFC Act] . . . ."[27]

In addition to this exclusive responsibility for action with strategic and critical materials, the RFC was soon directed to purchase or subsidize other commodities when requested by the Price Administrator.[28]

Rather curiously, the broad authorization for direct subsidy payments contained in the Emergency Price Control Act of 1942 was added almost as an afterthought and aroused little interest in Congress. Neither the House version of the original bill,[29] passed in November 1941 before Pearl Harbor, nor the Senate version passed in January 1942 contained this authorization. It was added by the conference committee. In the House debate on the final bill, the complete list of changes was presented. But this one was no more than mentioned. The verbal report of the Senate conferees was limited to what were considered the important changes. The subsidy authorization, although subsequently mentioned in the debate, was not included in this category.[30]

The distribution by product of the cumulative direct subsidies paid by the RFC as of June 30, 1946, is as follows:[31]

	(millions of dollars)
Livestock—to slaughterers	1,537
Petroleum transportation compensatory adjustments, net	356
Flour—to producers	349
Butter—to producers	183
Copper, lead, and zinc—to producers who exceeded quotas	293
Other[a]	263
Total	2,981

[a] Principally on production from stripper oil wells, on coffee, and on transportation of coal and sugar.

These figures exclude the substantial subsidy payments made by the Commodity Credit Corporation. To some extent there was product overlap in the subsidy payments made by the two agencies. The figures also exclude any indirect subsidies involved in the processing or purchase for resale of various commodities by the RFC subsidiaries.[32]

[27] Between February 1942 and February 1945 the powers and duties of the Federal Loan Administrator relating to the RFC were exercised by the Secretary of Commerce.

[28] Executive Order 9250, October 3, 1942.

[29] *H.R. 5990*, 77th Congress, 1st Session.

[30] *Congressional Record*, 77th Congress, 2nd Session, pp. 656–88, 693–725.

[31] Reconstruction Finance Corporation, *Consolidated Balance Sheet and Operating Statement*, June 30, 1946.

[32] From July 1943 to October 1945 the Rubber Development Corporation, the U.S. Commercial Company, and the Petroleum Reserves Corporation were under the jurisdiction of the Foreign Economic Administration. On November 15, 1945, the Petroleum Reserves Corporation became the War Assets Corporation.

The above RFC payments included both general and differential subsidies. The livestock subsidy, instituted with some others at the time of the price rollback in 1943, was largely in the form of specified payments per hundred pounds of weight. Differential costs within a species were, in general, disregarded. Under the copper premium price plan a specified subsidy per pound was paid for all production in excess of designated quotas. The use of quotas afforded some leeway in the recognition of differential costs. The transportation subsidies, for petroleum as an example, allowed compensation for higher costs due to greater war risks, or for shifting to a more expensive means of transportation without an increase in product price. The type of subsidy paid was, under the law, an administrative determination.

The control over subsidy payments which Congress delegated in January 1942 was not recovered until after the war period. In 1944 a deadline of June 30, 1945, was established, after which ". . . neither the Price Administrator nor the Reconstruction Finance Corporation nor any other Government corporation shall make any subsidy payments, or buy any commodities for the purpose of selling them at a loss and thereby subsidizing directly or indirectly the sale of commodities unless the money required for such subsidies, or sale at a loss, had been appropriated by Congress for such purpose."[33] Before the deadline arrived, however, Congress exempted the RFC from these provisions with respect to (a) obligations incurred prior to July 1, 1945, referring to 1945 and prior fiscal year activities; and (b) payments and purchases during fiscal 1946 involving direct and indirect subsidies of up to $1.5 billion.[34]

The published information on the RFC subsidy payments does not lend itself to an analysis of operations under the limitations imposed. The

[33] Amendment to the Emergency Price Control Act of 1942 contained in section 102, Stabilization Extension Act of 1944, approved June 30, 1944 (58 Stat. chap. 325, p. 632).

[34] Act approved June 23, 1945 (Public Law 88, 79th Congress). The act specified the following product limitations:

	(millions of dollars)
Foreign rubber and rubber products	60
Other foreign products	80
Domestic products	
Meat	595
Butter	100
Flour	190
Petroleum and its products	290
Copper, lead, and zinc	88
Other	100
Total	1,503

It was provided that in the event the entire amount of any of the above allocations was not required for its purpose, the unused portion, not to exceed 10 per cent of such allocation, might be used for making payments and purchases for any other items enumerated.

available figures on direct subsidies are on a payments-made basis rather than an obligations-incurred basis for any period. The somewhat flexible product limitations set up by Congress for fiscal 1946 applied to both direct and indirect subsidies. For some products the RFC was engaged in both types of subsidies. Perhaps the most that can be said is that direct payments of $1,020 million, or slightly more than one-third of the total up to June 30, 1946, occurred during fiscal 1946.[35] During 1946, as in prior years, the subsidies were paid from funds borrowed by the RFC from the Treasury.[36]

In summary, it may be said that from the passage of the Emergency Price Control Act of 1942 through fiscal 1945 the control of subsidy programs in furtherance of the war effort was an administrative matter. There were no substantial congressional controls over the selection of domestic products for subsidy payments, over the types or rates of the subsidies, or over the total costs of any or all programs. For fiscal 1946 an over-all limitation and flexible product limitations were imposed. Within these limits, however, administrative discretion was still large. There was no requirement that any or all programs be continued. The types and rates of payments were not specified, and there was still leeway for discretion over the products to be subsidized. Thus the authority delegated by Congress during this period was indeed broad.

By the end of 1946 the subsidy program was largely complete. Net payments in fiscal 1947 amounted to $213 million, including liquidation of liabilities incurred in prior years.[37] In the Government Corporations Appropriation Act 1949,[38] the Secretary of the Treasury was directed to cancel notes of the RFC in the amount of $9,314 million plus accrued interest. Relatively minor amounts were included in other acts passed in 1947 and 1948 to bring the total amount of RFC notes canceled to over $10 billion. This amount represented the net loss of the RFC due to national defense and war activities. Charges for direct subsidies amounted to $3,089 million, or not far from one-third of the total.[39]

[35] *The Budget of the United States*, 1948, p. 1061.
[36] See Table 43 above.
[37] *The Budget of the United States*, 1949, p. 1108.
[38] Approved June 30, 1948 (Public Law 860, 80th Congress).
[39] Reconstruction Finance Corporation, *Annual Report and Financial Statements*, June 30, 1947, p. 18.

CHAPTER VIII

The Requirements of National Security and International Aid

In Chapter VI we considered the factors making for an increase in federal net debt resulting from following a countercyclical fiscal policy during a business contraction, and deferred to the present chapter questions relating to retirement of the added debt after the economy has recovered from the contraction. Conditions making for or against retirement of the debt incurred in the 1930's and conditions making for or against retirement of the war debt must obviously be considered together. And it will prove advantageous to have considered them before we attempt to examine the possible significance of a countercyclical fiscal policy for future changes in federal debt.

It will doubtless be conceded that a countercyclical fiscal policy necessarily requires net borrowing during a business contraction. If one asks why or how far a war should be financed by borrowing, or why or how far international aid should be so financed, the answer can hardly be such a clear-cut statement. But war financing has proverbially meant deficit financing, and the limited experience we have had to date with international aid suggests that at least in wartime such aid is likely to be financed in substantial part by borrowing.

In this chapter we will first note some factors making for wartime deficits that have hitherto received inadequate attention, next examine the bearing of international aid programs on federal financial requirements, and then turn to questions relating to debt retirement.

1. Would It Be Feasible to Pay for a War as You Go?

It has often been suggested[1] that from a purely theoretical economic viewpoint a war, even an all-out war, could be entirely financed by raising taxes and other revenues as fast and as far as expenditures are increased. Among the arguments advanced against such a pay-as-you-go program are: that it would be more dampening to the ardor of patriotism than some measure of deficit financing; that it would be likely to employ taxes that would entail discouragements to maximum production increases; that

We are here concerned neither with the case for this suggestion nor with that against it. In particular we are concerned neither to affirm nor to deny the proposition that a perfect pay-as-you-go policy—if one were feasible—would avoid price inflation.

borrowing is a simpler, often a more equitable way to mop up the last dregs of excess purchasing power; and that price increases, if limited in extent, may be the easiest way to accomplish some of the necessary reallocations of resources.

TABLE 45

Federal Receipt and Expenditure Increases and Deficit Financing
in Four Wars

Year	Receipts	Expenditures	Receipts	Expenditures	Percentage of Deficit Financing
	(millions of dollars)		(per cent increase per year)		
	(1)	(2)	(3)	(4)	(5)
1811[a]	14.42	8.06			
1814[a]	11.18	34.72	−7	110	68
1860[b]	56.1	63.1			
1865[c]	333.7	1,297.6	99	392	74
1916[b]	1,080.0	1,040.0			
1919[b]	5,500.0	18,380.0	136	557	70
1940[a]	8,600.0	10,800.0			
1944[a]	58,200.0	109,000.0	144	227	46.5

[a] Calendar year figures.

[b] Fiscal year figures.

[c] Fiscal year figures for Union only.

NOTE: Data for 1811–65 are from *Historical Statistics*. Data for 1916–44 are from Table 5.

These contentions have been dealt with extensively in various studies of war finance, and it would be in the nature of a digression to go into them here. For our present purpose it seems sufficient to note that, to the extent they are valid, they make a full-fledged pay-for-a-war-as-you-go policy both economically inexpedient and politically improbable.

But even if all these contentions were to be summarily rejected, there is reason to think some lag of revenues behind expenditures would be very difficult to avoid, and that an important part of the explanation of war deficits lies in the rapidity of wartime expenditure increases. Table 45 compares roughly computed rates of increase of receipts and of expenditures in four wars. It also shows the percentage of deficit financing in the year taken as the terminal year of each war. Nonfinancial expenditures rose rather more rapidly during World War I than during the Civil War, despite the fact that price increases were somewhat restrained. Taxes and other nonfinancial receipts were stepped up most rapidly during World War II. If there is a substantial problem of developing the techniques of stepping receipts up rapidly—and we argue below that there

148

is—Table 45 is consistent with the hypothesis that these techniques have been improving. At all events tax rate increases were prompt enough and large enough during World War I so that the percentage of deficit financing in 1919 was less than that in 1865; and tax rate increases during World War II were prompt enough and large enough so that the percentage of deficit financing in 1944 was markedly less than that in 1919.

It is evident that there was no real effort to make revenues increase with expenditures during the War of 1812. And apparently William G. McAdoo, Secretary of the Treasury in 1913–18, after studying the Civil War experience, concluded that that experience was of negative help only, "teaching him what not to do" to finance World War I.[2]

In respect to tax sources conditions were distinctly favorable in 1917 to a sharp step-up of tax receipts such as would be needed to implement a pay-as-you-go policy. The inheritance tax (along with stamp taxes on various business documents) had been successfully levied as a war emergency measure in 1898–1901; and it had been reimposed in the 1916 Revenue Act. The Payne-Aldrich Act (1909), had established a corporate income tax. And promptly after ratification of the 16th Amendment an individual income tax had been included in the Underwood Tariff Act (1913). But before our entry into the war the rates were modest. Only 16 per cent of 1916 budget receipts came from income and profits taxes, and the inheritance tax did not yield anything during that fiscal year.

It might seem that Congress, with these almost untapped tax sources at its disposal, could have enacted tax increases as rapidly as it enacted the appropriations. As we have seen, in an emergency Congress has been willing to adopt short cuts in the appropriation process. On the other hand, when it comes to a revenue bill even during a war Congress is apt to take its own time. In September 1916 to meet the expenditure increases involved in the preparedness program a revenue act had been passed that imposed moderate tax increases, and this had been followed by another in March 1917 which raised inheritance tax rates and imposed an 8 per cent excess profits tax. But despite the sharp increases in expenditures after our entry into the war, agreement in Congress on a war revenue act was not reached until more than three months after the armistice.[3]

But the fact that making war appropriations seems to be a more expeditious process than levying taxes is probably only a minor part of the explanation of the need for deficit financing during World War I. Anything approaching a pay-as-you-go policy would have required leadership from the executive; the administration never seriously entertained the idea

[2] Paul Studenski and Herman E. Krooss, *Financial History of the United States*, p. 286.
[3] Under the Act of February 24, 1919, taxes on 1918 incomes were sharply increased. The effective rate on individual incomes of $3,000 to $5,000 was 0.86 per cent for 1917, 2.35 per cent for 1918, and 1.67 per cent for 1919 and 1920.

of such a policy. And even if it had, in the absence of an executive budget, a planned balancing of receipts against expenditures would have been very difficult, particularly since to an important extent—$4.7 billion in fiscal year 1918—United States war expenditures were planned in the first instance by allied foreign governments. Table 46 shows how far expenditures were underestimated for 1917–19. Of course the fiscal 1917 estimates went to Congress late in calendar 1915; and the fiscal 1918

TABLE 46

Estimated and Actual Federal Expenditures, 1917–20
(millions of dollars)

Fiscal Year	Estimated Expenditures (1)	Actual Expenditures (2)
1917	909	2,086
1918	1,269	13,792
1919	13,019	18,952
1920	7,443	6,142

NOTE: Prior to the Budget and Accounting Act of 1921 estimates were transmitted to Congress rather more than six months before the beginning of the fiscal year. These estimates were reprinted in Secretary of the Treasury, *Annual Reports*.

estimates were submitted several months before the United States entered the war.[4]

One aspect of fiscal procedures that complicates the problem of balancing revenues against expenditures is the lag of expenditures behind the incurring of the obligations to make them. No doubt this complication was more in evidence during World War I than in the 1920's and 1930's. But partly because so large a part of the war expenditures—those for loans to allied governments—were not particularly subject to this lag, it was not a major complication. However, it became so during World War II, as Table 47 makes clear. Column 2 shows not obligations incurred, but the newly enacted authority to incur them—that is, new appropriations and contract authorizations.[5] Total new obligational authority in

[4] Much as at present, revised (midyear) estimates were submitted some twelve months later. These midyear estimates for 1918–20 all erred significantly on the high side.

[5] Contract authorizations, like appropriations, convey authority to an agency such as the Department of Defense to incur obligations to spend money. The Constitution provides that "no appropriation of money [to support armies] . . . shall be for a longer term than two years." The contract authorization is used to authorize contracts involving expenditure commitments (not necessarily military) that run more than two years into the future (for naval vessels these were formerly expressed in tons rather than dollars). A contract authorization must be followed by an appropriation to provide for liquidating the obligations incurred under it. (Congress is morally but not legally bound to make such appropriations.) In addition to the appropriation and the contract authorization Congress has in recent years conveyed new authority to obligate funds in the form of "authorizations to expend from public debt receipts," e.g. for making loans.

1941–45 exceeded total expenditures by more than $130 billion. Evidently one way Congress in effect delegated a part of its discretion over expenditures during this war was through granting somewhat more new obligational authority than the executive actually used.

Another fact that can be deduced from the table is that there must have been a number of years during the 1940's (probably 1942–45) for which the total of unliquidated obligations to spend money outstanding on July

TABLE 47

Federal Budget Expenditures, Appropriations, and Other Obligational
Authority Enactments, 1941–47
(billions of dollars)

Fiscal Year	Expenditures (1)	New Obligational Authority (2)	Re-enacted Obligational Authority (3)
1941	12.7	41.0	a
1942	32.4	124.6	a
1943	78.2	81.0	22.0b
1944	93.7	102.1	36.9
1945	100.4	54.6	51.2
1946	65.0	70.6	36.1
1947	42.5	39.0	1.1

a Not shown in the *Budget.*
b Appropriations to liquidate contract authorizations.
NOTE: Column 2 represents new appropriations plus contract authorizations plus authorizations treated as public debt transactions minus recisions. Column 3 represents reappropriations plus appropriations to liquidate contract authorizations.
All figures refer to general and special account totals excluding debt retirement. Figures for 1941 and 1942 are from *Receipts, Expenditures and Balances of the United States Government;* figures for each other year are from the Budget for the second following year.

1 was larger than total estimated expenditures for the year ahead. But the amount of unliquidated obligations can only be roughly inferred from Table 47, and from data presented in the wartime budgets. It was not until after the great disparity between estimated expenditures and estimated new obligational authority developed during the war that the need for presenting a reconciliation between them in the Budget became urgent. And then it took time and experience to develop a satisfactory way to present such reconciliation in detail without adding greatly to the bulk of an already exceedingly bulky document.[6] But beginning with the 1953 Budget a reconciliation has been given.

With information on unliquidated obligations incurred at hand it would seem that the making of short-term expenditure estimates should be considerably facilitated. Indeed, a quarterly release of unliquidated

[6] Among other things it took time to develop the concept "new obligational authority."

federal obligations giving well-chosen detail might prove to be a highly significant addition to our current business information. But for Congress during World War II the disparity between expenditures and new obligational authority must have been a very confusing one. In fact, this disparity seems to have caused a good deal of confusion ever since the Budget began giving figures on it. Presumably, though, it will cease to be a source of confusion once it comes to be generally understood. But general understanding will not necessarily make prompter tax increases any easier. Indeed, since the new obligational authority conferred on the executive stepped up more rapidly than expenditures in 1941–44, mistaking the former for the latter may have helped to encourage prompter and sharper tax increases.

On the whole in respect to both the information and the procedures available the situation in World War II was far more favorable to making prompt tax step-ups than it had been in World War I. By 1940 the executive budget system had been in operation for nearly two decades. This provided the expenditure estimates needed for a planned relation between expenditures and taxes. Under it, too, important progress had been made in the technique of estimating tax yields, so that the executive branch was in a much better position to give some leadership in the development of tax bills. Perhaps more important, however, was what had been learned since 1918 about the problems of financing a major war effort and the increased influence of economists in dealing with these problems. Throughout World War I Treasury officials, ignoring the effect of government spending on private incomes, based their financing plans on the assumption that with the government in the bond market on so large a scale the total demand for funds was likely to outrun the supply. If not by 1940, then not long after that, Treasury economists had come to understand that "the income earned in producing output is necessarily equal to the value of output produced .... Any level of production is potentially self-financing at any level of prices."[7]

Table 48 compares for 1939-54 the budget estimates of expenditures submitted nearly six months before the beginning of each fiscal year, the midyear estimates, and the actuals. If there are still serious errors in the budget figures in 1941–43, 1946, and 1953–54, the record is clearly a considerable improvement over that of World War I. And the midyear figures are in general quite good.

Between July 1, 1940, when the defense effort may be said to have begun, and V-J Day, Congress passed six main revenue acts. During the

[7] Committee for Economic Development Research Staff, *Jobs and Markets*, p. 12. In other words, for all economic sectors (including the rest of the world) total nonfinancial sources of funds equal total nonfinancial uses; hence, if the government has a nonfinancial deficit, other sectors, taken collectively, must have an equal nonfinancial surplus and be adding this amount to their net financial assets.

defense program, while unemployment was still high, the administration recommended tax increases and the imposition of an excess profits tax, but qualified its recommendations with a caution against taxes that might "restrict general consumption." Congress responded in three acts, delaying the imposition of a tax on excess profits until the second and in

TABLE 48

Total Federal Budget Expenditures, Actual and Budgeted, 1939–54
(billions of dollars)

Fiscal Year	Budget Estimate (1)	Midyear Estimate (2)	Actual[a] (3)
1946 basis			
1939	6.9	9.5	8.7
1940	8.5	9.1	9.0
1941	8.4	13.2	12.7
1942	17.5	30.6	32.4
1943	58.9	80.4	78.2
1944	104.1	96.0	93.7
1945	98.0	98.9	100.4
1946	82.5	67.4	65.0
1947	35.1	42.7	42.5[a]
1952 basis			
1948	34.2	35.2	33.8
1949	37.5	40.2	40.1
1950	41.9	43.3	40.2
1951	42.4	47.2	44.6
1952	71.6	70.9	66.1
1954 basis			
1953	84.7	73.9	73.6
1954	77.9	67.1	67.8

[a] This figure is on a 1947 basis. The difference between this and the 1946 basis was apparently small for 1947.

NOTE: There were three main changes during the period covered by this table in the definition of budget expenditures (formerly called general and special account expenditures excluding debt retirement). On the adjustments made in the figures appearing in the budget documents because of these changes see Appendix A.

general enacting smaller increases than those recommended by the President. After Pearl Harbor the executive recommendations became more categorical and in various messages President Roosevelt vigorously stated the case for tax increases as an anti-inflationary measure. The first of the war revenue acts, approved October 21, 1942, raised taxes substantially, but far less than he had proposed. The main accomplishment of the second, approved June 9, 1943, was shifting the individual income tax to a current-payments basis, which added to tax collections in a year when individual incomes were increasing. The third was considered so inadequate by the President that he vetoed it (this was the first revenue act ever to be vetoed). But Congress passed it over his veto February 25, 1944.

These comments on the experience during World War II make it clear that some of the factors that hindered moving toward a pay-for-the-war-as-you-go policy were primarily political. President Roosevelt never proposed anything like a full pay-as-you-go policy—his most famous anti-inflation message (April 1942) advocated no more than reducing the budget deficit to 50 per cent of total budget expenditures—but Congress could not see its way clear to going this far.

By way of giving some indication of the extent of the tax increases during the defense program and the war we may note the following:

	1939	1940	1941	1942	1943	1944	1945
Ratio of individual income taxes to personal income, per cent[a]	1.2	1.3	1.7	3.2	9.4	10.5	11.5
Ratio of corporation taxes to corporation net income, per cent[b]	14.0	22.9	39.7	51.2	55.3	54.9	48.7

[a] Based on *Survey of Current Business; 1954 National Income Supplement*, Table 3; and *Flow of Funds in the United States, 1939–1953*, Table 17.

[b] For corporations reporting net incomes. Taxes comprise income and property taxes levied on income of year indicated (fiscal year most nearly coinciding with calendar year, including fiscal year ending the following June 30). Figures are based on *Statistics of Income for 1948*, Part 2, Table 11.

During the defense program the expenditure increase was not so very sharp—nonfinancial expenditures were $10.25 billion in 1939, $22.2 billion in 1941. Yet over 43 per cent of the 1941 outlay was deficit financed. In 1942 nonfinancial expenditures totaled $64.5 billion, and since tax collections did not yet fully reflect the rates of the 1942 act, 63 per cent of this amount was financed by borrowing. But in the following war years the ratio of deficit to nonfinancial expenditure declined; the $50.8 billion deficit in 1944 was only 47 per cent of the $109 billion expenditure total.[8]

Improved procedures and improved information helped to make the proportion of expenditures financed by taxes and other current revenues larger in World War II than in World War I. Presumably the proportion would have been higher still had Congress been more favorably impressed with the pay-as-you-go idea.

Let us imagine another occasion, and one on which Congress is persuaded that a pay-as-you-go policy is desirable. Even in such a situation it

[8] These statements are based on Table 5.

seems probable that present legislative procedures would be so slow that tax receipts could not be pushed up fast enough to keep pace with expenditures. However, if Congress could somehow divorce its consideration of tax rates from its concern with amendments to the tax structure, the legislative process required to raise rates might be considerably expedited. A more radical possibility would be a tax statute authorizing and directing the executive to make specified changes in tax rates to accord with specified changes in economic conditions. In form this would be a delegation of taxing power; but if the changes in rates and changes in economic conditions were properly specified in the statute, there might well be less delegation of tax policy-making power than was involved in letting the executive plan and put into operation the various subsidy programs it did in World War II.

2. How Far Need International Aid Be Financed by Borrowing?

During and after both world wars the United States contributed large amounts of aid to other countries. The amounts are summarized in Table 49. Nearly all of the aid during and after World War I took the form of loans, although viewed in retrospect we are well advised to call the unpaid ones grants. Also, most of the international aid advanced during World War II was part of what has commonly (and somewhat misleadingly) been called the lend-lease program. But, subject to one exception of consequence and one qualification, we can say that operations under this program up to V-J Day ought in general to be regarded as grants rather than as loans or as lease agreements. The one exception is the silver loans— the 335 million ounces of silver "lend-leased" to foreign countries are classified in the table as credits. The qualification is that to date some 5 per cent of the grants have in retrospect been converted into credits (i.e. into debts of the countries receiving the aid). Since V-J Day the bulk of international aid has been quite frankly labeled "grants". And the total of net new grants and credits extended to other countries, July 1, 1945, to December 31, 1953 (line M), was nearly 10 per cent larger than that of the grants and credits extended during the five preceding war years, only about a quarter of the $44.3 billion for the postwar period being net new (and in-retrospect-converted) credits.

During the 1920's it became doubtful whether the debts of the allied governments to the United States could be collected. However, in the funding agreements (the war loans had been payable on demand) only limited concessions were made—concessions in amount of interest and in lengthened payment periods rather than in principal. Then with the coming of the recession, 1929–33, one country after another ceased making payments; and in June 1932 President Hoover issued a statement offering

TABLE 49
International Aid during and after the Two World Wars, 1917–53
(billions of dollars)

	April 6, 1917 to November 30, 1918 (1)	After November 30, 1918 (2)	World War I Total (3)	July 1, 1940 to June 30, 1945 (4)	July 1, 1945 to December 31, 1953 (5)	World War II through 1953 (6)
A. Gross new grants						
B. Military	0	0	0	a	10.5	a
C. Other	0	0.1	0.1	a	26.4	a
D. Total	0	0.1	0.1	47.5[b]	36.9	84.4
E. Less reverse grants and returns	0	0	0	7.8[c]	1.4	9.2
F. Less prior grants converted into credits	0	0	0	0	2.3	2.3
G. Net new grants	0	0.1	0.1	39.7	33.2	72.9
H. New credits	7.3	3.0	10.3	1.2[d]	11.5	12.7
J. Plus prior grants converted into credits	0	0	0	0	2.3	2.3
K. Less principal collections	0	0.8[e]	0.8[e]	0.4[d]	2.7	3.1
L. Net new credits	7.3	2.3[f]	9.6[f]	0.8	11.1	11.9
M. Net new grants and credits	7.3	2.4	9.7	40.5	44.3	84.8

[a] Not available.
[b] Lend-lease $46.1 billion.
[c] Reverse lend-lease.
[d] Lend-lease $326 million less principal collection $47 million plus loans held by government corporations, June 30.
[e] To November 15, 1940.

[f] The principal amount of the debts was increased under refunding agreements by the inclusion of nearly $1.9 billion of accrued and unpaid interest, making the net principal amount $11.4 billion as of November 15, 1940.

Source: See Appendix A.

a moratorium. Most of the payments after the moratorium (there were revisions in some of the debt agreements) came from Finland. Finland paid $3.1 million, 1935–40. Total payments on principal account by all countries from the start up to November 15, 1945, came to $758 million. There is little prospect that any substantial part of the remaining principal—or of the accrued interest—will ever be paid.[9]

It is interesting to compare the $11.9 billion of net new credits extended during and after World War II with the $9.5 billion of unpaid principal of the earlier war period, despite the fact that the list of countries is not entirely the same in the two cases. One naturally wonders how much of the $11.9 billion, if any, will go the way of the World War I credits.

It would not be easy to say just what part of the international aid recorded in Table 49 involved deficit financing. In retrospect we have reconstrued $9.5 billion of net credits extended during the earlier war period as grants, and since grants are here treated as nonfinancial expenditures, this amount contributes to the financial requirement shown for the period. But we have—perhaps wrongly—treated the $11.9 billion as credit extended and hence as an addition to the financial assets we deduct from gross debt in computing net debt.

Some of the aid extended after World War I and a major portion of that after World War II was extended during years in which the federal government had a nonfinancial surplus. On the other hand the aid advanced during both wars contributed to the sharp expenditure increases that were in substantial part financed by borrowing. There appears to be no reason why international grants-in-aid as such should require deficit financing, particularly in the case of an aid program spread more or less evenly over a number of years. Indeed, while a series of annual extensions of credit aid in which year-to-year variations are no wider than in the decade following World War II might well be excluded from a revised concept of budget expenditures, some would argue that the funds so advanced to other countries should in general be provided by taxes rather than by internal borrowing.

It happens that the net federal debt was decreased from its 1920 peak during the next eleven years by an amount not very different from $9.5 billion of the net new credits on line L that have since been reconstrued as grants. But this approximate equality is doubtless a coincidence. If at some future time several billion of the credit aid extended after World War II were in retrospect to be reconstrued as grants, it is doubtful that the consequent increase in the net federal debt figure would occasion the retirement of a like amount of internal debt. But this possibility suggests the broader question which is the topic of the following section.

[9] But these "loans" are still carried as debts due the United States in the *Annual Reports* of the Secretary of the Treasury.

3. *On the Retirement of Emergency-Incurred Debts*

After the War of 1812 and to a large extent after the Civil War the war debts were retired; but the retirements do not seem to have been the result of a vigorous debt retirement policy. Table 50 indicates the course of the debt (net of the general fund balance) after the two wars. At the end of 1815 the net debt stood at $114.2 million. In all but three of the next twenty-one years there was a surplus, a major contributing factor to these

TABLE 50

Federal Debt Less General Fund Balance after Two Wars
(millions of dollars)

December 31	Net Debt	June 30	Net Debt
1811	44.5	1860	60.9
1814	98.1	1865	2,651.5
1815	114.2	1866	2,643.3
1817	88.5	1873	2,091.5
1818	94.1	1875	2,093.0
1830	34.4	1893	836.6
1836	−45.4		

NOTE: Figures on gross debt are from *Historical Statistics;* on general fund balance from Secretary of the Treasury, 1920 *Annual Report*, p. 776.

surpluses being the protective tariff. Although the rates imposed under the 1816 tariff act were in general below wartime levels, they were high enough so that the 1816 tariff has sometimes been considered the beginning of protectionism. Duties were increased in 1824 and again in 1828, then reduced in 1832 and 1833. Despite the duties, imports grew; the value of imports was 11 per cent higher in the decade ending 1836 than in that ending 1825.[10] And of the total federal revenues[11] from December 31, 1815, to December 31, 1836, customs duties constituted almost 80 per cent. At the end of this period the general fund balance exceeded the small amount of obligations outstanding by more than $45 million.

The process by which most of the Civil War debt was paid off was not so very different. In both cases debt retirement was in large measure a by-product of protectionism. Customs duties were increased during the Civil War, particularly by the acts of 1862 and 1864. The ratio of duties to value of total imports had been 15.7 per cent in 1860; it was 38.5 per cent in 1865.[12] A good deal of consideration was given to downward revision of the tariff in the next twenty-five years. But the principal results

[10] *Historical Statistics*, M-54. Figures refer to years ending September 30.
[11] Total in the sense of total nonfinancial receipts other than postal revenues. See *Historical Statistics*, P-89.
[12] 1923 *Statistical Abstract*, p. 799.

were a 10 per cent horizontal reduction enacted in 1872 and repealed
in 1875; a mixture of upward and downward adjustments in the act of
1883; and the McKinley Act of 1890, which increased some duties and
conferred on the President limited power to levy certain duties on a
reciprocity basis by proclamation but substituted a subsidy on domestic
sugar for the previous duty on raw sugar imports. The following ratios of
customs duties to value of total imports indicate in a general way the
changes in the level of the tariff from 1870 to 1895:[13]

Year	Ratio of Duties to Total Imports (per cent)
1870	44.9
1875	29.4
1880	29.1
1885	30.8
1890	29.6
1895	20.4

Again despite these postwar tariff levels imports grew. In the decade
ending 1876 they totaled $5.0 billion; in that ending 1893, $7.4 billion.[14]
So during the twenty-eight years following the Civil War customs receipts
were 43.5 per cent of total federal revenues.[15] In every one of these years
there was a surplus, and by June 30, 1893, the net federal debt had been
reduced to $836.6 million.

After both world wars political pressure to cut taxes was strong. It is
much easier to maintain customs duties at high wartime levels than
internal revenue rates. But there were other circumstances, too, that
militated against a policy of retiring all or most of the emergency-incurred
debt. During the 1920's, indeed, there was a good deal of discusssion of
such a policy, but the approximately $10 billion incurred in connection
with World War I to finance external loans was considered to be a
justifiable debt. If we were to count all of these loans—including the
uncollectable ones—as federal credit in 1929, and if we were to adjust
the net debt figures on line J of Table 51 accordingly, the record would
show a net debt of over $15 billion as of June 30, 1919, about half of which
was paid off during the next decade. Still this debt retirement—it amounted
to about $8 billion on the Table 51 basis—was accomplished somewhat
inadvertently. As we noted in Chapter III, tax yields grew, reflecting
the rapid growth of GNP during the 1920's, while nonfinancial expenditures were somewhat stable and the several cuts in tax rates were little

[13] *Ibid.*
[14] *Historical Statistics*, M-54. Figures refer to years ending June 30.
[15] See footnote 10.

enough and late enough to give us a decade of surpluses. Thus the process of partial debt repayment after World War I has something in common with the debt repayment processes after the War of 1812 and the Civil War; it was a by-product of a legislative procedure that was slow in making downward revisions in wartime tax rates.

After World War II there was little sentiment in favor of retiring any substantial part of the net debt accumulated during the war and the great depression preceding it. Indeed, there was a good deal of sentiment against

TABLE 51

Federal Debt and Financial Assets at Selected Dates, 1919–54
(billions of dollars)

		1919 (as of June 30)	1929 (as of June 30)	1945	1950 (as of December 31)	1953 (as of December 31)	1954
A.	Cash balance	1.25	0.33	27.2	5.2	5.7	6.0
B.	Federal obligations held by federal funds	0.59	1.02	37.8	44.7	58.3	61.4
C.	Foreign loans and securities[a]	b	b	1.6	13.4	14.2	15.1
D.	Other federal credit	0.75	1.62	7.4	8.4	10.5	11.4
E.	Total financial assets (A + B + C + D)	2.59	2.97	74.0	71.7	88.7	93.9
F.	Direct and agency obligations outstanding	25.95	18.80	292.6	266.4	289.3	294.4
G.	Net accounts payable	c	c	1.5	0.7	0.6	0.0
H.	Total obligations and accounts payable (F + G)	25.95	18.80	294.1	267.1	289.9	294.4
J.	Net debt (H − E)	23.36	15.83	220.1	195.4	201.2	200.5

[a] Includes capital subscriptions to IMF and IBRD.

[b] World War I obligations of foreign governments are not counted here as financial assets. See Table 35, line L.

[c] No estimate available.

SOURCE: See Appendix A.

debt retirement on any considerable scale, sentiment that was rationalized by the contention that government surpluses would be likely to reduce aggregate demand and cause unemployment.

Nonetheless net debt (see Table 51) decreased by some $19 billion during the eight years ending December 31, 1953. And it seems highly probable the decrease would have been greater had it not been for the Korean War. Further, despite the contention regarding the depressing effect of government surpluses, it seems fair to say the decrease that did occur in some sense reflects a deliberate fiscal policy. However, as Table 51 makes clear, if there has been debt retirement since World War II it has mainly taken the form of a decrease in net debt. In 1946, indeed, as we noted in Chapter I, some $20 billion of gross direct debt was retired by drawing down the general fund balance. But since 1948 the gross direct debt has been increasing.

If one tries to explain how it happened that net debt decreased by $19 billion during eight years in which there was a decrease of only about $4 billion in total obligations and payables outstanding, both the $16 billion expansion of federal credit and the more than $20 billion increase in federal obligations held by federal funds should be taken into consideration. Also if one tries to construe the changes in debt during these years as reflecting fiscal policy, presumably it is the budget surplus or deficit rather than the $19 billion nonfinancial surplus toward which that policy was immediately directed—and there was a budget deficit of some $17 billion during these eight years. Most of the $36 billion difference between these two computations is mainly the result of the expansion of federal credit (including the IMF and IBRD, it was chiefly external credit that was expanded) and the growth of social insurance funds. Thus the postwar decrease in net debt should be regarded as the joint product of a number of factors, principally a budget deficit of $17 billion, a social insurance funds surplus of some $21 billion, and a credit expansion of $16 billion.

A comparison of the four periods of postwar debt retirement we have been reviewing strongly suggests two propositions. First, anything like complete debt retirement is a policy objective that commands relatively little political support. And second, there has been a marked downward trend in the degree of debt retirement achieved.

If there has been little political support for a program of retiring emergency-incurred federal debt, particularly since the 1930's, no doubt a part of the explanation is that while there have in recent years been no specific political interest groups that stood to gain by such a program there have been specific interest groups that would have opposed it had one been attempted. Such a program would have meant either substantially lower expenditures or substantially heavier taxation. And a considerable cut in expenditures almost inevitably would have meant a cut in objects of expenditure that someone had a special interest in seeing maintained. Likewise substantially heavier taxes obviously would have meant opposition from those who would have had to pay them.

However there is one kind of tax that a special interest group can be counted on to favor, namely, a "protective" tariff. We have noted that maintenance of import duty rates played a major role in debt retirement after the War of 1812 and the Civil War. No doubt the downward trend in the degree of retirement of emergency-incurred debt reflects in part the declining relative importance of customs as a source of federal tax revenues.

But special interest groups are not the whole story. Those who have been concerned in recent years about the possibility that retirement of any considerable part of the federal debt might mean depressed business and a large volume of unemployment have been right to this extent. A decrease in the government's nonfinancial deficit or an increase in its surplus exerts a cyclically depressing influence on the level of aggregate demand. If the concern about this depressing influence was stronger after World War II than after World War I—and if accordingly there was less disposition to advocate war debt retirement—this was a natural consequence of the fact that federal fiscal operations had become so much larger in relation to the other parts of our economy.

These comments are pertinent to the circumstances influencing the prospects of retirement of our present federal debt. Of course different considerations apply in the case of a debt of a country that is held externally. The creditors are not a domestic special interest group.

Many writers, in discussing a countercyclical fiscal policy, have assumed an approximate balance of receipts and expenditures over the period of the cycle. But in our analysis of the circumstances influencing federal debt retirement no distinction has been drawn between war debt and the debt incurred in the 1930's. And this suggests a question: With both special interests and a general interest aligned against debt retirement, is it not more likely that the nonfinancial deficits incurred in periods of relatively slack business would tend to exceed the surpluses of the periods of brisker business? If so, the federal debt might continue to grow, cycle after cycle. But we cannot entirely rule out the contrary possibility. During the 1920's government revenues grew with the growth of the economy, and grew fast enough so that there was a series of surpluses. This could conceivably happen again.

What seems clear is that there is nothing in present fiscal procedures that constitutes a mechanism for achieving a balance of receipts and expenditures over the cycle, and that, in the absence of any such mechanism, a substantial imbalance one way or the other is far more likely than an approximate balance. But there is also the possibility that the government might develop a form of capital budget that would provide just such a mechanism by taking most of the cycle out of the current budget and making it possible to balance every year's current budget approximately. A budget system under which countercyclical expenditures on works projects, state and local grants-in-aid, etc. would be charged to capital account and amortized over a subsequent period of years such as a decade would be a step in this direction, for it should be possible substantially to smooth the cycle out of budget expenditures in this way. And presumably an analogous deferred-credits procedure could be applied to a portion of tax and other receipts during the upper stages of the cycle in such a way as to smooth year-to-year variations out of budget receipts. If so, and if the receipts thus "smoothed" balanced the "smoothed" expenditures every year, there should be no secular trend either up or down in the cumulative total of the unsmoothed net budget expenditures. A well-devised budget system along these lines should provide a mechanism for implementing the idea of balancing the budget over the cycle.

4. Summary

One reason for deficit financing during World War I was the primitive nature of the then existing budgetary procedures. During World War II the lag of expenditures behind appropriations became extremely important. This complicated the problem of relating receipts and expenditures, but it may have done something to keep down the deficits. Shifting the individual income tax to a pay-as-you-go basis in mid-1943 undoubtedly helped thereafter to keep deficits down. The slowness of the legislative process in the case of tax bills worked in the opposite direction during both wars. This process might be expedited if Congress dealt separately with tax rates and tax bases. Also there is the possibility of what has been called formula-flexibility taxation.

The international aid extended during and after World War I and that extended during World War II involved extensive borrowing. The aid extended to other countries in the eight and one-half years following World War II did not. Even if all the more than $44 billion extended during this period were to be counted as grants—and this would mean adding some $11 billion to the nonfinancial expenditures shown in Table 5— there would still remain a substantial nonfinancial surplus. The difference in the time patterns of expenditures in these contrasting cases is undoubtedly the main significant one. Aid extended at a rate that does not vary too widely from year to year, no matter whether it takes the form of loans or of grants, can be financed by taxes. Aid that contributes to a rapid step-up of expenditures is likely to entail a resort to borrowing.

Such retirement of emergency-incurred federal debts as has occurred seems for the most part to have been inadvertent. And during the nineteenth century it was helped by the fact that import duties were the main source of federal revenues.

The lack of support for a debt retirement program, particularly after World War II, reflects in part the fact that special interest groups would have opposed such a program while there were no special interest groups that stood to gain by it. But there is also a more general kind of opposition. With federal fiscal operations on the scale they have now attained, any large increase in nonfinancial receipts or large cut in expenditures would exert temporarily a marked cyclically depressing influence on the level of economic activity.

Our analysis of the influences making against a program of debt retirement raises a question regarding the possibility that a counter-cyclical federal fiscal policy might be followed in future in a fashion that would result in a long-run balance of receipts and expenditures. With present budgetary procedures an ever-growing federal debt seems far more likely. So does another period of persistent inadvertent surpluses like that of the 1920's. But an appropriate form of capital budget might provide a mechanism for achieving a long-run balance of receipts and expenditures.

CHAPTER IX

Trends and Prospects

This inquiry into government capital requirements has departed from the general plan for the broad study of capital formation and financing of which it is a part because of the distinctive characteristics of the economic sector with which it deals. We have been primarily concerned with the financial capital requirements of governments.

We have, with one exception noted below, taken those requirements to be the funds governments have actually raised, not the funds they required (in the sense of justifiably required).

In summarizing our findings it will be convenient first to restate some distinctions that we have found it important to insist on, next to recapitulate what seem to be the main trends in state and local financing, and then to review our analysis of federal financing. Finally we will attempt to draw some inferences from our findings that we consider pertinent for an appraisal of the prospects for future government financial requirements.

1. *Some Basic Distinctions*

Particularly for the federal government since World War I it is urgent to distinguish and to have in mind the difference between the budget deficit and what we have called the nonfinancial deficit. The concept of the federal budget surplus or deficit is, of course, the one that receives primary attention in the budget document and in Treasury financial reports. It has been gradually developed since the passage of the Budget and Accounting Act (1921), and especially since the 1930's by a process of study and experiment to serve broadly the purposes of legislative control in levying taxes and in making appropriations and the purposes of administrative management. Hence budget receipts and expenditures do not include the receipts and expenditures of federal trust funds (except that, in the case of transactions between general government funds and trust funds, the trust account receipts appear as budget expenditures, the trust account expenditures as budget receipts).

The deficit computation with which we have been principally concerned is not the budget deficit but one which is designed to serve another fiscal policy objective—the objective of economic stabilization. It is also especially appropriate as a measure of federal financial requirements. It is the excess of the nonfinancial uses of funds over the nonfinancial sources shown for the federal government in the Federal Reserve *Flow of Funds* compilations—or the excess of financial sources over financial uses.[1] Nonfinancial receipts and expenditures, in contrast to budget receipts and expenditures, include both trust account transactions and general government transactions with the public (but not transactions between one government fund and another).

In addition to trust account operations there is another main category of nonfinancial transactions that are not classed as budget receipts and expenditures. These consist of certain transactions of government corporations and other business-type and lending activities. Just how to draw the line between the inside-the-budget and the outside-the-budget transactions of these federal agencies has proven a difficult problem. The solution adopted in 1951 has the effect of treating net funds provided each such corporation or activity by the rest of the government during the year as a net budget expenditure.[2]

Not only are there important categories of nonfinancial transactions in the FOF compilations that do not count as budget receipts and expenditures; there are also budget transactions of a financial nature that do not count as nonfinancial receipts and expenditures. These consist chiefly of budget expenditures for acquiring loans and securities and budget receipts from the sale or redemption of the loans and securities in government agency portfolios.

As a result of all the various differences in transactions included and excluded, there can be a substantial budget deficit when there is a nonfinancial surplus. In 1946 there was a budget deficit of $2.5 billion; a nonfinancial surplus of $5.0 billion.

Before the considerable expansion of federal functions and agencies that took place in the 1930's, budget receipts and expenditures were not distinguished from other federal agency transactions. Total expenditures minus total receipts equaled the increment in federal debt minus the increment in the general fund balance.[3] Of course this is not true today of budget expenditures and receipts alone; balancing Treasury financial

---

[1] *Flow of Funds in the United States, 1939–53.* Figures for more recent years have been published in the *Federal Reserve Bulletin* as they have become available.

There are two other deficit computations that are useful for the fiscal objective of economic stabilization: (a) One is the deficit in the account for the federal government in the National Income and Product Accounts. (b) The other, in the compilation of which the Treasury Department and the Bureau of the Budget cooperate, has had various names. We refer to it here as net cash operating outgo. For our present purpose the FOF nonfinancial deficit is distinctly better than either of these. It spells out financial details as (a) does not. It consistently identifies all financial transactions as financial while (b) does not and it provides more clean-cut detail by object of expenditure.

[2] Technically the language here used applies to the way the Post Office is treated in the budget accounts. But in many respects the Post Office continues to be treated as a part of the general government rather than as a business-type activity.

[3] Except for a technical float discrepancy.

statements include figures on the transactions of trust and other accounts too.

When we speak of the financial requirement of a government during a particular period we mean (unless otherwise indicated) the excess of its nonfinancial expenditures over its nonfinancial receipts. This is equal to the increment in its net debt,[4] where by net debt we mean the excess of its outstanding debt over its total financial assets. These financial assets consist mainly of its cash balance and the loans and securities it holds. In the case of the federal government we have included in the minuend of this net debt computation, in addition to the direct debt, the bonds, notes, and debentures of and the privately held proprietary interest in government corporations, government accounts payable, and certain government trust and deposit liabilities.[5] Federal financial assets other than the general fund balance are held chiefly by the Old Age and Survivors Insurance Fund and other social insurance funds and by credit agencies like the Commodity Credit Corporation and the Export-Import Bank. Both social insurance funds and federal credit started in the 1930's on a period of rapid growth. The assets of the social insurance funds—these are almost entirely government bonds—increased from around $0.5 billion in 1929 to practically $45 billion in 1954. Federal credit increased during this period from $1.7 billion to $28.2 billion.[6] Mainly because of these two developments, gross direct debt less the general fund balance exceeded net debt by some $73 billion as of December 31, 1954. It has become very important when speaking of federal debt to say whether one means gross debt outstanding, debt held by the public (i.e. by holders other than federal agencies), or net debt.

What has been said about federal finances applies on the whole also to the finances of state and local governments. The distinction between the budget surplus or deficit and the nonfinancial surplus or deficit is much the same. Current Bureau of the Census compilations of government financial data use the terminology "general revenues and expenditures" instead of "budget receipts and expenditures," and they report in addition to these the transactions of government enterprises and social insurance trust funds. The Federal Reserve *Flow of Funds* compilations include a statement of state and local nonfinancial receipts and expenditures and financial sources and uses of funds.

The parallel to federal finance goes farther. With the rapid growth of their financial assets in recent years the distinction between gross state

---

[4] There can be a technical discrepancy in this equation too.

[5] But not insurance policy reserves or state balances in the Unemployment Compensation Fund.

[6] As of June 30. The figures on federal credit do not include World War I international debts to the United States. They do include small amounts of veterans' loans also included in the social insurance funds.

and local debt, debt net of sinking funds, and net debt has become extremely important. In addition to sinking funds and social insurance trust funds, there have come to be substantial endowment and investment funds. Total cash and security holdings of state and local governments were $7.4 billion at the close of their 1937 fiscal years; $38.0 billion nineteen years later.[7] General expenditures exceeded general revenues in the 1956 fiscal year compilation by $3.0 billion; the 1956 calendar year nonfinancial deficit is estimated at $2.5 billion.[8]

2. The Record of State and Local Financial Requirements

It will be convenient to summarize our findings regarding state and local financial requirements under the following six headings: (a) geographical debt patterns, (b) construction indebtedness, (c) orderly and disorderly finance, (d) financing by different units of government, (e) emergency borrowing, and (f) the general trend.

a. Geographical debt patterns. The borrowing practices of communities of different size have been sufficiently distinctive so that there has been at least until quite recently a very striking pattern of per capita local government indebtedness. Likewise there has been a somewhat definite, though gradually changing, regional pattern of per capita indebtedness.

In general the tendency has been for per capita gross debts to vary with community size—the larger the community, the larger the per capita debt. It is true the rapid growth of the financial assets of some of the larger cities during the last few years has made the net debt pattern for cities of more than 25,000 inhabitants a distinctly irregular one and even impaired the regularity of the gross debt pattern. But the tendency of per capita debts to decrease with community size is still clearly discernible.

The available information on the trends of per capita debts by community size is mostly on a gross basis. The growth of per capita gross debts in the smaller communities has shown a tendency to catch up with the growth in the larger cities. We think this catching-up process likely to continue, particularly if rural communities continue to acquire more urban characteristics. But the recently developed irregularities in the community size pattern raise the question whether uniformity on a net basis may not eventually be achieved by a leveling-down rather than a leveling-up process.

Regional differences in per capita state and local debts (gross debts less sinking fund assets), 1890–1942, have reflected a very rough correlation with per capita incomes. Between 1890 and 1922—the impact of the

[7] This figure does not include the Unemployment Compensation Fund.

[8] See Bureau of the Census, *Summary of Government Finances in 1956*, Tables 1 and 6, and October 1957 *Federal Reserve Bulletin*, p. 1192.

industrial revolution on state and local government capital outlay seems to have been particularly strong during this interval—these regional differences widened. But the longer-term trend of 1890–1942 seems to have been toward narrowing them. In large part this trend was probably due to the growth of cities in regions that were relatively little urbanized in 1890.

b. Construction indebtedness. Most state and local long-term debts can be identified by purpose of issue, and the purposes that account for the bulk of these debts are capital formation financing purposes. Further, most of the capital outlays—and the only capital outlays on which a reasonably satisfactory statistical time series is available—are construction outlays. Still the relation between construction expenditures and financial capital requirements is not a very close one. The ratio of the aggregate nonfinancial deficit for state and local governments to their new construction expenditures (excluding expenditures financed by federal aid) is extremely variable. On an annual basis in 1929–52 it varies between about 2 : 5 in 1950 and about −6 : 1 in 1944 (the 6 is negative because there was a surplus in 1944). Even on a quinquennial basis this aggregative ratio is highly erratic. The quinquennial ratio of new long-term debt issues to new construction is a good deal more stable. It varies between 45 and 77 per cent for 1915–53.

The volume of new security issues reflects new construction expenditures somewhat more closely than do the increments in net indebtedness. No doubt this is partly because nonfinancial surpluses can be used to finance debt retirements. But perhaps a more important consideration is that differences between the net surplus or deficit and the volume of securities issued are in considerable measure absorbed by changes in cash balances, in short-term debts, and in sinking fund assets.

Since state and local public buildings and other public works are in substantial part financed by borrowing, we might expect a somewhat stable relation between the investments in such structures and the debts they have occasioned. There are three categories of public capital assets and of debts specifically incurred to finance them for which it is possible roughly to determine what has been happening in recent years to the ratio of debt to depreciated value: highways, school buildings, and enterprise structures. These ratios both for highways and for schools show marked variations reflecting both changes in the financial condition of governments and the growing importance of federal and state grants-in-aid. Since accrual accounting conventions presumably exert more influence in the case of capital formation by public enterprises than in other state and local capital outlays, one might have expected more stability in the debt to value ratio for enterprise structures (including sewage systems, for these cannot readily be separated out). The expectation does not appear to be well founded.

169

c. Orderly and disorderly finance. In general we have not inquired whether the borrowings governments have engaged in have been justified. But it has seemed necessary to note that there have from time to time been various instances of clearly unjustified deficits and thoroughly disorderly finance. And in some of these there has been outright corruption. Among the most extreme instances of disorderly finance during the last fifty or sixty years are those that accompanied the Florida land boom of the 1920's; and the Coral Gables case stands out as one that was clearly characterized by corruption.

From time to time there have been instances of disorderly finance; but on the whole there has been a definite tendency toward greater orderliness. Indeed, there have been very substantial improvements in fiscal and other administrative procedures; and the quality of the personnel responsible for financial administration at all levels of government has been raised to a point that warrants saying public financial administration seems in process of becoming a profession.

One aspect of improved fiscal procedures is improvements in government accounting. Perhaps it is reasonable to look forward to future progress in accrual accounting for state and local enterprises—conceivably even for general government—that will make the connection between new capital expenditures and the increment in net debt more like that in the field of private business.

d. Financing by different units of government. During the nineteenth century disorderly state finance, especially during the 1830's and in the South after the Civil War, led first to serious financial distress and then to measures designed to prevent its recurrence. These measures in general took the form of constitutional restrictions on state borrowing. State borrowing during the first fifty years of the nineteenth century had apparently been a great deal more important quantitatively than borrowing by local government units. One unintended result of the constitutional restrictions was that local debts grew so rapidly during the second half of the century that by 1902 they were seven-eighths of the total.[9] And municipal debts alone were such a large fraction of this total—nearly three-quarters—that "municipal bonds" became a synonym for all state and local obligations.

With the rapid growth of local government borrowing came instances of disorderly local government finance. Many of these were followed by financial distress, particularly after the crisis of 1873; and again there followed measures to restrict borrowing, this time the borrowing of local governments. Some of these restrictions were written into state constitutions, some were incorporated in state statutes, and some in municipal charters.

[9] That is, of total gross state and local debt less sinking fund assets.

170

The special district is, among other things, a device for considerably relaxing restrictions on borrowing power. It also serves to relax other restrictions, notably restrictions on taxing power. And it serves as a means of realizing the main advantages of consolidating specific functions of local government units—schools, water supply, sewage and fire protection systems, ownership of levees, bridges, toll highways, etc.—while avoiding the various serious political and legal obstacles to outright consolidation of the municipalities or other units involved. It is little wonder that school and other special districts, though of almost negligible importance at the turn of the century, have come to account for nearly a third of the total indebtedness of all local governments and about two-thirds of the long-term school debt as of 1951.

If the special district makes it possible to realize important economies of large-scale operation without outright consolidation of the local units involved—even when the units are in different states—it has also made possible a great deal of small-scale operation. Of the nearly 114,000 local government units in the United States in 1952, school and other special districts accounted for almost 80,000. Still there was a substantial amount of consolidation during the two preceding decades; the number of school districts was reduced by almost 50 per cent.

Economies in borrowing and in collecting taxes are among the significant economies resulting from large-scale operation. The past forty or more years have seen the development of another device for realizing this kind of economy—the grant-in-aid. No doubt the advantages of borrowing and taxing on a larger scale have contributed significantly to the growth of both federal and state aid programs. Another factor, more important in the case of federal than of state programs, is that the grant-in-aid has proven a convenient way to promote standards in the performance of functions by the aid-receiving governments and to decrease inequalities in performance among them. In 1950 federal aid to states represented some 17 per cent of state nonfinancial receipts,[10] while state aid to local governments amounted to about two-ninths of local government nonfinancial receipts.[11] Aid seems to have been a smaller proportion of the receipts of the larger cities than of other local units ever since the start of state programs. Federal aid has tended in a general way to be a larger proportion of state revenue in those states where per capita personal incomes are relatively low.

e. Emergency borrowing. Most, but not quite all, long-term debts of state and local governments have been incurred to finance capital outlays. Non-capital-formation borrowing has in general been occasioned by

[10] State withdrawals from the Unemployment Compensation Fund are excluded from both numerator and denominator of this ratio.

[11] This computation includes state-collected, locally shared taxes.

various emergencies. There was borrowing after both world wars to finance veterans' benefits. There was borrowing during the 1930's made necessary by the depression. Also there has been some borrowing—a quite small amount in the aggregate—in connection with floods, hurricanes, and other disasters.

Table 8 gives total nonfinancial receipts and expenditures of state and local governments and the aggregate net deficit. The deficit does not show any clearly cyclical variation except during the 1930's. Before this decade the property tax provided so large a part of total nonfinancial receipts that it is not surprising these receipts were cyclically quite insensitive. And while for states cyclically sensitive taxes have since become important, their influence on the total of nonfinancial receipts was not sufficient in 1949 and 1954 to make these two stand out as recession years in Table 8. Even if state and local governments assume no further responsibilities for countercyclical fiscal operations than they have to date, increasing reliance on cyclically sensitive taxes may conceivably involve them in recession deficits in future.

f. The general trend. It is tempting to say that there has been a long-term upward trend not only in state and local total debt but also in debt per capita. We think the most significant question in regard to trend relates to net debt, and particularly for this basis it is difficult to be definite about the trend on either an aggregate or a per capita basis.

From the 1890's to 1930 certainly both trends were markedly upward. The immediate response of state and local governments to the industrial revolution was a vast increase in expenditures, both capital and current. And with their total expenditures growing somewhat more rapidly than total gross national product, state and local governments had extensive recourse to borrowing.

During the great depression of the 1930's, borrowing was often difficult; pressure for small and balanced budgets was strong; and after 1933 federal aid helped to finance a moderate increase in expenditures. There was little increase in net debt during the decade.

Then during the war receipts grew; expenditure increases were restrained. By 1945 aggregate net debt was reduced to a negligible amount. And at the end of 1954 it was only $6.5 billion, about what it had been thirty-four years earlier.

3. *The Record of Federal Financial Requirements*

In times past there have been federal debt issues identified as serving to finance particular capital expenditures, like the issue of bonds that helped finance the purchase and construction of the Panama Canal. But there have been no such issues since the 1930's. As of December 31, 1954, more than 90 per cent of the federal net debt had been incurred during war emergencies and practically all the rest of it had resulted from the contra-cyclical nonfinancial deficits of the 1930's. No doubt both the war expenditures and the depression expenditures that were financed in part by these debts include physical capital formation outlays. But obviously this is not the main fact about the debts. The main fact is that they were incurred during emergencies to finance very rapid increases in expenditures on a wide variety of objects.

The proportion of expenditures that were deficit financed was smaller during the Civil War than during the War of 1812,[12] smaller during World War I than during the Civil War, and smaller still—though more than half—during World War II. This general downward trend reflects in part improved fiscal procedures.

But, if the United States were to have another major war-financing problem to deal with, and if there were to be, as there was not during either world war, a firm administration policy of pay-as-you-go in which Congress acquiesced, there would still be difficulties in fiscal procedures that would make it unlikely such a policy could be fully realized. In particular there is the difficulty that while Congress has shown a willingness during an emergency to relax its control over appropriations so as to expedite the legislative process, it has not been willing to expedite the process of handling revenue bills. Conceivably this kind of legislative process could be expedited by putting tax rate changes and tax base changes in separate bills; or, if Congress were prepared to accept a more radical approach, the need for legislative speed could be diminished by formula-flexibility taxation.

The international aid extended during and after World War I and during World War II added to the emergency expenditure totals that were financed in part by borrowing. Aid can be expected to involve recourse to borrowing when it contributes to a sharp increase in expenditures; and so far as the borrowing is concerned, it makes no difference whether the aid takes the form of grants and adds to the nonfinancial deficit, or the form of loans that add to the federal portfolio of financial assets. But an aid program that is not too unevenly distributed over a period of years, as has been the case in the years following World War II, need not occasion borrowing.

The federal government has gradually come to assume some measure of responsibility for "recovery and relief" in connection with business recessions, even for maintaining a high and stable level of employment. The degree to which such a responsibility is recognized seems itself to be inversely correlated with the cycle, but there has been a definite trend toward making the responsibility broader and more categorical.

During the 1930's federal recovery and relief activities took a wide variety of forms. There were moves that were largely of a noncyclical

[12] This statement does not include the deficit financing of the Confederacy.

character, principally some of the financial reforms, labor relations and labor standards legislation, and the establishment of an old age insurance system and three broad special public assistance programs. There were moves allegedly relevant to promoting economic recovery whose effectiveness was questionable: monetary nostrums including a plan for varying the price of gold, autarchic measures designed to encourage a more favorable trade balance, and organizational arrangements for price and wage maintenance.

The principal measures and programs that were really pertinent to the objectives of recovery, relief, and economic stabilization were: the steps taken to bolster up the economy's credit structure and to relieve the distress of defaulting debtors by assuming their debts; direct and work relief programs for the unemployed and special benefits to veterans and farmers; increased public construction; and increased grants-in-aid to state and local governments. To the extent that these measures and programs meant additions to federal purchases of gross national product or transfer payments to state and local governments and to individuals which added to the funds they had available for national product purchases, they provided a fiscal countercyclical bolstering of aggregate demand. But fiscal policy vacillated between the objective of an annually balanced budget and the objective of an effective countercycle, even though there was, on the whole, somewhat greater emphasis on the latter.

In three minor recessions since World War II the chief federal countercyclical activities and developments have been: countercyclical easing and tightening of Federal Reserve credit (but until 1951 Federal Reserve obligations to maintain government bond prices largely precluded an effective tight credit policy); the easing of housing credit underwriting terms, particularly in 1954; the operations of the Commodity Credit Corporation, particularly in 1948–49 and 1953–54; the "built-in" increases and decreases in the volume of unemployment compensation benefits; tax cuts effective in 1949 and 1954; and an increase in national security expenditures in 1949. The national security expenditure increase and, in large measure, the tax cuts may be characterized as not intended countercyclically.

During the decade of the 1930's federal net debt increased by about $16.0 billion. In 1949 the federal government had a nonfinancial surplus of $0.5 billion; in the previous year a surplus of almost $10.0 billion. There was a nonfinancial deficit of $4.8 billion during the five quarters ending September 30, 1954, but less than $2.0 billion of this can be definitely attributed to the 1953–54 recession. During the two years ending June 30, 1959, there was a nonfinancial deficit of $11 billion; this compares with a surplus of $11 billion during the two years ending December 31, 1956.

174

4. *A Postscript on Prospects*

The expenditures that have been responsible for most government borrowing in the past—wars, recessions and depressions, and state and local capital formation—will probably continue to be responsible for most borrowing in the future.

What can be said about the prospects for state and local capital formation requirements is quite limited. We may note first five conditions to which it seems likely the total volume of this kind of financing will conform. None of them gives a clear-cut clue regarding the total volume.

One of these relates to community-size and regional debt patterns. It seems reasonable to look forward, though perhaps some time forward, to a gradual trend toward greater uniformity in per capita debts both regionally and by size of community. Whether this will mean a leveling-up process, and a consequent upward trend in net debt, or a leveling-down will depend somewhat on the growth of government financial assets.

The second condition relates to the development of more businesslike accounting and budgetary procedures for government enterprises. It is reasonable to expect that such developments will gradually make the relation between enterprise debt and depreciated value of enterprise assets more like the corresponding relation for nonfinancial private enterprises. Conceivably, too, capital budgeting will develop in a way that will give something of a push in this direction for general government debts and capital investments.

The third condition also relates to the trend toward improvements in the fiscal procedures. This condition involves short-term debt and other elements in liquidity position. The proportion of short-term borrowing that is budget borrowing can quite possibly be expected to increase. More generally, variations in the liquidity position of the individual government unit can be expected, as time goes on, to be dominated more by short-term influences—differences in the seasonal pattern of nonfinancial receipts and expenditures and other differences that are purely temporary, particularly differences between the time pattern of receipts from long-term debt issued to finance a capital outlay and the time pattern of the capital outlay.

The fourth condition relates to taxation. It seems likely that the tax exemption which state and municipal bonds have enjoyed heretofore will continue to constitute an encouragement to such financing.

The fifth condition involves the purposes of borrowing. In the past a major fraction of long-term indebtedness has been incurred to finance road and school construction projects. But in recent years a considerable part of such capital expenditures has been financed by federal and state grants-in-aid and as a consequence put on more or less a pay-as-you-go basis. Any forecast of future state and local borrowing must therefore take account of the extent to which the further development of grant-in-aid programs may obviate the need for bond flotation financing.

But subject to these conditions, what is the prospect for a definite upward trend in the per capita state and local government indebtedness incurred to finance capital outlays? The upward trend from the 1890's to 1930 was interrupted first by the depression, then by World War II. However, there would seem to be no reason to think that these interruptions are permanent, no reason to suppose that they have permanently reduced the proportion of capital expenditures likely to be financed by borrowing. Still that proportion has been a decidedly variable one in the past. And if one tries to list considerations one should take into account in attempting to project it into the future, two such considerations stand out in our analysis. The proportion of debt-financed capital outlays seems to reflect the ratio of the rate of growth of government expenditures to the rate of growth of gross national product. A high ratio makes for a high proportion. And the proportion can be expected to be smaller to the extent that the capital expenditures are financed by federal—and perhaps also by state—grants-in-aid.

We can be a little more definite about the considerations one should take into account in appraising the prospects for government borrowing in connection with business recessions and depressions.

The effect of the 1929–33 recession on the aggregate deficit of state and local governments shows clearly in Table 8. Apparently the effects in 1949 and 1954 were quite minor. If one asks about the likelihood that some future recession may entail a considerable increase in state and local net debt, there are two main considerations to be taken into account, one that tends to increase the likelihood of such a development, the other working in the opposite direction. We have attributed the fact that there is so little evidence of the cycle in Table 8 largely to the insensitivity of the major tax source to most business fluctuations. But sensitive sources have been becoming relatively more important, and if this trend continues, as it probably will, it will make a future depression deficit more likely.

However, the other consideration may at least in the longer run prove to be overriding. During the 1930's the federal government came to assume practically the whole depression deficit burden. True, it has taken no steps since then that would more fully eliminate cyclical variations in state and local receipts. But the unemployment insurance system means that state payments into the Unemployment Compensation Fund are large when times are good and that state withdrawals are large when unemployment is high. We think it not unlikely that other intergovernment flows of funds will be developed that will help to take the cycle out of state and local surpluses and deficits—perhaps, for example, promptly

176

and markedly flexible grant-in-aid programs. Quite conceivably such intergovernment flows that vary in volume with the cycle may presently make any considerable amount of depression borrowing—except perhaps for borrowing from the federal government—an extremely unlikely development. But this prospect is hardly an immediate one.

During the decade of the 1930's the federal net debt increased by $16 billion, the federal loan and security portfolio by $9 billion. We think that even a minor recession might in future entail a comparable net debt increase. If the federal government should assume a fuller responsibility for keeping the economy operating at a high and stable employment level, this would make such a debt increase all the more likely, particularly if the federal government should come to rely more heavily on a counter-cyclical fiscal policy in discharging this increased responsibility. Also, such a debt increase during a minor recession would become more likely if the federal government were to assume something like the whole coun-tercyclical deficit burden for all levels of government through some system of cyclically flexible intergovernment nonfinancial flows of funds.

In this latter connection we note that during fiscal 1958 and 1959 the federal government's nonfinancial deficit totaled $11 billion. But pre-sumably this deficit would have been larger had there not been a pre-recession nonfinancial surplus of $11 billion in calendar 1955 and 1956. The size of the deficit incurred during the lower stages of a cycle—and of the increment in net debt—must obviously depend in part on whether the federal government has been operating at a deficit before the recession began.

On one assumption these comments, with appropriate modifications, would seem to apply also to the possibility of a severe and prolonged business contraction. We think net debt might increase by a number of times $16 billion. Also that the amount of federal credit extended to promote recovery and relieve financial distress might be considerably more than $9 billion. In this connection we should note that there were some $40 billion of federally underwritten loans outstanding on June 30, 1954. The likelihood of such federal debt and credit increases should be greater the larger the responsibility assumed by the federal government for keeping the economy operating at a high employment level—or for restoring it to a high level—and the larger the extent to which it engages in a counter-cyclical fiscal policy. The likelihood should be greater, too, in proportion as it assumes more fully the entire countercyclical deficit burden of all levels of government. And in appraising the possible size of the deficit we would need to consider whether the government sector's nonfinancial transactions account was in balance when the contraction started.

But an assumption underlies these comments, and indeed also the comments on the deficit prospects for minor recessions. It will doubtless

177

be agreed that the deficit incurred would increase with the degree of the business contraction that federal actions have to cope with. Yet we assume that federal actions, including countercyclical operations that involve running a deficit, can reduce the degree of contraction, even convert it into a business upswing. If so, the degree of contraction attained at the trough of the cycle and consequently the amount of the countercyclical deficit depend upon how promptly and how vigorously the antirecession actions are taken.

We noted that during the 1930's there was a conflict between the objective of a balanced budget and the objective of an unwavering, sizable fiscal countercycle. No doubt this conflict of objectives continues. And, to the extent that it does, prompt and vigorous actions during the early months of a cyclical downswing are made less likely. So are actions that might involve a $16 billion nonfinancial deficit, especially if this should mean a substantially larger budget deficit. It is easy to understand why the prospect of such deficits would generate opposition to a countercyclical program that involved tax cuts or works program and grant-in-aid step-ups. The idea of alternating budget deficits and surpluses with the downs and ups of the cycle so as to achieve a balance over the cycle could only avoid opposition to such countercyclical actions if there were some way to implement it. At present there are no fiscal procedures to implement such a balance-over-the-cycle fiscal plan.

However, a capital budget system under which the additional countercyclical works and grants expenditures during the lower phases of each cycle would be charged to capital account and amortized over, say, the next ten years would help to implement a balance-over-the-cycle fiscal plan. And it is at least conceivable that a capital budget system could be devised that would smooth the cycle out of budget receipts as well as budget expenditures, so that, if the "smoothed" receipts balanced the "smoothed" expenditures every year, the difference between the cumulative total of "unsmoothed" budget receipts and that of "unsmoothed" budget expenditures would have no secular trend either up or down.

Such a capital budget system would make prompt borrowing during a recession more likely. But if it facilitated countercyclical action that proved effective, it would not necessarily increase the total amount of recession and depression borrowing.

What can be said about the prospects of future wartime borrowing is necessarily entirely hypothetical, except that we can confidently predict that state war-connected borrowing will be confined to financing veterans' bonuses. Should there be another war, or other wars, the amount of borrowing entailed would obviously depend on the size of the conflict or conflicts. Federal net debt increased by about $175 billion during World War II, but scarcely at all during the Korean War. Beyond this not a

178

great deal can be said. It is reasonable to expect that the pay-for-more-of-it-as-you-go trend would continue, but it would be extremely unlikely that all or nearly all the cost of a major war would be met out of current receipts. And of course wars have been getting more expensive and the value of the dollar is less than it was in 1940.

These considerations regarding the prospects of wartime borrowing and countercyclical borrowing do not by themselves throw much light on the question whether the prospect is for an upward or conceivably for a downward trend in federal net debt. This question is largely one of the influences making for and against a program of debt retirement.

In Chapter VIII we concluded that such retirement of emergency-incurred federal debt as has occurred seems for the most part to have been inadvertent. And we noted that a program of retiring the existing federal net debt would be likely to arouse both special interest group opposition and a more general opposition to the cyclically depressing influence the inauguration of such a program would entail.

Inadvertent debt retirement has been possible in the twentieth century as it was in the nineteenth. Thus the tax cuts during the 1920's were so slow they did not prevent a decade of surpluses. But, since income taxes have replaced customs duties as the main revenue source, it has become less likely. And the same considerations that make it improbable that any substantial part of existing federal net debt will be retired make it probable that, in the absence of fiscal procedures which might prevent such a cumulative tendency, future business cycles will often add to the net debt total.

We do have one such fiscal procedure now—the exclusion of social insurance fund transactions from budget receipts and expenditures. Because of this exclusion the increment in net debt since 1937 has been less than the cumulative budget deficit would otherwise have made it by the amount of the growth in social insurance fund balances. That these balances will continue to grow is by no means certain. But if and insofar as they do, the exclusion of social insurance funds will help to keep down the net—but not the gross—federal debt.

Another possible development that could work in the same direction is that of a federal capital budget system that not only would make an annual provision for debt retirements to implement an approximate balance-over-the-cycle program but would also include provisions to implement a gradual retirement of at least all emergency debts incurred after the inauguration of this capital budget system. In the absence of such provisions the most likely prospect would appear to be a gradual accumulation of emergency debts.

APPENDIX A

Additional Notes on the Tables

34. Loans Guaranteed or Insured by Federal Agencies, 1939 and 1954
35. Federal Credit at Selected Dates, 1920–53
36. Countercyclical Fiscal Influences in Recent Minor Recessions, 1945–54
38. Assets in Federal Social Insurance Funds at Selected Dates, 1929–54
39. Cash and Securities in Various State and Local Government Funds at Selected Dates, 1915–50
40. Federal Recovery and Relief Funds and Expenditures, 1934–38
42. Government Corporations and Credit Agencies—1940 Balance Sheets and Operating Incomes
43. Total RFC Sources and Uses of Funds, from Inception to June 30, 1946
48. Total Federal Budget Expenditures, Actual and Budgeted, 1939–54
49. International Aid during and after the Two World Wars
51. Federal Debt and Financial Assets at Selected Dates, 1919–54

Table 1. Government Gross and Net Debts, Selected Years, 1890–1950

Federal gross debt is (a) direct only, 1890 and 1913, (b) direct plus agency debt, 1929, (b) plus (c) private interest in government corporations, 1939, (b) plus (c) plus (d) accounts receivable from government by business corporations, plus (e) trust and deposit liabilities of government corporations and business-type agencies (excluding interagency items), 1950. Net debt is gross minus (f) general fund balance, 1890 and 1913; minus (f) and (g) direct and agency obligations owned (other than those owned by the Postal Savings System and Exchange Stabilization Fund), and (h) other loans and securities held by government funds and minus agencies, 1929; and minus (f), (g), (h), and (j) accounts receivable of government corporations and business-type agencies, 1939; and minus (f), (g), (h), (j), and (k) other post-World War II international credits, 1950.

All state and local gross debt is (l) all direct. Net debt is gross minus (m) cash balances, (n) all government obligations owned, and (o) the small amount of other securities owned.

(a), (f), and (g), also (c), (j), and (n) for 1939 and 1950 and (d) and (e) 1950 are from Treasury *Annual Reports* and *Treasury Bulletin*. (b) and (l), 1929–50, are from *Survey of Current Business*, October 1950 and September 1952, (l) by interpolation. (m) see Table 3. (h) for 1929 is from reports of War Finance Corporation and Federal Farm Loan Board, and Treasury *Annual Reports*. (h) for 1939 and 1950 and (j) and (k) are from Federal Reserve *Flow of Funds* study. (l), (m), and (n) for 1890 and 1913 are from censuses plus estimates for omissions. (o) is estimated on incomplete census data.

In the case of the 1929 figure on line D the estimate was made for 1928, using data from *Financial Statistics of States and Cities*, the Treasury data on sinking funds and debts of territories and possessions, and *Survey of Current Business* data on gross debt. The 1929 deficit was added to this estimate. (See Table 8.) For 1939 and 1950 (m), (n), and (o) are from Federal Reserve *Flow of Funds* study.

Lines G through M, 1890, are from the 1890 *Census of Wealth, Debt and Taxation*; other years from Bureau of the Census, *Government Debt in the United States*, 1942 and 1951.

Table 2C.   Functional Distribution of City Government Debt, Selected Years, 1905–51

The principal sources are *Financial Statistics of Cities, 1905–41*, and *Large-City Finances, 1951*. Details refer to funded and special assessment debt, 1905; funded, floating, and special assessment debt, 1929; long-term debt, 1941 and 1951.

The figure on line A for 1951 was estimated by adding utility borrowing to and subtracting utility debt redemption from the 1950 figure.

The figure on line M for 1941 was estimated on the assumption that the gross debt ratio for cities over 25,000 to that for cities of 100,000 was the same in 1941 and 1942.

See also notes on Table 20.

Table 3.   State and Local Government Gross and Net Debt, 1946 and 1950

Figures for 1946 were derived as follows:

Line A. Total shown in September 1952 *Survey of Current Business*, p. 12, plus interest-bearing debts of territories and possessions (average of two fiscal years), 1951 Treasury *Annual Report*, p. 938.

Lines B and C. 1951 Treasury *Annual Report*, pp. 938–39; average of two fiscal years.

Line D. Federal Deposit Insurance Corporation 1946 *Annual Report*, p. 123, plus $100,000 estimated currency holdings.

Line E. Conservatively estimated as one-half the assets other than cash, government securities, and real estate held by state sinking, trust, and investment funds in 1941. See *Financial Statistics of States*, 1941.

Figures for 1950 are from the *Federal Reserve Bulletin*, April 1957, p. 382.

Table 4.   Federal and State and Local Debt Growth Compared to Increase in Capital Assets and Construction

Increases in capital assets (lines A and D) are computed from Solomon Fabricant's estimates, *Studies in Income and Wealth*, Vol. 12, pp. 527ff.

Federal net debt before 1916 equals total direct debt minus the general fund balance. Net debt at other dates was determined by using the annual data in the third column of Table 5 to interpolate on Table 1, line B (federal net debt). State and local net debt was determined similarly by interpolation. See Table 8, A and B, and Appendix Table A-1.

The construction figures are from Department of Commerce, *Construction and Building Materials Statistical Supplement*, May 1952.

Table 5. Federal Government Nonfinancial Receipts, Expenditures, and Deficits, 1890–1954

Figures prior to June 30, 1929, are for fiscal years and are based mainly on the official Treasury report of total receipts and expenditures (other than those arising from direct public debt transactions), and the deficit (excluding debt retirement). The receipt and expenditure figures cover the general and special accounts and the trust accounts; the deficit equals the increment in gross direct debt minus the increment in the general fund balance.

Two sets of corrections were applied to these basic series: (a) The postal deficit was eliminated from the expenditure series (or the postal surplus from the receipts series in years when there was one), and postal revenues were added to receipts so adjusted, postal expenses to expenditures so adjusted. This set of corrections was made for every fiscal year 1890–1929. (b) Figures on federal government portfolios and federal agency debt were used to develop a rough second correction to eliminate credit and agency transactions from the receipt and expenditure series and to estimate the cash deficit. The figures on agency debt outstanding and the government obligations component of portfolios are as shown in Treasury *Annual Reports*. Other portfolio components are: (i) railroad obligations and miscellaneous securities held by the Treasury, (ii) farm credit as reported by the Federal Farm Loan Board, (iii) loans held by the War Finance Corporation, and (iv) loans to veterans held by the U.S. Life Insurance Fund. Annual increments and decrements in the excess of portfolios over agency debt were computed. The cash deficit estimate which appears in the third column equals the budget deficit minus this increment or plus this decrement. The increments were also subtracted from expenditures; the decrements from receipts. This second set of corrections was applied 1916–29; such corrections would have been of no consequence for earlier years.

The resulting series on receipts and expenditures are slightly too net in some respects, slightly too gross in others. However, they are believed to give an approximately correct general picture.

Calendar year figures are given for 1929–50. Those for 1936–42 are, in the first instance, from *A Study of Moneyflows in the United States*. Estimates from the Federal Reserve *Flow of Funds* study were used to carry the table forward through 1950. The *Flow of Funds* series and the 1936–42 series overlap for four years and were spliced.

184

Total ordinary receipts, 1929–36, were estimated as the sum of the following items:

    i.   Customs duties, taxes, fees, fines, etc. collected (as reported in Treasury Daily Statement)

    ii.   Interest (National Income and Product Accounts)

    iii-a.   Estimated operating revenues of enterprises

    iii-b.   One-half of nontax receipts (National Income and Product Accounts)

    iii-c.   Sales to abroad (National Income and Product Accounts)

    iv-a.   Employee contributions for social insurance, other than payroll tax and state and local contributions (National Income and Product Accounts)

    iv-b.   Federal Deposit Insurance Corporation assessments

Total ordinary expenditures, 1929–36, were estimated as the sum of the following items:

    vi.   General and enterprise compensation of employees (National Income and Product Accounts)

    vii.   Interest (National Income and Product Accounts)

    viii.   Grants-in-aid (National Income and Product Accounts)

    ix.   Tax refunds (National Income and Product Accounts)

    x-a.   Transfer payments (National Income and Product Accounts) minus the increment in the U.S. Life Insurance Fund portfolio of adjusted service certificate loans

    x-b.   Farm benefits (*Agricultural Statistics*)

    xi-a.   Purchases of goods and services from business and from abroad (National Income and Product Accounts)

    xi-b.   An estimate of enterprise procurement charged to current account. These estimates were spliced at 1936.

After 1933 the difference between nonfinancial receipts and nonfinancial expenditures does not fully explain changes in net debt. There was a capital gain of $2.8 billion on the monetary gold stock in 1934. This is not counted as a receipt but it is a deduction item in computing net debt. During the 1940's there were three main ways in which government debt increased without causing a cash deficit: (i) The accrual of interest on savings bonds and Treasury bills adds to the debt; it is not a cash expenditure. Net accruals during the eleven years 1940–50 totaled $3.8 billion. (ii) The issue of terminal leave bonds adds to the debt but is not a cash expenditure. The redemption of the bonds is treated as a transfer payment (nonfinancial expenditure). There were some $300 million of these bonds still outstanding at the end of 1950. (iii) The sale of excess profits tax bonds is here treated as a tax collection. Substantially all of these bonds had been redeemed by 1950. They do not need to be considered in relating the eleven-year deficit, 1940–50, to the increase in debt during these years. The debt at the end of 1950 equals the debt at the end of 1939 plus the eleven-year deficit plus $3.8 billion plus $0.3 billion (apart from rounding discrepancies).

Table 8. State and Local Government Nonfinancial Receipts, Expenditures, and Net Deficits, 1910–54

The figures used in Table 8 are the result of splicing together three receipts and expenditures series—one for 1909–36, one for 1936–42, and one for 1939–50. The method of estimating the series for 1909–36 is described below. The 1936–42 series is from *A Study of Moneyflows in the United States* except that unemployment compensation benefits have been added to both receipts and expenditures. The 1939–50 series is from the Federal Reserve *Flow of Funds* study.

Because the estimates 1909–28 are necessarily rough ones, the table shows three-year moving averages for this period.

The deficit column is computed from the other two columns throughout.

Expenditure estimates 1909–29 were obtained by interpolation and extrapolation, applying an annual indicator series to benchmarks at 1913 and 1929.

The 1913 expenditures benchmark equals total general government expenditure including aid paid to other governments (*Historical Statistics*, series P-195 and P-197), plus enterprise expenditures for operation, interest, and capital outlays (1913 census data), plus estimated general and enterprise expenditures of "municipalities" having less than 2,500 inhabitants (based on a comparison with the 1902 and 1932 censuses), plus estimated pension payments (W. I. King, *The National Income and Its Purchasing Power*, p. 369).

Receipt estimates were made by applying a state and local annual indicator series to benchmarks at 1902 and 1913; and by applying a local annual indicator series to benchmarks at 1913 and 1929, and adding total revenue receipts of states (estimates for 1914, 1920, and 1921; as reported in *Financial Statistics of States* for other years). The resulting 1922 figure agreed closely with an independent estimate based on the incomplete census for that year. Receipts for the benchmark years include total tax and other receipts of general departments including aid from other governments, enterprise operating revenues, and pension assessments. As with expenditures, the local government figure for 1913 was adjusted to correct for the omission from the census of "municipalities" having less than 2,500 inhabitants.

The 1929 receipt and expenditure estimates explained below were used as the benchmarks for this year.

The expenditure indicator series was obtained by adding (a) payrolls plus pensions plus interest (estimates by Kuznets, 1919–29, and King,

1909–19); (b) new construction expenditures (estimates by Commerce, 1915–29, carried back to 1909 on the basis of Harold Wolkind's estimates of capital outlays in 145 cities, *Historical Statistics*, H-58); and (c) one-half the operating expenses of municipal enterprises of cities of more than 30,000 inhabitants (*Financial Statistics of Cities*).

The local receipts indicator series was the total receipts of the 146 largest cities as reported by the census, including enterprise and trust fund receipts. This series was used as an indicator for state and local receipts before 1913. For the period 1914–28 both the estimated expenditures and the estimated receipts series have been adjusted, the expenditures being revised upward by 2 per cent, the receipts revised downward

TABLE A-1

State and Local Government Nonfinancial Receipts, Expenditures, Deficits, and Net Debts, 1909–50
(millions of dollars)

Year	Receipts	Expenditures	Deficit	Cumulative Deficit	Net Debt	Year	Deficit	Cumulative Deficit	Net Debt
1909	1,850	1,850	0	2,900		1930	550	11,450	
1910	2,000	2,050	50	2,950		1931	700	12,150	
1911	2,100	2,200	100	3,050		1932	250	12,400	
1912	2,200	2,300	100	3,150		1933	150	12,550	
1913	2,250	2,450	200	3,350	3,350	1934	−300	12,250	
1914	2,400	2,650	250	3,600		1935	−350	11,900	11,900
1915	2,450	2,750	300	3,900		1936	−100	11,800	
1916	2,600	2,850	250	4,150		1937	−100	11,700	
1917	2,800	2,950	150	4,300		1938	−100	11,600	
1918	3,000	3,100	100	4,400		1939	300	11,900	
1919	3,300	3,650	350	4,750		1940	100	12,000	
1920	4,050	4,450	400	5,150		1941	−600	11,400	
1921	4,700	5,650	950	6,100		1942	−1,500	9,900	9,100
1922	5,400	6,250	850	6,950		1943	−2,500	7,400	
1923	5,700	6,400	700	7,650		1944	−2,800	4,600	
1924	6,250	7,050	800	8,450		1945	−3,300	1,300	
1925	6,800	7,650	850	9,300		1946	−800	500	0
1926	7,500	8,000	500	9,800		1947	−500	0	
1927	8,100	8,700	600	10,400		1948	500	500	
1928	8,650	9,050	400	10,800	10,750	1949	1,600	2,100	
1929			100	10,900		1950	1,900	4,000	4,900

by 2 per cent, so that the cumulative deficit would agree approximately with the estimates of net debt (Table 1).

The figures for 1929–36 were obtained by adding the following six items to the National Income and Product Accounts receipt and expenditure series:

a. Interest received
b. Enterprise current surplus

    c. Compensation of enterprise employees

    d. State alcoholic beverage monopolies, cost of goods sold

    e. Other enterprise procurement charged to current account

    f. Aid to other governments

The first three items are from National Income and Product Accounts; (d) is from *Financial Statistics of States*; (e) is estimated; (f) is based upon *Historical Statistics of the United States*, series P-197 adjusted to exclude shared taxes.

    Table A-1 shows the relation between the cumulative deficit and estimated net debt. Net debt estimates for 1935 and 1942 are from *A Study of Moneyflows in the United States*. For the other net debt estimates see notes on Tables 1 and 3.

    There are indications that the receipt and expenditure figures from the GNP accounts used in making the estimates for 1929–36 are too low during this period; but it did not seem feasible to revise them upward, and this would not have improved the deficit estimates. One of these indications is that the splicing required a progressive upward adjustment for 1934–36. Another is that the 1932 figure here shown on line A of Table 15 is higher than that in Table 8.

Table 11A. *Federal Nonfinancial Expenditures, Fiscal Years 1890, 1916, and 1929*

    This table is based chiefly on the Treasury *Annual Reports* for the years 1890, 1916, and 1929.

    Line A excludes War Department nonmilitary expenditures.

    Line D includes rivers and harbors, Panama Canal, Alaska Railroad, Inland Waterways Corporation, Interstate Commerce Commission, Bureau of Public Roads, Bureau of Lighthouses, Steamboat Inspection Service, National Advisory Committee for Aeronautics, and Aeronautics Branch (1929).

    Line E includes department expense.

    Line F excludes Library of Congress, Government Printing Office, and Botanical Gardens.

    Line G reported in 1890 under "foreign intercourse"; 1890 Treasury *Annual Report*, p. cxiii.

    Line L excludes Bureau of Public Roads, Forest Service, and loans.

    Line N includes national parks in the District of Columbia, and (in 1929) Arlington Memorial Bridge.

Table 11B. *Federal Nonfinancial Expenditures, Calendar Years 1929, 1940, and 1950*

    Lines D, E, and F are from the National Income and Product Accounts.

    Line A is from the balance of international payments.

    The total of lines A and B is from the President's *Economic Report*.

Line C was estimated by deducting two items from gross interest, National Income and Product Accounts (i) interfund interest payments— average interest rate on obligations times obligations owned, June 30; and (ii) accrued interest on savings bonds and Treasury bills. Data for (i) and (ii) from Treasury *Annual Reports* and *Treasury Bulletin*.

Line G is from *Agricultural Statistics*.

Line H is computed from *Treasury Bulletin* data.

Line J is amount shown in the National Income and Product Accounts plus withdrawals from the Unemployment Compensation Fund.

Line K, 1940 and 1950, is from the Treasury *Daily Statement*; 1929 is partly estimated.

Line L is from the Postmaster General's *Annual Reports*. It is an average of two fiscal years.

Line M equals civil general government and enterprise wages and salaries, National Income and Product Accounts, minus (i) defense agencies payrolls and (ii) Post Office payroll, *Handbook of Labor Statistics*.

Some of the items are not on a strictly cash basis, especially line B. Line N is a residual. A direct estimate of miscellaneous procurement and construction, excluding force-account wages, comes out significantly larger than the residual in all three years.

Table 12. *Federal Employment at Selected Dates, 1900–1950*

The sources used in this table are: (i) Solomon Fabricant, *The Trend of Government Activity in the United States since 1900,* (ii) the National Income and Product Accounts, and (iii) *Handbook of Labor Statistics*.

All figures for 1900, 1910, and 1920 are from (i). Lines B, D, and F, 1930–50, are from (ii); and line A for these years is from (iii). The rest of federal employment, 1930–50, is distributed between C and E on the basis of (iii). Fabricant's figures for 1930 for lines A, B, C, and E agree closely with those here shown. Apparently his total, 820,000 is lower because of the exclusion of miscellaneous enterprise employees.

Line C covers the War and Navy Departments, 1900–1920. Line C, 1930–50, covers the national military establishment, Maritime Commission, National Advisory Committee for Aeronautics, Panama Canal, and, until the abolition or amalgamation with a peacetime agency, the agencies created specifically to meet the World War II emergency or the problem of reconversion.

Table 13. *State and Local Government Nonfinancial Receipts, Selected Years, 1890–1950*

The principal sources used in compiling this table are *Census of Governments* (formerly *Wealth, Debt and Taxation*); *State Government Finances* (formerly *Financial Statistics of States*); *City Government Finances* (formerly

Financial Statistics of Cities); *Historical Statistics of the United States: Survey of Current Business*, July 1952, and *National Income Supplement*, 1951 edition.

Except for 1890 the totals on line T are from Table 8. The figure for 1890 is from the 1890 census (p. 410); it includes a small amount of loans, but omissions were probably larger than such financial receipts.

The following items, 1932–50, are from the National Income and Product Accounts: lines C, D, L, P, and Q. Line L for 1913 is from *Historical Statistics*.

Lines A, E, F, G, H, J, and K, 1890 and 1913, are based on the *Censuses of Wealth, Debt and Taxation*. Figures for 1913 were adjusted to cover places of less than 2,500 inhabitants. The income tax figure in *Financial Statistics of States* for 1915 indicates that such taxes in 1913 were less than $5 million. A, B, E, F, G, H and J, 1932 'and 1942, are based on the censuses. Tax details have been adjusted to make total property taxes, line A + line G, and total taxes, line K, agree with calendar year amounts shown in the National Income and Product Accounts. Lines A, B, E, and F for 1950 are from *State Government Finances*. Lines G, H, and J are residuals based on the National Income and Product Accounts figures for line A + line G and line K.

Lines M and R and the state component of line N are from *State Government Finances*. The city component of line N is from *City Government Finances*.

Table 14. State and Local Government Nonfinancial Expenditures, Selected Years, 1915–50

The principal sources used in compiling this table are: *State Government Finances* (formerly *Financial Statistics of States*); *City Government Finances* (formerly *Financial Statistics of Cities*); *Survey of Current Business*, July 1952, and *National Income Supplement*, 1951 edition; May 1951 *Statistical Supplement* to *Construction and Building Materials*; *Historical Statistics of the United States*; *Biennial Surveys of Education*; W. I. King, *The National Income and Its Purchasing Power*.

The totals on line T are from Table 8.

Line A is from the *Biennial Survey of Education*.

Lines B, C, D, and U are from the *Statistical Supplement* to *Construction*.

Lines H, N, and R and the state components of lines E, F, and G are from *State Government Finances*. The city components of lines E, F, and G are from *City Government Finances*. The basic data for 1915 and 1929 are for cities of over 30,000 population; for 1939 for cities of over 100,000 population. Expenditures by cities of 25,000 to 30,000 population in 1915 and 1929 were estimated from population data on the assumption that per capita expenditures by these cities were the same as per capita expenditures by cities of 30,000 to 50,000 population. Expenditures for 1939 were estimated from 1942 data on the assumption that the percentage change, 1939–42, was the same for cities of over 100,000 population and those of 25,000. The city estimates for 1915, 1929, and 1939 were reduced to exclude computed portions of expenditures of overlying counties and special districts on the basis of the ratios for 1940.

Lines J, K, L, M, P, and Q are from the National Income and Product Accounts.

Table 15.   State and Local Government Expenditures by Level of Government, Selected Years, 1890–1950

Most of the basic data for this table are from *Historical Statistics of the United States, State Government Finances in 1950*, and *City Government Finances in 1950*.

Line A in general represents P-195 plus all aid shown in P-197, *Historical Statistics*. The 1913 figure includes an estimate for places of less than 2,500 inhabitants, based on a comparison of the 1902, 1913, and 1932 censuses, and population data. The 1950 figure for P-195 was estimated on the assumption that it would bear the same ratio to total nonfinancial expenditures in 1950 as in 1942 (see Table 8).

Line B 1890, 1902, 1932, and 1942, is P-197, *Historical Statistics*. The figures for 1913 and 1950 represent line A minus P-197-B and minus P-191-C respectively.

The figure in the third column on line D is for 1912. The method of splicing the data for line D at 1940 and 1942 is explained in the note under the table.

The population data used in computing lines F and G are based on B-146, B-148, and B-159, *Historical Statistics*. Figures for 1902-42 are linear interpolations adjusted to equal B-31 (*ibid.*). B-31 figures were used in computing line J.

Table 16.   State and Local Government Employment at Selected Dates, 1900–1950

The sources used in this table are (i) Fabricant, *The Trend of Government Activity in the United States since* 1900; (ii) the National Income and Product Accounts; (iii) *Public Employment in January, 1951;* (iv) the censuses of occupations.

Lines A, F, and L are from (i) for 1900 and from (ii) for the other years.

Lines B, C, D, E are based on (iii) for 1950 and on (i) for the other years. Small discrepancies in the total of these four categories, 1930 and 1940, were prorated. (iii) gives total and permanent full-time employees at four dates during the year. Temporary employees were converted to a full-time equivalent by dividing by three. The discrepancy between total employment so computed and line F was prorated among the four categories.

Line G, 1900, is the total for all levels of government from (i) minus the number of postal employees. For other years G is from (ii).

Lines H and J are based on (iv). The 1910 and 1930 censuses lump public and private policemen and detectives together. The percentage of public employees in these two categories was assumed to be the same in 1910 and 1930 as in 1940. The 1900 census lumps watchmen and guards with these categories. One estimate for 1900 was made on the basis of the percentage change, 1900–1910, for this broad group. A second estimate was made by blowing up the number of officers, detectives, and patrolmen in cities of over 30,000 in 1905, using general revenues for these cities in 1905 and all places of over 8,000 inhabitants in 1902 for the blow-up ratio. The two estimates were averaged.

Table 18. Per Capita State and Local Debt at Selected Dates, 1920–50

Two estimates were made of the overlying debt for cities of more than 100,000 population for 1946 and 1950. One assumed that for each of five groups of cities the ratio of overlying debt to city corporation debt was the same in 1940, 1946, and 1950. (The groups were New York; other cities of over 1,000,000; cities of 500,000 to 1,000,000; cities of 250,000 to 500,000; cities of 100,000 to 250,000.) The other estimate assumed that the overlying debt was equal to 37.9 per cent of total gross county and school district debt in each of the three years. The two estimates were averaged.

In analyzing the figures on total gross local debt and on gross debt (including overlying debt) by city size groups, 1923 and 1931, two assumptions were made: (i) that the per capita debt for cities, towns, and villages of 2,500 to 30,000 population was less than that for cities of 30,000 to 50,000; and (ii) that the per capita debt for cities, towns, and villages of 2,500 to 30,000 population was greater than that for rural areas. The second condition sets lower limits to the per capita figure for the smaller urban communities. The upper limits set by condition (i) are:

$$\left. \begin{array}{ll} 1923 & \$ \ 79.00 \\ 1931 & 116.50 \end{array} \right\} \text{per capita debt of cities of 30,000 to 50,000}$$

Estimates were made assuming that the per capita figure for places of 2,500 to 30,000 was (a) 95 per cent of the upper limit, and (b) 83 per cent of that limit. The results were:

	1923		*1931*	
	(a)	(b)	(a)	(b)
Per capita debt, places of 2,500 to 30,000	$75.00	$65.50	$110.67	$96.70
Per capita rural debt	42.10	45.70	90.75	96.00
Per capita debt, places of 2,500 to 100,000	80.20	73.40	118.20	108.75

Table 19. State and Local Debts by Census Regions, 1890, 1922, and 1942

The total debt figures (gross debts less sinking fund assets) used in computing the per capita amounts for each region and year are from the censuses of governments. The 1922 census gives per capita computation but because errors were discovered it was necessary to make new computations. Population figures, urban and rural, for each region were estimated for 1922 and 1942 by interpolation between the decennial population census figures. The results were adjusted to total to the July 1 estimates for the continental United States.

Per capita figures for columns 4 and 5 of the table were computed by weighting the urban population 3, the rural population 1. Each of the two resulting figures for each year was then multiplied by a factor such that the 1922 figure would equal the 1922 per capita debt as in column 2. A similar procedure was followed for columns 5 and 6 with the urban population weighted 2 1/2, the rural 1. See line K of Table 18 for these weights.

Table 20. State and Local Short-term Debt, Expenditures, and Cash Balances at Selected Dates, 1922–53

Column 1 is from *Governmental Debt in 1951* except for 1929. The 1929 figure was estimated from total gross interest bearing debt of all state and local governments and short-term and total debt data from *Financial Statistics of States* and *Financial Statistics of Cities*. For cities of less than 30,000 population the ratio of short-term debt (floating and current except interfund items) to total debt was assumed to be the same as for cities of 30,000 to 50,000 population. For other units of government the ratio for states and cities combined was used.

The figure in column 2 for 1922 is an average of two fiscal years. See Table A-1.

Column 3, 1929-42, is from S. Shapiro, "*The Distribution of Deposits and Currency in the United States, 1929–1939,*" *Journal of the American Statistical Association,* 1943, pp. 438ff, and *A Study of Moneyflows in the United States* (figures for 1929, 1932 and 1942 are averages of two calendar years). On more recent figures see Table 3 notes. The 1922 figure was estimated on the assumption that the percentage increment, 1922–29, was seven-sixths of that for states plus cities of over 30,000 population, 1923–29. States plus these cities accounted for about two-thirds of the 1929 total.

Figures on sinking fund assets for 1922–32, column 4, were estimated from holdings of government securities in sinking funds (Secretary of the Treasury *Annual Reports*), and such holdings and total assets of the sinking funds of states and the larger cities (*Financial Statistics of States* and *Financial*

Statistics of Cities). For more recent years figures are from *Summary of Governmental Finances in* 1953.

Table 23.   State and Local Debt and Depreciated Construction, a Rough Three-Function Comparison, Selected Years, 1922–51

Figures on construction, except for the earlier years, are from *Construction and Building Materials Statistical Supplement,* May 1952. For the earlier years (before 1915 for lines B and H, before 1920 for line E) construction was estimated on the basis of *Historical Statistics,* H-58 to H-63.

State and larger city components of lines A, D, and G are from *State Government Finances, Large City Finances* (1951), and *Financial Statistics of Cities* (1922–42). Smaller city debt for each of the four years was apportioned among the three functions and all other on the basis of the percentages for the smallest city size group for which information was available for the year. Line D includes total school district long-term debt. There is no satisfactory basis for determining county and township highway debt. It was assumed to be 50 per cent of total long-term county debt in 1922 and 40 per cent in 1949. Figures on debt issue and retirement from *Highway Statistics, Summary for 1945* and from subsequent annual issues of *Highway Statistics* were used for interpolation and extrapolation. The state and city components of line A are somewhat lower than those shown in *Highway Statistics* for recent years. The latter source gives a long retrospect only for state issues, and the total for these for 1915 is lower than that in *Financial Statistics of States.* The total it shows for county and township highway debt as of the end of 1949 is 44 per cent of the grand total outstanding. On the other hand the Bureau of the Census compilations are presumably understatements of the debt for the various identified purposes, because of the large amount—apparently chiefly refunding issues—classified as not allocable by purpose.

Table 28.   Intergovernmental Aid Compared to Nonfinancial Receipts, Selected Years, 1913–50

The principal sources used in this table are the various Bureau of the Census publications; *Federal Grants in Aid,* Council of State Governments, 1949; and Treasury *Annual Reports.*

Line B for 1913 is from *Historical Statistics;* for 1929–50 from the National Income and Product Accounts.

Lines C and G were computed from Bureau of the Census data. Line G, 1912 and 1929, covers what were formerly called total revenue receipts (including enterprise revenues and various trust account receipts). Line C, 1913 and 1929, covers such revenue receipts plus state-collected, locally shared taxes (see *Historical Statistics*). The components included in these totals for line G—so far as they could be identified—were tabulated to give the figures for line G, 1940 and 1950. This involved some estimating, particularly to arrive at the figure for 1940. Line C, 1942 and 1950, is total general, alcoholic beverage, and social insurance trust fund revenues less state contributions to employee retirement funds.

Lines D, F, and V through Y are from *Historical Statistics, State Government Finances*, and *City Government Finances*.

Line E was computed by subtracting line C from the receipts column of Table 8.

Lines N through U, 1912–42, are from *Federal Grants in Aid*. The 1950 figure was compiled from the Treasury *Annual Report*.

Table 31. Various Federal Expenditure Programs and Federal Credit, 1929–33

Line A is from Table 36, 1954 *National Income Supplement* to the *Survey of Current Business*, 1954 edition. It covers life insurance benefits; pension, disability and retirement payments; and adjusted compensation benefits. The adjusted compensation benefits include all loans on the security of adjusted service certificates (such loans by the United States Government Life Insurance Fund are not included in line E).

Line B is from 1954 *National Income Supplement*, Table 9. The figure for 1933 excludes work relief construction.

Line C is from the 1952 *Statistical Supplement* to *Construction and Building Materials*.

Line D is from 1954 *National Income Supplement*, Table 15.

Line E is from text Table 5.

Line F, 1929–31, is from the *Third Annual Report* of the Federal Farm Board, p. 102. Line F, 1932–33, is from *Senate Report No. 1456*, 74th Congress, 1st Session, pp. 1 and 32. Figures include delinquent loans. However the figure for 1933 is evidently net of a loss write-off. (See *ibid.*, footnote 30.) The estimate of $345 million of losses (footnote d to Table 31) includes $88 million out of $125 million of loans outstanding to cooperatives as of June 30, 1935, but classed as probably uncollectible.

Line G includes: farm mortgage loans to cooperatives other than Agricultural Marketing Act revolving fund loans, federal intermediate credit bank loans, production credit association loans, regional agricultural credit corporation loans, and emergency crop and drought loans. Figures for 1929–31 for emergency crop and drought loans are as of June 30. (See 1935 *Statistical Abstract*, p. 253.)

Line H is from *ibid.*, p. 261.

Table 32. Federal Countercyclical Programs Related to Personal Income and Farm Income, 1929–39

Lines A, C, and E are from Table 36 of the 1954 *National Income Supplement* to the *Survey of Current Business*.

Lines D and G are from *idem*, Tables 15 and 3 respectively.
Line B is computed from *Federal Grants in Aid*, pp. 32 and 36.
Line H is from 1947 *Agricultural Statistics*, p. 535.
On line J see notes *c* and *d* to Table 31 and Table 31 source notes, above, to lines F and G.
Line K is from 1950 *Statistical Abstract*, p. 584.

Table 33. Federal Countercyclical Programs Related to Aggregate Demand, 1929–39

Lines A and G are from the 1954 *National Income Supplement* to the *Survey of Current Business*, Table 15; Line B is from *ibid.*, Table 9. Line E equals total grants, *ibid.*, Table 8, minus the grants for public assistance shown in Table 32 above. Line C was computed from data in the *Treasury Bulletin*, July 1940, p. 56. Lines D and E are residual computations.

Table 34. Loans Guaranteed or Insured by Federal Agencies, 1939 and 1954

Lines A, B, C, and D, 1939, are from Saulnier, Halcrow, and Jacoby, *Federal Lending and Loan Insurance*.

Data for lines A, B, C, and D, 1954, except for loans guaranteed or insured by the Veterans' Administration, are from the 1956 *Budget of the United States*, p. 1167.

Home loans underwritten by the Veterans' Administration, as of 1954, and data underlying line E are from *Federal Reserve Bulletin*, May 1955, p. 541. Other loans underwritten by the Veterans' Administration, as of 1954, are from the 1954 *Annual Report*, Administrator of Veterans' Affairs, pp. 96-97. All farm credit outstanding (the denominator of the ratio on line F), 1954, includes Commodity Credit Corporation loans outstanding (other than loans to government agencies) minus reserves for losses (see *Treasury Bulletin*, October 1954, p. 58), and farm real estate debt and other debt, estimated from January 1 figures (see October 1954 *Agricultural Finance Outlook*, p. 3). For denominator of ratio on line E see *Federal Reserve Bulletin, loc. cit.*, and December 1953, p. 1369.

Table 35. Federal Credit at Selected Dates, 1920–53

For line A, 1920 and 1929, see 1935 *Statistical Abstract*, p. 253. For lines E and J, 1920 and 1929, see tables on securities owned by the United States, Secretary of the Treasury, *Annual Reports*.

For line F see Administrator of Veterans' Affairs (and Veterans' Bureau), *Annual Reports*, balance sheets of United States Government Life Insurance Fund and National Service Life Insurance Fund.

For 1939 lines A, B, and K are from Morris A. Copeland, *Concerning a New Federal Financial Statement*, Technical Paper 5, National Bureau of Economic Research, p. 5. Line E and the loan component of line C are from *Banking and Monetary Statistics*, p. 517. The preferred stock component of line C is from Treasury *Daily Statement*, January 31, 1940. Line D is from Secretary of the Treasury, 1945 *Annual Report*, p. 697 (average of two June 30 figures). Line J is a residual computation.

Figures on Exchange Stabilization Fund capital included in line G are from Secretary of the Treasury, *Annual Reports* for 1940 and 1954. Subscriptions of capital, International Monetary Fund and International Bank for Reconstruction and Development, are from the 1954 Treasury *Annual Report*, p. 656.

For 1953 lines A, B, C, E, and J are from the balance sheets of government corporations and certain other business-type activities, *Treasury Bulletin*, April 1954, pp. 62-78. Line H was computed as follows:

	millions of dollars
Foreign loans of government corporations, June 30, 1945	511[a]
Lend-lease credits less repayments before June 30, 1945	279[b]
New foreign credits less repayments, July 1945 through December 1953	11,093[b]
Total	11,883

[a] See 1947 *Statistical Supplement* to *Survey of Current Business*, p. 79.
[b] See 1954 *Statistical Abstract*, p. 898, and 1950 *Statistical Abstract*, p. 831.

Table 36.   Countercyclical Fiscal Influences in Recent Minor Recessions, 1945–54

Line A, lines D through J, and the totals for line B plus line C are National Income and Product Account figures. Line B includes state unemployment compensation law benefits, railroad unemployment insurance benefits, and Servicemen's Readjustment Act benefits. Figures are based on reports of the Bureau of Employment Security and Railroad Retirement Board. Line C is a residual computation.

Figures for line L appear currently in the *Federal Reserve Bulletin*. Figures for June 30, 1945 and 1946, March 31, 1946, and September 30, 1948 and 1949, were estimated by interpolating between year-end figures on the basis of data on loans insured or, in the case of earlier FHA figures, on the basis of Title II Loans outstanding.

Table 38.   Assets in Federal Social Insurance Funds at Selected Dates, 1929–54

Lines A, B, and C and the National Service Life component of line D are from the *Treasury Bulletin*. The Government Life component of line D is from Administrator of Veterans Affairs, *Annual Reports*. The component of line D, 1954, was estimated by adding net receipts to the 1953 figure.

Line E, 1929, is from Secretary of the Treasury, 1929 *Annual Report*. The figure for 1939 represents special issues of federal securities held (see *Treasury Bulletin*) plus 0.68 per cent for other assets. (On June 30, 1940, the ratio of other assets to special issues held was 0.68 per cent;

see Secretary of the Treasury, 1940 *Annual Report.*) Figures for other dates represent special issues of federal securities held (see *Treasury Bulletin*) plus 1.33 per cent for other assets. (On June 30, 1954 the ratio of other assets to special issues held was 1.33 per cent; see Secretary of the Treasury, 1954 *Annual Report.*)

Table 39. Cash and Securities in Various State and Local Government Funds at Selected Dates, 1915–50

The chief sources used in this table are *State Government Finances, Large City Finances* (and *Financial Statistics of Cities*), and Treasury *Annual Reports.*

Line A, 1915–37, was estimated by applying the ratio of general fund cash to total cash for states plus reporting cities to estimates of total cash. The estimates of total cash were from various sources. (See notes to Tables 1, 3, and 20).

Lines A and B, 1942–50, are as reported by the Bureau of the Census. The earlier figures for line B were estimated by interpolating the ratio of government obligations in sinking funds as estimated by the Treasury to total sinking funds, 1913, 1922, and 1932.

Line C, 1929, was estimated by capitalizing investment income. Assets for 1937–50 were estimated by adding the cumulative surplus (National Income and Product Accounts) to the 1929 figure. The ratio of assets to benefits (1915 benefits figure from King, *op.cit.*) was assumed to be the same in 1915 and 1929. Preliminary estimates of line C plus line D, 1915–37, were made from data on retirement, investment, and miscellaneous trust fund assets plus other assets and on debts for states plus reporting cities by applying the ratio of total gross debt to gross debt for states plus reporting cities. A small, constant percentage reduction was made in these preliminary estimates to make the final 1937 figure coincide with that already obtained as explained below for 1937–50. The large government securities component of line C was estimated from the total by applying the ratios for government securities to government securities plus other assets for states plus reporting cities. The resulting figures were deducted from the Treasury estimates of government securities held by trust and investment funds to obtain the government securities component of line D. The cash and nongovernment securities component of line D, 1937–42, was estimated on the basis of the ratio of such assets to government securities in the funds of states and reporting cities. The 1950 figure for the cash and securities component of line D is a guess.

Table 40. Federal Recovery and Relief Funds and Expenditures, 1934–38

The main source for columns 1 through 5 was Secretary of the Treasury, 1938 *Annual Report,* Table 23; $605 million there shown as a specific appropriation to the FERA, and $332 million to the CWA, appear in Table 40 in column 1; the act of February 15, 1934, gave the President discretion to allocate the funds to any agencies he saw fit. Three captions of Table 23 have been altered to identify the agencies receiving and spending the funds. Details on the NYA and Puerto Rico Relief Administration have been added from Table 24. Funds provided in the Act of June 21, 1938, have been excluded as being substantially unavailable during fiscal 1938. The following agencies and financial institutions were excluded on the ground that they received no funds by allocation of the appropriations covered by column 1: HOLC; home loan banks; RFC (direct loans and expenditures); FFMC; federal land banks, federal savings and loan associations, and FDIC. FHA and Export-Import Bank received less than $1.5 million each; these two agencies have been combined with all others on line T.

The following specific appropriations for the Civilian Conservation Corps have been added to line C:

	millions of dollars
June 22, 1936	308
July 1, 1937	350
April 25, 1938	22
Total	680

Total general and special account emergency expenditures for each agency to which footnote *j* is attached and for all agencies combined, and total non-emergency general and special account expenditures for each agency listed in column 6, have been compiled from the 1940 United States Budget, Informational Table No. 5. The figures in column 5, lines A and C, are from this source. In general the entries in column 6 reflect the difference between total expenditures, 1934-36, as shown in the 1940 Budget (1933-36 for lines A and C) and column 5. The 1940 Budget table distinguishes emergency from other (or "general") expenditures, and the distinction there drawn is accepted here with two exceptions. The 1940 Budget table treats Civilian Conservation Corps and AAA expenditures as "general," they are here considered "emergency" expenditures.

Table 42. Government Corporations and Credit agencies—1940 Balance Sheets and Operating Income

Columns 1 through 8, and except as otherwise noted column 12, are based on the Treasury compilation of balance sheets (see *Daily Statement* for July 31, 1940). For each corporation the following were computed:

    a. U.S. securities and agency obligations held plus cash with the Treasurer of the United States plus interagency assets

199

b. Interagency liabilities plus those bonds, notes, and debentures outstanding appearing in the compilation as assets of other corporations or agencies

c. Other bonds, notes, and debentures plus privately held capital stock (column 6)

d. Other cash plus accounts and other receivables plus accrued interest receivable plus other assets (column 4)

e. Accrued interest payable plus other liabilities plus deferred income (column 7).

Column 1 equals (a) minus (b), where positive; column 8 equals (b) minus (a) where positive. Other loans and securities and tangible assets are net of valuation reserves (reserves for uncollectible items and, except in the case of the FDIC, operating reserves).

Column 9 is derived from Secretary of the Treasury, 1940 *Annual Report*, pp. 115 and 790–92; column 10 from the 1938 *Annual Report*, pp. 462–63. For several of the items in column 11 it was necessary to identify the appropriation acts involved.

Column 13 for FHA is from the 1942 Budget; for TVA from the TVA 1940 *Annual Report*; for USMC from MC 1940 *Annual Report*.

For the following agencies operating income was taken to be "interest, dividends, assessments and property income" as reported in the *Treasury Bulletin* for August 1940, p. 28: FDIC, EIB, FNMA, RFCMC, HOLC, FSLIC, federal home loan banks, USHA, CCC, FFMC, REA. For the other corporations and agencies, operating income represents estimated interest income from portfolios.

Table 43.   Total RFC Sources and Uses of Funds, from Inception to June 30, 1946

Sources and uses of funds from February 2, 1932, to June 30, 1940, were computed by adding to the balance sheet items for the latter date certain data on capital reimbursements and certain data from the sources and uses statement in the *Treasury Bulletin* for August 1940, p. 30. The balance sheet was published in the Treasury *Daily Statement* for July 31, 1940. The source and use data added were: (a) interest expense, lines D and S; (b) administrative expense, lines D and T; (c) expenditures n.e.c., lines F and U. The capital reimbursement data added relate to RFC notes held by the Treasury that were canceled (reported in Secretary of the Treasury, 1941 *Annual Report*, p. 51). The entries were as follows:

millions of dollars

Dr. Line L	260	Cr. Line A	2,734
Line N	1,782		
Line P	18		
Line S	33		
Line A	132		

Sources and uses from June 30, 1940, to June 30, 1946, were computed by adding to the balance sheet increments the following items and then deducting items a, b, and c above: (d) $348 million to line S; $143 million to line T; $34 million to line U; and $525 million to line D a/c lending activities. (e) $2,981 million to line P; $2,142 million to line Q; $315 million to line R; $267 million to line S; $105 million to line T; $48 million to line U; and $5,858 million to line D a/c nonleading war programs. (f) $1,741 million to line Q; $18 million to line R; $1,365 million to line B; and $394 million to line D a/c 1946 balance sheet valuation reserves. The 1946 balance sheet and the data for the (d), (e), and (f) adjustments are from the 1946 annual report of the RFC.

Lines V and W are from the Secretary of the Treasury, 1954 *Annual Report*, p. 653.

It is believed that Table 43 reveals the operations of the RFC far more clearly and adequately than do the sources and uses statements filed with the Treasury (these are standardized for all government corporations and business-type activities).

Table 48. Total Federal Budget Expenditures, Actual and Budgeted, 1939–54

During the period covered by this table five important changes were made in the definition of what was formerly called total general and special account expenditures excluding debt retirements and is currently called total budget expenditures. It is convenient to identify these changes in terms of the Secretary of the Treasury, *Annual Reports*.

a. The 1937 Secretary of the Treasury, Annual Report, shows the following general and special account expenditure items under the main caption "Revolving funds (net)" in Table 5:

	millions of dollars
Commodity Credit Corporation—RFC funds	−112
Export-Import Banks—RFC funds	−3
RFC—direct loans and expenditures	−334

In the 1938 *Annual Report* these items appear as checking account transactions under the main head "Trust accounts, increment on gold, etc."

b. The Social Security Act amendment of August 10, 1939, had the effect of excluding the tax receipts appropriated to the OASI account from general and special account receipts and expenditures effective July 1, 1940.

c. Under the definition of general and special account expenditures adopted during the 1930's most transactions of or involving government corporations were shown as "Transactions in the checking accounts of government agencies, etc. (net)." This meant they were outside the budget. (However, appropriations for subscriptions to capital stock and for the "restoration of capital impairment" were included in the budget.) The Government Corporation Control Act of 1945 aimed to bring specified corporations fully under budgetary control and also under audit by the General Accounting Office. To effectuate the purposes of this act the net checking account transactions of government agencies and wholly owned corporations were subdivided into: (i) redemptions minus sales of the obligations of the corporations in the market and (ii) "other activities (net)." And beginning with the 1947 Secretary of the Treasury, *Annual Report*—and the 1949 Budget—(ii) for each agency and wholly owned corporation has been reported as a general and special account or budget expenditure.

d. Effective July 1, 1948, payments to the Treasury, principally by wholly owned government corporations for retirement of capital stock and for disposition of earnings, have been excluded from both budget receipts and budget expenditures. Also, effective January 3, 1949, amounts refunded by the government, principally for the overpayment of taxes, have been excluded from budget expenditures (and reported as a deduction from receipts).

e. Effective July 1, 1952, appropriations of tax receipts to the Railroad Retirement Account have been excluded from both budget receipts and budget expenditures.

To put the budget estimate, midyear estimate, and actual for each year on the same basis the following changes have been made in the figures shown in the various budget documents:

Budget Document for	Midyear Estimate	Budget Estimate
1939		(a) deducted
		(b) and estimated
1940	(b) deducted	(b) deducted
1948		(d) deducted
1949	(d) deducted	(d) deducted
1953		(e) deducted
1954	(e) deducted	(e) deducted

While the effect of c on the 1947 budget estimate was apparently small, this change involved substantial revisions in several earlier year figures on actual expenditures.

Table 49. International Aid during and after the Two World Wars

World War I figures:

Expenditures for European food relief (line C) Secretary of the Treasury, *Annual Reports*, 1920, p. 264; 1921, p. 142.

New credits to November 30, 1918 (line H, col. 1) from 1920 *Annual Report*, p. 340, and subsequent and total new credits (line H. cols. 2 and 3) from 1928 *Statistical Abstract*, p. 209.

Principal collections to and unpaid principal as of November 15, 1940, Secretary of the Treasury, 1940 *Annual Report*, p. 795.

World War II figures:

July 1, 1940 to June 30, 1944, 1950 *Statistical Abstract*, p. 831.

July 1, 1945 to December 31, 1953, 1954 *Statistical Abstract*, p. 898.

Table 51.   Federal Debt and Financial Assets at Selected Dates, 1919–54

For 1919 and 1929 line A equals general fund balance; line B is direct and agency obligations held by federal funds other than the Postal Savings System (see Secretary of the Treasury, *Annual Report* for 1945, p. 696, and *Banking and Monetary Statistics*, p. 519); line D is farm credit as reported by the Farm Credit Administration plus War Finance Corporation loans and policy loans by the U.S. Government Life Insurance Fund plus miscellaneous domestic securities owned by the United States as reported in Secretary of the Treasury, *Annual Reports*; line F is gross direct debt plus agency obligations (on the latter see Secretary of the Treasury, *Annual Report* for 1945, p. 695).

For 1945–54 line F is from the May 1955 *Survey of Current Business*, p. 10. Other items are from the Federal Reserve *Flow of Funds* study.

APPENDIX B

Statistical Compilations, Books, and Other Documents Cited

PART I. FEDERAL DOCUMENTS AND PUBLICATIONS

NOTE: In addition to those here listed, the annual reports of a number of federal government agencies are referred to in Appendix A.

Agriculture, Department of. *Agricultural Finance Review.* Semiannual.

Agriculture, Department of. *Agricultural Statistics.* Annual.

Budget, Bureau of the. *The Budget of the United States Government.* Annual.

Census, Bureau of the. *Census of Wealth, Debt and Taxation.* 1880, 1890, 1902, 1913, 1922, 1932, 1942. Note: The somewhat limited 1942 compilation was called *Governmental Finances in the United States: 1942.*

Census, Bureau of the. *City Government Finances.* Annual. Prior to 1942 this publication was entitled *Financial Statistics of Cities.*

Census, Bureau of the. *Government Debt in the United States.* Annual.

Census, Bureau of the. *Historical Statistics of the United States, 1789–1945.*

Census, Bureau of the. *Historical Statistics of the United States, 1789–1945, Continuation to 1952.*

Census, Bureau of the. *Public Employment.* Quarterly.

Census, Bureau of the. Special Studies. Among the particularly useful studies in this series are:

Historical Statistics of State and Local Government Finances, 1902–53. No. 38.

Revised Summary of State and Local Government Finances in 1942. No. 26.

Governments in the United States in 1952. No. 31.

School Districts in the United States in 1954. No. 40.

Census, Bureau of the. *State Government Finances.* Annual. Prior to 1942 this publication was entitled *Financial Statistics of States.*

Census, Bureau of the. *Statistical Abstract.* Annual.

Census, Bureau of the. *Summary of Governmental Finances.* Annual.

Commerce, Department of, n.e.c. "Balance of Payments of the United States, 1919–53." July 1954 *Survey of Current Business,* pp. 11ff. Also "United States Balance of Payments in 1954." *Ibid.,* March 1955, pp. 9ff.

Commerce, Department of, n.e.c. *Construction and Building Materials, Statistical Supplement.* Annual.

Commerce, Department of, n.e.c. *Foreign Grants and Credits by the United States Government.* Quarterly.

Commerce, Department of, n.e.c. *Highways Statistics.* Summary issue, annual.

Commerce, Department of, n.e.c. *International Transactions of the United States during the War, 1940–1945.*

Commerce, Department of, n.e.c. See Wolkind under Part II.

Congress. *Congressional Directory.* Annual.

Council of Economic Advisers. *Economic Report of the President.* Annual.

Federal Reserve System, Board of Governors. *Banking and Monetary Statistics.* Washington, 1943.

Federal Reserve System, Board of Governors. *Federal Reserve Bulletin.* Monthly.

Federal Reserve System, Board of Governors. *Flow of Funds in the United States, 1939–1953.* Washington, 1955.

General Services Administration. *United States Government Organization Manual.* Annual.

Labor Statistics, Bureau of. *Handbook of Labor Statistics.* Issued at intervals of three or more years.

National Income Division. "Debt and Borrowing in 1954." May 1955 *Survey of Current Business*, pp. 6ff. Also previous annual debt articles in the *Survey of Current Business.*

National Income Division. *National Income 1954 Supplement to the Survey of Current Business.*

National Income Division. "Personal Income by States, 1929–54." September 1955 *Survey of Current Business*, pp. 12ff.

Office of Education. *Biennial Survey of Education.*

Securities and Exchange Commission. *Net Working Capital of U.S. Corporations.* Quarterly.

Social Security Administration. *Social Security Year Book.* Formerly annual, now a special issue of the *Social Security Bulletin.*

Treasury Department. *Daily Statement.*

Treasury Department. *Receipts, Expenditures and Balances of the U.S. Government.* Annual.

Treasury Department. *Statistics of Income.* Annual.

Treasury Department. *Treasury Bulletin.* Monthly.

Treasury Department. Secretary of the Treasury, *Annual Report.* Annual.

PART II. PRINCIPAL OTHER REFERENCES CITED

Barger, Harold. *Outlay and Income in the United States, 1921–1938.* (Studies in Income and Wealth, Vol. 4.) National Bureau of Economic Research, 1942.

Brown, Josephine C. *Public Relief 1929–1939.* New York, 1940.

Burns, Arthur F., and Mitchell, Wesley C. *Measuring Business Cycles.* National Bureau of Economic Research, 1946.

Committee for Economic Development. Staff of the Committee. *Jobs and Markets.* New York, 1946.

Copeland, Morris A. *A Study of Moneyflows in the United States.* National Bureau of Economic Research, 1952.

Copeland, Morris A. "The Capital Budget and the War Effort." *American Economic Review*, March 1943, pp. 30ff.

Council of State Governments. *Federal Grants-in-Aid*. Chicago, 1949.

Dewey, Davis R. *Financial History of the United States*. 8th ed. New York, 1922.

Durand, Edward Dana. *The Finances of New York City*. New York, 1898.

Fabricant, Solomon. *The Trend of Government Activity in the United States since 1900*. National Bureau of Economic Research, 1952.

Goldsmith, Raymond W. *Financial Intermediaries in the American Economy since 1900*. Princeton University Press for the National Bureau of Economic Research, 1958.

Grebler, Leo; Blank, David; and Winnick, Louis. *Capital Formation in Residential Real Estate*. Princeton University Press for the National Bureau of Economic Research, 1956,

Halcrow, Harold G; Saulnier, R. J.; and Jacoby, Neil. *Federal Lending and Loan Insurance*. Princeton University Press for the National Bureau of Economic Research, 1958.

Hillhouse, A. M. *Municipal Bonds*. New York, 1936.

Huse, Charles P. *The Financial History of Boston*. Harvard University Press, 1916.

International City Managers' Association. *Municipal Year Book*. Chicago. Annual.

Kilpatrick, Wylie. *State Supervision of Local Finance*. Chicago, 1941.

King, Wilford Isbell. *National Income and Its Purchasing Power*. National Bureau of Economic Research, 1930.

Kuznets, Simon. "*Annual Estimates of National Product, 1869–1949*." Memorandum prepared for the Capital Requirements Study, 1951.

Mendelson, Morris. *The Flow-of-Funds through the Financial Markets*. National Bureau of Economic Research, 1959.

Mitchell, Wesley C., and Burns, Arthur F. *Measuring Business Cycles*. National Bureau of Economic Research, 1946.

Ratchford, B.U. *American State Debts*. Durham, N.C., 1941.

Roose, Kenneth D. *The Economics of Recession and Revival*. New Haven, 1954.

Ross, Earle D. "Emergence of Agricultural Regionalism," in H. F. Williamson, ed. *The Growth of the American Economy*. New York, 1944.

Ruggles, Catherine F. "American Public Finance 1789–1943," in H. F. Williamson, ed. *The Growth of the American Economy*. New York, 1944.

Secrist, Horace. *An Economic Analysis of the Constitutional Restrictions upon Public Indebtedness in the U.S.* Bulletin of the University of Wisconsin, Economics and Political Science Series, Vol. 8, No. 1, April 1914.

Shapiro, S. "Distribution of Deposits and Currency in the United States, 1929-1939." *Journal of the American Statistical Association*, December 1943, pp. 438ff.

Sowers, Don C. *The Financial History of New York State from 1789 to 1912.* New York, 1914.

Studenski, Paul. *Public Borrowing.* New York, 1930.

Studenski, Paul and Krooss, Herman E. *Financial History of the United States.* New York, 1952.

Wolkind, Harold. *Fluctuations in Capital Outlays of Municipalities.* Bureau of Foreign and Domestic Commerce, Economic Series, No. 10. Washington, 1941.

Young, Marilyn. "A Reconciliation of Alternative Budget Concepts." In *Problems in the International Comparison of Economic Accounts.* (Studies in Income and Wealth, Vol. 20.) Princeton University Press for the National Bureau of Economic Research, 1957.

INDEX

Accounting and budgetary practices: accrual accounting, 6, 170; Budget and Accounting Act of 1921 and, 21, 131, 165; capital budget, 6, 23, 83–84, 86, 162–163; change in mint price of gold, 21, 23; in federal budget statements, 20–23, 27–36; in federal cash income and outgo statements, 23–24, 30–36; government compared to private, xxiii, 5–6, 19, 73–74; of government corporations, 22–23, 28–32, 133–146; Government Corporation Control Act of 1945 and, 28; for social insurance funds, 21–22, 25–29

Assets, *see* Financial assets

Barger, Harold, 110 n.
Blank, David M., xv n., xvi n., 118 n.
Borenstein, Israel, xv n., xvi n.
Borrowing, government: relation to capital formation, xvii, xxiii–xxiv, 5–6, 8, 13–16, 64–66, 77–80; relation to total borrowing, xvi–xvii; *see also* Debt; Deficits and surpluses
Burns, Arthur F., 105

Capital formation: concepts and definitions, 5; and borrowing by federal government, xvii, 14–16; and borrowing by state and local governments, xvii, 5–6, 8–9, 13–16, 64–66, 72–73, 75–80, 83–84, 86, 169; community size and, 64–66; concepts and definitions, 5; military expenditures in, 5
Capital requirements: concepts of, 3–6; financial vs. physical, xvi–xviii, 3–6, 14–46; *see also* Borrowing, government; Debt; Deficits
Copeland, Morris, 23 n., 84 n.
Countercyclical policies: credit underwriting programs as, 117–118; depression of 1930's and, 112–118, 120–122, 127; early development of, 107–111; emergency relief programs in, 114–117; Employment Act of 1946 and, 111; and farm income, 126–127; federal lending programs as, 108, 118–121; and Federal Reserve System, 107, 112 n., 117, 128; in recent recessions, 123–128
Creamer, Daniel, xv n.

Debt, federal: depressions and, 9, 12, 14, 16, 18; growth in, 6–16; relation to total or private debt, 13–14; retirement of, 4, 158–163; war expenditures and, xviii–xix, xxiv–xxv, 9, 11–12, 14, 16, 18, 39–40, 62, 147–155

state and local: changes in, compared with federal debt, 12; community size and, 64–69, 168; disorderly finance and, 80–83; of enterprises, 8, 10, 11, 13; functional distribution of, 8–13; gross vs. net, 12; growth of, 7–16, 87–90, 92; and income levels, 168–169; by level of government, 7, 97; per capita, 65–72; regional data on, 69–72, 168–169; repudiations and defaults on, 7–8, 88–90; restrictions on, 80–83, 88, 90–93, 98, 170; urbanization and, 71–72; war expenditures and, 10–11, 49, 87

Deficits and surpluses, federal: capital budgeting and, 162–163; capital expenditures and, 14–15; cash income and outgo concept, 23–24, 30–36; concepts and definitions of, xviii, 19–36; countercyclical policy and, xix, xxi, xxiv, 106–126; cyclical fluctuations in receipts and, 104–106; depressions and, 9, 40–41, 73; federal budget concept of, 20–23, 27–30, 31–34, 43–45, 165–167; flow of funds nonfinancial concept of, 23–27, 30–33, 36, 43–45, 165–167; international aid and, 155–157; National Income and Product concept of, 26, 30–33, 35; trend in, 37–38

state and local: and capital formation, 9, 15, 72–73, 75–80, 169; cyclical fluctuations in receipts, 73; depressions and, 48, 73, 74; emergency borrowing for, 73–74, 77, 171–172; short-term borrowing and, 74; trend in, 45–46; *see also* Borrowing; Debt

Dewey, Davis R., 88 n.
Dobrovolsky, Sergei P., xv n.
Durand, E. Dana, 82 n.

Employment and payrolls: federal, 53–54; state and local, 59–60
Expenditures: growth compared to GNP and deficit financing, 47, 61–62; growth in federal, 37–43, 51–54; growth in state and local, 45–49, 56–60; industrialization, and growth of, 9; by level of